THE CAMINO IS NOT JUST FOR WALKING

THE CAMINO IS NOT JUST FOR WALKING

PILGRIMS, HOSTS AND GHOSTS ALONG THE WAY

DANIELLE AIRD

Dedication

This book is dedicated to every friend I made along the way, and to all the wonderful hosts and volunteers, backbone of the Camino.

I thank first and foremost my son Anthony Aird whose graphic design, art, computer skills, and inexhaustible fountain of patience transformed my prose into this beautiful object. I am grateful to my husband Neil and my daughter Katie for not minding my frequent escapades and for holding the fort while I am away. I thank my son Robin for making me fall in love with nature from his Golden, B.C. home. A special thank you to Chloë without whom I might never have ventured onto the famous path.

A book is never a solitary enterprise. A very special thank you goes to my friend Gabrielle Henry for helping edit and for her productive comments. I look forward to reading her fascinating memoir about life in New Zealand, the U.S., Tanzania, Guyana, and Canada.

And I would like to thank you, my readers. Without readers, there can be no writers. I hope my book will bring back some of your Camino memories or inspire you to take that first step. Buen Camino.

Almonds

Contents

Portomarín

Introduction

Dad captivated us with tales of hopping on trains with his buddies. He was not a hobo. He loved adventure. I dreamt of the day when I could ride all the way to the other end of the country.

I was six years old when Mom put me, my seven-year-old sister Michèle, and eight-year-old Lucie who would be in charge of us during the three hundred and forty mile journey, on an overnight train from Val d'Or in Northern Quebec, to Ste Ursule, in the south. We were going to the Sisters of Providence's convent, where I would attend school for five years. My sisters knew the ropes. We would see our parents at Christmas and come back home for the summer holidays. It was the happiest day of my life. I waved cheerfully as my parents, standing on the platform with our three younger sisters, waved goodbye to us. Dad's eyes must have been misty. Mom must have sighed with relief. My love of adventure had just begun. I can still feel the excitement today.

By the age of fourteen, totally unbeknownst to my parents, after school, a friend and I were hitch-hiking from Val d'Or to another small town an hour away, joining other friends for a soda in a restaurant, and thumbing back home in time for dinner. Years later, while at university, in Kingston, my roommate Marg and I spent many weekends on the road to Toronto, Montreal, or perhaps to the Winter Carnival in Quebec City. At dinner Friday in the cafeteria, one would turn to the other, "Where shall we go?" The next morning, our thumbs, and perhaps Marg's good looks for tickets, we would be bouncing on the seat of a transport truck, cheerful company for a lonely driver. Only once or twice did we find ourselves in danger in a car. Never in a truck. Fortunately, although stupid enough to hitch-hike, we were clever enough to get out of trouble when needed.

My feet never stopped itching. When I met Neil, my Scottish husband, he had already travelled to forty-nine of the U.S. States. Marrying him meant trips to Britain and Europe. Closer to home, children in tow, we explored Canada from coast to coast, and beautiful areas of the United States. Neil loves pristine scenery. He loves flying over icebergs, mountains, rivers. The bird's-eye view was invented for him. Looking at his exquisite photos,

I understand. He also needs bland, familiar food, hotels with at least a few stars. He was happy with his head in the clouds; I wanted to learn about different cultures, languages, history, architecture, sample different foods, stay in a cabin, anywhere. I loved the idea of roughing it. Having slept in youth hostels during his solo bicycle trips through Britain and the Continent in his teenage years, Neil had 'been there, done that'.

After our kids had flown the coop, we started punctuating our travels together with separate trips. In Turkey, I discovered international hostels where I met like-minded travellers and explored with them. That was the way for me. While my husband's lifelong hobby, (a website about the Beaver airplane) took him to Australia, New Zealand, Alaska, the Southern U.S., I indulged my wanderlust across Central America, Europe, Morocco, Turkey, India, sometimes with a friend, sometimes solo. I especially enjoyed exploring India and Spain. In the spring of 2001, my sister Nicole at the wheel and I, a map on my knees, we travelled from Barcelona, across the Pyrenees, to Santiago de Compostela, and down the Portuguese coast before crossing over to Morocco. Santiago meant nothing to me then.

A few years ago, when it was time for Neil to renew his passport, he announced: "I have seen all I want to see; I am perfectly happy at home." I, too, am happy at home, but like the Eveready Bunny, I plan to keep going until I drop. I was hearing more and more about a certain 730-kilometre trail. I joined a local group of hikers and met them for short hikes, intending to go on the longer ones if I felt capable. They walked to stay fit. I wanted to stop and listen to the birds, examine a plant, a flower, a patch of moss, look at the sky, slow down when tired perhaps take a photo or two. It reinforced my feeling that no matter how friendly, groups are not for me. Rumour had it the Camino could be walked in segments and at one's speed, and a person like me would never be lonely along its path. There could be no stopping me now.

Horreo in Galicia

Stepping stones

The Beaten Track

Pilgrims have walked to Santiago for almost as long as to Jerusalem or Mecca. The most beaten path to the famous city, the one I would follow, is the Camino Francés. A thousand years ago, they came from as far away as Northern Europe and Ireland, the south of Italy and everywhere in between. Now, one is just as likely to find oneself alongside a pilgrim from Seattle as from Buenos Aires, Los Angeles, Seoul, Timbuktu, Pretoria, Canberra, or even Mumbai. One might even meet an occasional Spaniard.

What is perhaps less known about the 730-kilometre trail is that it is highly addictive. There is no *caveat emptor*. The number of pilgrims along the Camino has tripled in fifteen years to over 340,000 a year. Some walk a part each year, others, the entire length in one go. Many come back again and again, sometimes along the same path. More often, they choose an alternate trail, either from the south near Seville, or from Portugal, or they might try the Camino del Norte closer to the sea, or one of the lesser-known ones, almost always with Santiago de Compostela or even, a few days' walk further, to Finistere (Land's end) as their ultimate destination. There are also those who walk back home along the Camino. I have met pilgrims who walked from their home in the north of Germany. One woman had walked from Helsinki.

A repeat pilgrim will not be surprised to meet an eighty-year-old or a family with a toddler or two. One might even stumble upon a handicapped person being helped along in a wheelchair, even lend a hand to get chair, pilgrim and belongings over the crest of a challenging hill. Inspired by the Americans Justin Skeesuck and Patrick Gray's compelling book, *I'll Push You* is an association of volunteers helping the handicapped reach Santiago. I have seen dogs, horses, and a donkey on the Camino. Cycling pilgrims pass us occasionally along stretches of road or even on some rough trails. One cyclist had his dog in a basket. I even met a man pulling a home-built cart with his belongings.

The pilgrimage to Santiago used to be for Christians intent on earning indulgences to atone for their sins, or asking the Almighty for a particular favour. Nowadays, the hikers are still called pilgrims, (*peregrinos* in Spanish). Few of us would fit that definition. Many have never set foot inside a church.

No one can accuse me of being religious or spiritual. I have even been called pragmatic. My sins are much too numerous for my slate to be wiped clean from a mere walk in the woods. The thought of spending several weeks on a nature trail listening to the birds' early morning songs, the bleating of sheep, the sound of raindrops splashing off my brand new poncho were quite enough to lure me onto the Camino. Visions of venturing into mysterious groves, past warbling brooks, fields of wheat waving in the wind, vines, orchards... had been filling my daydreams for a while now. What more could a vagabond old lady wish for? Wouldn't it be enough to sit in the shade of an olive tree, cool my Camino-weary toes in an icy brook under an old stone bridge? When I recited this to my husband, he couldn't help but add, "Or listen to the snoring of thirty pilgrims in a stuffy dorm at night." One thing was for sure: I wasn't looking for transformation. Isn't life itself an ongoing metamorphosis?

I get immense pleasure strolling along Lake Ontario in Kingston where I live. The Camino would provide an orgy of nature, a whole month of hills and valleys, fields and forests, nature in all its elements, wind, rain, sun, cold, escape from the real world. And I would never, for one second, forget that this was a privilege only someone from a rich country could afford. All my problems on the way to Santiago would be Rich People's problems.

When exactly did I start being interested in the Camino? I cannot tell. It had wiggled its way up to the top of my Bucket List. I was spending a lot of time secretly watching pilgrims' experiences on YouTube. Little by little, the Camino took front seat amongst my obsessions. Some of the tales I had heard were not encouraging for a person my age going alone. I should never have read Bill Bryson's *A Walk in the Woods*. About the Camino also, there were a few stories floating about of people getting lost, being attacked by mean dogs. Or worse. I have passed the age of being afraid of dying, but I would prefer to do it peacefully, and I have a terrible fear of certain big dogs. Safety in numbers. I would wait until I found a partner to hike with.

Of course, there was also an abundance of tales about snorers, farters and other stinkers, bed bugs, thieves, cold water showers, no room at the inn... most of which would turn out to be untrue or grossly exaggerated. Having slept in an eighty-bed dorm for five years as a child, dorms did not worry me. I had often stayed in hostels, and once even had to share a bed with two women in a friend's home in India. As for bed bugs, the cow dung and mud floors in Karnataka had left me unblemished.

Diane, the Temptress

Several years ago, I attended a presentation by Diane Ricard, an energetic woman who had walked the Camino Francés to Santiago de Compostela where, through a tremendous leap of faith, some believe the bones of Saint James, Jesus' disciple murdered by King Herod, lay entombed. I have not seen it related anywhere how or where he actually died the second time around after a bishop resuscitated him in the year 844, as Santiago Matamoros (Saint-James the Moor Killer). Did he pop out of the coffin and then sneak back in? This remains one of the mysteries of the Camino.

Diane was bubbling with enthusiasm. Ask a pilgrim how she or he liked the experience and you are in for a couple of hours. Some will go as far as writing an entire book about it. I was fascinated by her presentation but appalled at how much gear she had lugged. Empty, her backpack weighed more than I could carry for five hundred metres. Since then, more lightweight backpacks have sprouted on the market in all good sports equipment stores. These are fitted to the buyer by knowledgeable staff. Discomfort is minimized.

Our presenter's gear was state-of-the-art and expensive: sturdy hiking boots, hiking sticks, special socks, a sleeping bag, the whole kit... And she had prepared for every eventuality: blisters, sprained ankle, sore muscles, headaches, fever, snorers...

I abhor lugging stuff around. Stuff makes me feel enslaved. I have often said I would love to live out of a backpack. It is perhaps a slight exaggeration, but not enough to make my nose grow longer. Except for the contents of her backpack, our speaker that day fanned the flames of my wanderlust.

Packing

In 2004, on a solo two-month trip around India, I had stuffed all my travel gear into the small backpack I used at home to pick up a few groceries. One underwear on, one in the bag. No 'just-in-case'... Other countries have stores. Everyone is dying to sell you something. After decades of solo travelling, it would be no challenge to reduce the list of suggested equipment to a minimum. I have never found myself in a situation when I wished I had taken more stuff with me.

Have you ever noticed how happy an over-packer is when you ask if he might have a knife, a corkscrew you could borrow, an aspirin he could trade for a Latte? "Aha! I knew there would be a need for that," he will say triumphantly as he rummages to the bottom of his twenty-gallon bag in the 'just-in-case' section. Sifting through his extras, he will ask if you could use an extra pair of socks, a notebook, (he is not sure why he brought two). "And how about this brown sweater?" he asks hopefully, comparing it to his other two.

It is now September 2019, and I am embarking on my fourth partial Camino hike. Chloë (my nineteen-year-old granddaughter) and I first walked from Pamplona to Burgos in May 2018. Two weeks after my return home, my mother died quite unexpectedly. Thus began a difficult summer. I had been named executrix. To add insult to injury, the day Mom had her last *rendez-vous* with Destiny was the first day of a hellish heat wave. It would last the whole summer. I live in a Victorian-era house with an unusable handkerchief-size backyard. Our only real outdoor space is a roofed-in balcony which my husband's green thumb turns into a colourful garden in the summer. Across the street, a historical school was being restored. Until the beginning of September, when I was not at Mom's lawyer's office or emptying her house and preparing to sell it, our days were filled with the racket of drills, compressors, jackhammers. In order to finish work before school started again, the workers sometimes put in long days and even worked on the weekend. That summer, my husband and I got a close glimpse of hell. First-world hell.

My Love Affair

In the fall, my granddaughter was back at university. I desperately needed an escape. It is a good thing my husband is not the jealous type. There was no use pretending otherwise: my love affair with the Camino was out in the open. I went back with Andrea, a woman of many talents who had been his jewellery-making student, and is our hairstylist. Yoga teacher, artist-painter, onetime bodybuilder, ten years younger than I, Andrea is hard-working, caring, compassionate, giggly, and young-at-heart. Yoga is something she started practising in her late thirties to help stall the growth of an inoperable brain tumour. For fifteen years, she had religiously celebrated the summer solstice along with tens of thousands of yogis in New Mexico; she had been to a yatra (a spiritual journey) to Patna in Bihar, India to celebrate Guru Gobind Singh's 350th anniversary. She was now ready for a different kind of pilgrimage, one where she would be her own guru.

When Andrea heard my stories, her eyes opened wide. Her dream of one day walking the famous trail grew with each tale I told. I hesitated when she asked if she could accompany me because we are so different. Gurus are not for me. Then I remembered how bored I felt in the company of people 'just like me'. When she produced a book about walking and breathing, I thought, I have been breathing and walking for seven decades, I have probably mastered both arts. But she and I usually get along with most people. She was willing to take a chance. So was I.

Since it would be her first time in Spain, and it didn't matter to me which part of the Camino I walked, it didn't seem fair to start in Burgos, where my granddaughter and I had stopped. We would walk from Pamplona. From there, we could hike for almost three weeks, enough time to make it to León where we could pick up the next time.

After indulging in Gaudi sights in Barcelona, Andrea and I took a train to the famous city known to most North Americans for Hemingway and for hundreds of macho guys running before the bulls every summer to show their bravery, perhaps getting gored or trampled to death under the eyes of delighted spectators. The blood and gore are all part of the fun. Miracles abound on the Camino: different as we are, we would return home as good friends.

Those who have not left everything behind and immersed themselves in nature for several weeks at a time might not understand the lure of the Camino. In May 2019, I went back for the third time, and hiked from Saint-Jean-Pied-de-Port over the border in France, with my granddaughter again, and with Janine, a Philadelphia artist about my age whom I had met on Casa Ivar's Camino website. Janine and I had much in common but not enough to bore each other. We both love languages and have similar lifestyles. Though I am no artist or gardener like Janine, I live with an artist and gardener and have great admiration for both skills.

Janine was with us for only two weeks when unexpected events called her away. We had by then become a solid group of six, including Vicki from Australia, and Randall and Joanna a Hawaiian couple. Apart from Chloë, we were all about the same age. We would leave the hostel (called *gîte* in France and *albergue* in Spain) together in the morning and, after each finding our own pace, end up in two or three separate groups, or sometimes on our own, and meet at destination. After Janine left, Chloë and I stayed with our new friends until the end of our hike at Terradillos de los Templaros, about halfway to Santiago.

Collecting Stories

This time, my fourth, I am going solo, skipping a part, hoping to finish in Santiago. I want to collect more stories along the way. I would be embarrassed if I were the only addict, but there are enough of us to warrant a Camino Addict Anonymous Society. On September 11, my train departs for Montreal at 9:11 a.m. in time for my flight via Frankfurt. Only after purchasing my ticket did I notice the time and date: 9:11, 9/11. Glad I am not superstitious.

In the Frankfurt transit lounge the next morning, trying to stifle my early morning yawns, I can easily spot the pilgrims: large, state-of-the-art backpacks; Gore-Tex, hiking boots or recently broken-in sneakers, a look of anticipation or nervousness on some faces, and perhaps a white shell dangling from a string from a previous pilgrimage. No hiking sticks: not allowed on the plane in case some of us might be terrorists. Amongst the passengers, I guess about ten of us will be on the trail, but social barriers have not come down yet. Except for those who are obviously travelling together, we all keep to ourselves.

Later, in the arrivals lounge in Pamplona, a quiet airport where probably less than a thousand passengers disembark daily from a handful of flights, I meet Barbro, a cheerful, reserved, Swedish woman with rosy cheeks and thick white hair. "Are you going to Saint-Jean-Pied-de-Port?" she asks. She has reserved a taxi which I could share. Unfortunately, I already have a bus ticket, but in the five minutes before her taxi arrives, we arrange to meet early tomorrow morning. We will hike to Orisson together. On the Camino, friendships strike quick as lightning. I was going to say faster than a speeding bullet, but eh, we are still in the airport.

Tourism is one of Spain's most important sources of income. Municipalities go out of their way to welcome pilgrims. We get free or reduced rates to museums. Restaurants everywhere offer a reasonably priced, hearty pilgrim's menu at hours to accommodate foreigners. We sleep in clean, comfortable establishments starting at €5 per night. Some places only ask for a donation (*donativo*) so penniless pilgrims can also have a bed.

Surprised to discover that the bus to downtown has been discontinued, upon inquiring, an airport employee points to a large sign posted by the Municipality, a number to call. A taxi will drop passengers off downtown for less than €1 each. (A regular taxi would cost about €25 plus €5 per bag.) The City of Pamplona picks up the tab.

Most travelers, unaware of the inexpensive service, have already hopped into regular taxis. Only two jolly German fellows and one young Italian woman are looking for the bus. Once I translate the poster to them, the Italian woman lets me borrow her cell phone. (I don't own one). The dispatcher asks for our names and how many bags we have; they will send a car of appropriate size. The Italian woman has disappeared to the loo and the two Germans are away from the building, puffing on cigarettes. I give my name. The dispatcher wants all four names so I blurt out, "Cynthia, Patricia and Rita." When the taxi arrives at the now almost deserted airport, there is a bit of confusion as the driver looks for a group of four women. The reason the dispatcher had asked for names was so it would be first come first served. Since we are the only four left, it is no problem.

In downtown Pamplona, after giving our driver tips larger than our fares, we soon scatter. The two puffy pink-cheeked Germans, who I guess to be in their early sixties, with respectable beer bellies, want to explore Pamplona before heading to Saint-Jean. I have a hunch they are as keen on Estrella Galicia and Estrella Damm as they are about the stars of the Milky Way straddling the Camino. I can picture them in front of beer steins during Oktoberfest in Munich. They are probably not true pilgrims either. As for the Italian girl, in the taxi, she had opened her notebook and attracted my attention to three lines: Cafe Iruña, Bar Txoko, and Hotel la Perla. She must be a Hemingway fan intent on finding some of his favourite haunts. I won't see her again, but in a few days in Zariquiegui before Alto del Perdón, and again in Torres del Río, I will bump into my beer-bellied friends.

Multilingualism takes down barriers; it is a wonderful key to new friend-ships. Spaniards often speak two languages: one regional, such as Catalán, Basque or Galician. Many of them don't speak French or English. I cannot claim to speak any language perfectly, not even French, which is my mother tongue, but with my imperfect skills I make many French, English, Spanish and German friends along the way. And armed with French and Spanish, it is easy to capture the gist of an Italian or Portuguese enquiry, usually about where to catch a bus, find a pharmacy, an ATM, a place to sleep. There are tricks to learning languages. Many years ago, when my husband and I drove across Canada, I took along my *Learn Portuguese in a month*. I did not come home anywhere near fluent, but I learnt to make the connections between it and Spanish. Languages weigh nothing and are valuable travel companions. Mind you, now with smart phones, translation apps, google maps, multilingualism will soon go the way of the dodo along with my two-inch thick Lonely Planet Guides.

On the Bus

We are over a dozen pilgrims at Pamplona's Alsa bus station. Many have come via Madrid. Some look wrinkled like me. We are mostly a jet-lagged posse speaking a cacophony of languages. I hear Australian accents. A couple sound South-American. Three women are talking about their exhausting long trip from Seattle, something I do not envy. Koreans, Germans, Dutch, Eastern-Europeans complete the picture. Students are back in school, workers at the grind. I am far from being the only white-haired pilgrim.

It would be tempting to fall asleep on the way, but I don't want to miss one second of the Pyrenees. The drive from Pamplona over the border into France must have been terrifying in the days before the N-135. It must have been a hassle when travellers had to produce passports at the border. And what must the crossing have been like from Nazi-invaded France to Franco's Spain during the war years when Jewish refugees were fleeing France in a desperate bid to reach Portugal where they might board a ship to a host country?

Despite our exhaustion, everyone seems in high spirits. Tomorrow morning starts our adventure. Are any of us religious pilgrims? Any would-be heroes? Or are we all loafers? Although few would call hiking the Camino a fancy holiday, not everyone can afford the flight and weeks on end of idling in a country half a world away. It is a luxury to choose an ascetic lifestyle for a short time when our comforts await. It is one thing to carry a heavy backpack for forty days on a sometimes difficult trail; it would be another to carry all the belongings we could salvage out of our country when bombs are falling and our home has been destroyed. Heroes can be found in refugee lines or packed in leaky boats on rough seas, rarely on the Camino.

On the hairpin curves, the sun keeps moving from side to side. Near the French border with the small pilgrim hub waiting to welcome us, we are treated to a spectacular orgy of scenery. It is thrilling to sit back and feast our eyes on the display of emerald-green hills and valleys in front of us. Tomorrow we will walk in the opposite direction on a trail used by pilgrims, invaders, refugees and adventurers over centuries. Our driver is calm and prudent. This ride is nothing like the hair-raising ones I have miraculously survived on pot-holed, or even half-washed-out roads on mountain passes in places like Mexico, Guatemala, or India.

The man next to me is Oriental. He does not speak English. We content ourselves with an occasional smile. We scored the front seats opposite the driver. I am in heaven with the panoramic view. What is in store for me this time? I am happy to have met Barbro at the airport, to have a companion to hike with tomorrow morning. I am thinking about Chloë. Last May, on my third and her second time, when we were on this bus, she could hardly contain her excitement. Before arriving in Saint-Jean we knew we had made the right decision in starting on the French side that time. Now, I am thrilled to go back. I wouldn't miss the hike from Saint-Jean to Roncesvalles for anything. At this end, it is my favourite stretch. Later, in Galicia, I will have to admit the beauty contest is fierce.

If Chloë and I started in Pamplona our first time, it was because I had heard many negative reports about Saint-Jean to Roncesvalles. One woman had been warned at her *gîte* the morning she left Saint-Jean: "Be very careful, this is the part where people die." Not too reassuring... Last September, however, Andrea and I met a woman in her seventies who had hiked alone from there. She raved about it. I figured if she can do it, I can do it. I wonder how different the trail will be from last May.

I carry an iPod, and promised my husband to message him when internet is available to let him know my plans for the next day. He and my children will be happy to know I am walking with Barbro starting at St-Jean. I have assured them one never needs to be alone on the Camino. On the other hand, it is nice to have an opportunity for solitude when the spirit craves it.

Saint-Jean-Pied-de-Port

Last May, with Chloë and Janine (my chat line friend from Philadelphia), we arrived in Saint-Jean on a later bus. Chloë's and my day had started before sunrise the day before in Canada. Janine had come on the train from the south of Spain, where she had been visiting her daughter. We first met in the flesh at the bus station in Pamplona. When our bus reached Saint-Jean, we all longed for a hot shower and a bed. Stupidly enough, it never occurred to us to visit this gem of a medieval town even in the morning before heading off to Orisson, only a few hours' hike up, and where we had prepaid reservations. Jet-lag will do that.

This time, from the bus drop-off point, even before shedding my bag, I take time to explore Rue d'Espagne called Rue de la Citadelle on the other side of the river. Elbowing my way along the narrow cobblestone passage teeming with hundreds of pilgrims and tourists, I climb up to the Citadel. In the valley below, hundreds of white houses with red roofs and shutters form the perfect jig-saw puzzle picture. Tomorrow morning, for the second time, I will be a moving speck in the folds of these mountains and valleys. But I have dallied too much. Jet-lag is gnawing at me. My backpack is getting heavy. I must find my *gîte*, the Bidean. I don't want the last bed in the dorm.

Down with the crowd, the ambiance is festive. In the pilgrim's office, they say four hundred of us are starting from here tomorrow. I am not alone! It's a good thing my bed is reserved for tonight and the next two nights. Rue de la Citadelle is lined on both sides with a multitude of *gîtes* amid deep, narrow, modern speciality shops of all kinds inside centuries-old buildings. Tourists and pilgrims from all over the world fill the street. The window displays are inviting. The aroma of the spice shop wraps its cloak around me, lures me inside. Irresistible. In the busy shop, I must keep reminding myself not to turn abruptly and smack anyone with my backpack. From dozens of large four or five-gallon open bags full of products with shapes and colours sometimes dazzling, a myriad perfumes waft up to my nose. There are herbs and spices, teas, grains, beans from all over the world, many with names I have never heard and redolent with scents that have never tickled my nose before. There must be twenty different mixtures of curry. Here and there, jutting out of the large spice and tea containers, are signs: 'Please don't touch. Natural Food Products: Look, smell and travel'. Along the windows, pepper grinders, salt shakers, and colourful ceramic tajines from Morocco cover every inch of narrow shelf. This shop is a magic carpet. I find myself in the spice markets of Mumbai, Istanbul, Casablanca... Even outside, the aroma of the shop clings to me. Who could have resisted its call? I envy the buyer who must travel the world in search of nature's wonderful treasures.

Rue de la Citadelle reminds me of the picturesque villages at the foot of ski hills near Mont-Tremblant in Quebec: Saint-Sauveur, Morin-Heights, or Banff and Lake Louise at the other end of the country, their vibrant little streets, their souvenir shops, luxury clothing and jewellery stores, fancy restaurants. They sell ski equipment. In Saint-Jean, one finds hiking poles and boots and all the other tempting, modern paraphernalia one might wish for the long hike. Alas, much of it will be found discarded, lying on benches, or hanging from fences or even at the end of tree branches, abandoned by overburdened pilgrims. A couple Chloë and I met confessed they had shed $500. worth of equipment a few days after St-Jean.

Shoulder to shoulder, through a cacophony of languages, with looks of anticipation, tourists and pilgrims are posing, snapping photos, pouring in and out of the small shops. And it is not even the weekend. What must it be like here on Saturdays and Sundays? What must it be like in a Holy Year when the number of pilgrims doubles?

Many are taking selfies in front of the stone arch and ancient clock tower lording it over the town. I love those old clocks. Will my great-grandchildren be able to read them? Was there a sundial in its place in times past? Or was it just the church bells that sounded the hours, calling people to prayers? Along the Camino, many sundials have been preserved. Last year, I had to explain to a younger pilgrim how come they seemed upside down.

By the river, I snap photos of the Basque houses, their long wooden balconies with turned spindles, teeming with dozens of flower pots full of colourful blooms jutting out over the river. The Nive is quiet. It is not like the canal in Bruges or Ghent where motor boats take tourists all day long, day after day, while tour guides recite their spiels, and residents are driven mad by the constant noise and fumes.

Gîte Bidean

Before I indulge my desire to explore the church, at Gîte Bidean, my host, Joe, shows me upstairs to my dorm. In the hallway, he points to an old couch. "This is in case we have a snorer. He can sleep here." He apologizes for giving me an upper bunk. "It's my last bed," he says. I don't mind. My fault. I shouldn't have dilly-dallied.

The accommodation is not luxurious but there is a warm, homey feeling about this *gîte*. If only I can remember to look down at my feet for the treacherous three-inch step between hallway and dorm. I should be used to these changes in floor height by now. How often have I tripped, sprained an ankle, fallen flat on my face, lost my dignity in Spain or in Cuba because of them? I must try to look down at my feet. I believe those minor changes in floor height between rooms are not allowed in public places in Canada where over-protective laws turn absent-minded citizens like me into accident-prone morons.

Joe asks if I will join them for dinner. He is cooking pasta. Unfortunately, I'm gluten intolerant. For some silly reason, I feel embarrassed mentioning it in a country where wheat makes up the major part of every meal. Undaunted, Joe offers to prepare a gluten-free meal, so I will join them. But first I want to explore a bit more of this XIII Century town.

Inside the church, I dip my fingers into the holy water stoup, make the sign of the cross, and genuflect. It has been many decades since I made those gestures. With reverence, I walk up to the apse to see more closely the high arched stained glass windows depicting who knows what saints. Three tall, slim pilgrims are kneeling together half-way down the nave, heads bent, elbows on the pews in front of them, hands joined in prayer. Praying mantises. Asking God for a safe crossing? The cold and damp interior with its vaulted ceiling seems an appropriate place to start on a pilgrimage. Feeling like an intruder, I move as inconspicuously as I can back to the vestibule.

Out into the crowd, jet-lag hits me suddenly like a raw-hide mallet so it's back to the Bidean, hoping supper will not be too late. The perfume of Thai chicken welcomes me at the door. Maya, an Israeli woman in her thirties, is the only other pilgrim at the table with our hosts Joe and Pascal. We share a generous plate of fresh *crudités*, melon and *jamón iberico* (delicious, paper-thin cured ham), followed by the perfectly seasoned chicken and rice. Joe had baked and iced a cake, so he kindly offers me yogurt, often served as dessert along the Camino.

Joe is from Thailand. He studied at a culinary school in Paris where he met Pascal, a geriatric nurse. Both in their early forties maybe, they loved their work, but since their different hours were not conducive to a steady relationship, they decided to have a new start together with this *gîte*. "Your patients must miss you," I tell Pascal. "I miss them too," he replies. I can tell he is sincere. He and Joe are kindness incarnate, a necessary quality

St-Jean-Pied-de-Port

Orisson

Roncesvalles

Viskarret

Zubiri

Larrasoaña

Pamplona

N

Pascal

Joe

Barbro

for success as hosts to pilgrims. I have no doubt their business will prosper. They are full of initiative, flexible with their guests' needs and both paragons of hospitality. And they are handsome, which never hurts. It is true the eyes are the mirror of the soul. That is where their handsomeness comes from. Pascal's patients must have loved him. Years ago, when my sister hired a companion for our ailing father, she found an attractive person with a sunny disposition. It makes a difference. The companion could not do much for Dad's physical comfort, but she brought a ray of sunshine into his life.

I could not have landed into a better *gîte*. Last May, Chloë, Janine and I had beds a few blocks away. The sleeping quarter was nicer than here because there were only beds, no bunks. Our host was very businesslike. She lacked the warmth I am experiencing here. This time, I wanted to try something different. I am not disappointed. Joe and Pascal only opened six months ago. Already their reputation is established. The French government gave them a boost with a Small Business grant. "We are booked for months ahead," says Joe proudly. And they have all kinds of plans for improvements.

What is the meaning of the name Bidean? I wonder. It is an obvious Basque word. "Is it Pascal's last name?" "Not at all," says Joe. "*Bide* means 'way', the '*a*' means 'the', the '*n*' means 'on'. 'Bidean' means 'On the Way.'" This is my first official lesson in Basque. From a Thai! I carry a sheet with a short list of words in Basque, French and English which Andrea and I picked up along the way last September. Eventually I hope to learn a few more words. Basque is not easy because it has no connection to any other language. This humble start will at least help me understand some names of places. "But," says Pascal, "don't forget there is French Basque and Spanish Basque. And we have a few dialects." I forgot to ask if he was kidding.

De Rerum Natura

At 8 o'clock in the morning, Barbro is waiting for me by the Clock Tower. "Where is your backpack?" she asks, surprised. Hers looks heavy. "I get it shipped," I explain. She was not aware of the service. Before we make it to Orisson, she knows she will not be carrying hers after today.

Blankets are provided in Orisson, so I have put only what I need for tonight into my daypack. Joe will ship my backpack to Roncesvalles tomorrow. The transfer service is perfect for wimps like me. Nevertheless since I know there might be times when I have to carry it, I have packed the minimum.

My Swedish companion is well rested. Not a good sleeper at the best of times, I was awake at all hours of the night. My jet lag clings to me, but although the path is steep today, the distance is short: only 8 kilometres. I will be fine.

There is a wonderful French expression: *atomes crochus*. It means atoms with little barbs. In his long poem, *De Rerum Natura* (On the Nature of things) the philosopher Lucretius, disciple of Epicurus, pictured everything made of tiny particles. Observing dust motes in the sun rays, he noticed they were in constant motion, thus his theory: when two people meet, particles emanating from them collide and either bounce back or hook together to form instant friendship. Although we only met briefly at the airport, it is as though Barbro and I have known each other for a long time. On the Camino, atoms move in all directions. Bonds form in minutes. How else to explain the camaraderie, often the lasting friendships that develop over a glass of wine, or even on a short stony dirt path, between perfect strangers? If friendship had a mass, few pilgrims could carry the accumulated load all the way to Santiago.

Immediately out of Saint-Jean, the climb is steep. Thinking we will have lots of time to get to know each other, Barbro and I talk sparingly. We move slowly, laboriously, saving our breath, through the lush mountain range. Even before we pass the arrow confirming we are on the right path, it is nature as those who wrote of Adam and Eve in paradise must have imagined it. The fog is slowly rising from the valleys. Each photo we take, each image we capture, is a visual poem. Here we are far from real life, from politics, economics, manipulation, arguments, lies, anger, fear and resentment. Here, nothing matters and we are nothing. And for a change, it is nice to be nothing.

I would have liked to hike with Barbro at least part of the way to Santiago, so I am disappointed to learn that she has been advised by a travel agent in Sweden to book beds for every single night along the way. The agent (who has obviously never walked the Camino) warned her that she might find herself without accommodation. Barbro is committed to walking a whole stage each day. Tonight, a bed is waiting for her on the other side of Roncesvalles. After Orisson, pilgrims face more hours of strenuous climbing followed by a steep, perilous descent. Even strong young men find Saint-Jean to Roncesvalles challenging. Most pilgrims break the 25 km stage in two at Orisson, a relatively short stretch, but itself no mere little stroll.

Between Orisson and Roncesvalles last May, the weather was fairly good, yet I remember how arduous a climb it was. Once in a while, I learn my lesson. I know from experience how insane I would be to attempt to walk all those kilometres up and downhill while still jet-lagged. That is why my bed is waiting in Orisson. I could, of course, skip Orisson to Roncesvalles and continue with Barbro tomorrow, but I don't want to miss that part. I have not been past León, but today and tomorrow the path cuts through some of the most breathtaking areas of the Camino, at least at this end. Neither do I want to commit to walking a whole stage each day. I rarely plan more than one day at a time.

From Saint-Jean, we follow an almost deserted road through rich pastureland. I am, like last May, transported to my husband's beautiful Scotland. We met soon after he came to Canada, but because he quickly adapted to the Canadian way of life, its food, its winters, I have always thought of him as Canadian. Although he was happy to leave haggis, bagpipes and kilt behind, he never forgot the beauty of his country. What a pair we are: he with his Scottish accent and I, with my French-Canadian one.

On the Camino, we are a Tower of Babel. Barbro and I exchange comments with others. Before even asking for names, we ask each other where we are from, and whether we started in Saint-Jean or further away in France. According to our different paces, we change walking partners after a few hundred metres, reconnect with a previous one, meet a new one, hike alone for a stretch, stop at our own whim, catch our breath, capture some scenes to share with friends back home. That is the way of the Camino. So it goes until Orisson. Barbro and I will reach our first stop separately.

Last month, I connected on the Camino chat group with Betty from Calgary who is turning sixty-seven today. I am keeping an eye open for an attractive woman with slightly greying short brown hair, bangs and eyeglasses.

About half-way to Orisson, a woman is carrying a folded, life-size cardboard cut-out of Ellen DeGeneres attached to her backpack. Not sure if I should ask her about it, I decide to wait and see. I will surely run across her again. Incidentally, she says she is turning 67 today. "What is your name?" I ask. "Alma." "Where are you from?" "Calgary." Now I am totally confused. Did I have the wrong name from the chat group? Am I remembering the wrong picture? How jet-lagged am I? Alma has piercing blue eyes and ash-blond hair half-hidden under her colourful knitted cap, no bangs, no eyeglasses. I don't have much of a visual memory, but I could swear she looks nothing like the woman on the chat line. The age is right, the town is right, the name is wrong, the face is wrong. It's a mystery.

Alma looks strong though I can tell she is not finding it easy. No wonder! Her backpack looks heavy. Her legs are much shorter than mine. Each of her kilometres requires many more steps than mine, but it's important for me to walk at my natural pace so after a *"Buen Camino,"* I move on ahead.

Apart perhaps from muscular young men with long bouncy strides, not too many people find this stretch easy. We look like a parade of masochists. Maybe that's what we are.

Refuge Orisson

Late morning, Refuge Orisson pops up in the distance welcoming pilgrims who stop for a hot drink, a bite to eat, and those of us, especially from overseas, who are breaking the first stage in two. It is a rare pilgrim who doesn't stop, if only to use the facilities, today only an outdoor loo, the last one for at least four hours. On the Napoleon route, Orisson is our last-chance Café before Roncesvalles,

At the top of a hill, in a restored shepherd's home, handsome Jean-Jacques Etchendy, the Basque owner, receives pilgrims with a warm welcome. A bit more expensive than most, Refuge Orisson is still extremely affordable if one compares it to an establishment like it in the Alps. One can tell right away it is a deservedly successful business. At first sight, it looks like one building and its patio across the road, but under the patio is a large dorm built into the hill. From a few dozen tables, pilgrims can take

The Birthday Twins

Carolyn and Kate

in the view over the mountains. The panorama is one of the most iconic of the Camino Francés. Last May, it was too cold and rainy to sit outside. The large parasols were at half-mast. Today the tables are almost all occupied. Across the quiet road, the restaurant is buzzing with activity. Servers go back and forth balancing large trays with beer, wine, and plates heaped with generous, appetizing fare.

After signing in and getting my *credencial* stamped, I am instructed to wait at the patio area. My *credencial* (the *sine qua non* little passport needed to get pilgrim's accommodation) is to be stamped at one stop during the day and everywhere I sleep, as proof I am walking and not just driving and taking advantage of inexpensive accommodation. I must also present it at Santiago to obtain the coveted certificate of completion: the Compostela. Restaurants, churches, museums, and sometimes local citizens selling small trinkets or food also offer stamps.

By the time Alma appears at the top of the hill, I have joined a group of women on the patio. We must be about fifty pilgrims enjoying some form or other of libation and food. "Let's sing Happy Birthday to Alma," I tell everyone, so we all stand and sing, stopping Alma in her tracks. She is still wiping tears from her cheeks when some of us go to meet her, lavishing her with hugs and good wishes, while others add a chair for her at our table.

Everyone is curious about the Ellen DeGeneres' cutout on Alma's back. She is raising funds for the mental illness section of the Children's Hospital in Calgary. She unfolds the cutout and asks everyone to sign it. When we pull out our wallets, she won't accept the money; it would be too big a responsibility. There is a website with a long URL we can capture with our cameras to which we can send a donation. By raising a large sum of money, and by her visibility on the Camino, Alma hopes to get an invitation to Ellen's talk show. That would certainly help her cause.

I love coincidences. It is not long before we all get to meet Betty from Calgary with dark, slightly greying hair, bangs, and eyeglasses. She is turning 67 today. I wasn't being stupid. Unfortunately, I did not spot Betty in time to give her the same spontaneous birthday acknowledgement as Alma, but I manage a photo of the Calgary twins as we repeat our Happy Birthday song.

After a while, Barbro surfaces. She looks tired. For a long time over lunch, she debates about walking all the way to Roncesvalles. Scrutinizing today's topographical map in my *vade me cum*: John Brierley's *A Pilgrim's Guide to the Camino de Santiago*, and seeing what we have accomplished so far and what lays ahead before Roncesvalles, she knows she would be pushing herself insanely on her first day. Only a few, younger women at our table are planning to walk at least up to the small hut on this side of Roncesvalles. In case of emergency, they can spend the night there. Barbro is hesitant to hike alone after the hut. She is enjoying the camaraderie, and lingers longer than she should. In mid-afternoon, resigned, she will take a taxi to destination, a very expensive proposition. We have exchanged contact information, and hope our paths will cross again. Sadly, they will not. At least, not on the Camino. Back home, we will reconnect online.

One woman who is staying in Orisson tonight started her pilgrimage in Le Puy-en-Velay in the Massif Central in France over twenty days ago. She is one of the hardy ones. I have seen that path in *Saint-Jacques La Mecque*, a 2005 French comedy. It seems much more challenging than from Saint-Jean, but the scenery is spectacular. For some who started there, Orisson is only a place to pause for a meal before Roncesvalles. But since this is our first day, many of us are keen to meet other pilgrims, make friends, listen to each other's reasons for being here. Atoms are flying everywhere. Bonds are forming. Friendships are blossoming. On the whole, pilgrims are a gregarious bunch. We will probably bump into each other here and there along the way. Where are we all from? Is it our first time? Are we planning to walk the whole way? Why are we here? And by the way, what are our names?

At our table, beside Barbro, Betty and Alma, there is Caroline, a writer from St. Albert, north of Calgary. What are the chances? We, Canadians, are apparently outnumbered by Koreans on the Camino. We are not even listed in the eight most frequent nationalities. There is also Connie, a retired psychologist from the U.S. who will be meeting two of her sisters and a brother-in-law in Pamplona. They plan on walking together for four or five days to Logroño, after which one sister will walk with Connie to Santiago. Karen Axelrod from Vermont is a musician, composer, accordionist and pianist who hosts concerts on Facebook. Kate Elliott from Seattle is the author of *A*

Camino of the Soul. Tall, athletic-looking, bright eyed, a spontaneous smile...
friendly, self-assured, she has words of kindness and wisdom for everyone.
I tell her I am gathering material for a book. She gives me encouragement.
Caroline says she was also thinking about writing a book. "But there are
already so many Camino books," she adds. "How many books have been
written about love?" I ask her. "How many pictures have been painted of
hills and valleys?" Her face lights up. She might reconsider.

Soon we are shown our accommodation in groups of eight or ten and
given the low-down. Our hosts have it down pat. Although they work long
days, probably without pause from April to October, they don't look stressed.
Do they spend the winter on the Costa del Sol? I hope so. They deserve it.

The modern facilities make everything easy. The stamp in my *credencial*,
a simple shell with black contour, reflects the no-nonsense, lucid yet warm
approach to hospitality for the daily invasion of tired pilgrims, neophytes
and old-timers alike. Our dorm has the same spectacular view as the patio
above. Along its outside wall past the water fountain are large hooks under
a wide overhang for dripping rain capes. Inside are an area for shoes and
hiking sticks, lockable boxes where we can recharge electronic equipment,
and lockers (a welcome convenience since, unfortunately, thieves also
frequent the Camino). Best of all are the long benches on which we can
deposit our bags while fishing from them. We are instructed never to put
our backpacks on beds for fear of spreading little creatures that might have
hitched a ride while we rested on a patch of grass. I know what they mean.
Last September, Andrea and Cathy (a friend we made along the way) had
the unfortunate experience of learning firsthand about bed bugs. I did not
envy their weeks of misery.

We are each given a shower token (five minutes of hot water). "Dinner
at 6:30. Lights off at 10. Breakfast from 7 to 8." In our dorm are four sets
of bunks and one bed. Eight women and one man. Brave man. This is one
place he will not forget. When I bump into him a week later, and tell him he
looks familiar, he replies, "Remember the pasha in the harem at Orisson?"

At dinnertime, we file into the restaurant at three parallel rows of long
tables placed end to end. I have not forgotten the wonderful fare they served
last May. At regular intervals on the tables, huge tureens of thick soup with

chickpeas and meat awaited us, hungry pilgrims, to be followed by roast chicken, vegetables, bread and dessert, all in generous amounts. Pity the vegan! To be fair, even they get a satisfying meal. This time around, I know what to expect. The menu is different, but I am not disappointed. And of course, the large carafes of regional red wine are appreciated.

Refuge Orisson works on a system of semi-pension. Everyone who has a bed here is present. After the meal, one by one, we stand up like jack-in-the-boxes, and introduce ourselves. We hail from Australia, South Korea, Japan, China, South Africa, Europe, the Americas. Only the Middle East, India and the islands between Australia and China don't seem represented. We are the lucky ones. We have all come here for this long challenge, and each one of us will experience a different Camino. Before dinner is over, we will meet the chef and applaud him. No one leaves the table hungry; no one leaves the table lonely.

Crossing into Spain

Last May, we were six coming out of Orisson together in the morning: Chloë, Janine, and I as well as Vicki the Australian, and Randall and Joanna, the Hawaiian couple we had met at our *gîte* in Saint-Jean. Realizing Janine and I spoke French and Spanish, they had asked if they could hike with us. We quickly became a six-some. The three of them could not get beds at Orisson so they had hiked with us from Saint-Jean and, mid-afternoon, taken a shuttle back; early the next morning, the shuttle drove them to Orisson where we started out together. I enjoyed every minute of their company in the spring. This time, I am looking forward to a different experience: hiking alone at least part of the way. I know what lies ahead. I feel like a pro.

Today again, I am met by the breathtaking vista I remember so well. Outside the *gîte*, pilgrims stare at the mountains, capturing the scene with iPhones. Excited exclamations echo in the otherwise silent morning. Dense fog hovers over the valleys. For long minutes, we stand, locking the scene in our reservoir of memories. I hope we will not be turned into pillars of salt. One moment, a distant hill pokes through a cloud below us. The next, it hides behind thick fog. Nothing is still. Only us, pilgrims. No one wants to leave. It is a hard heart that would not be touched by such beauty. Truly, we are all in paradise and it is almost with sadness that we eventually leave our Shangri-La behind. But there is more ahead. I must go on.

My path is dimly lit by horizontal pink streaks from the sky. I still turn around occasionally to capture the ephemeral view, to catch my breath. I can tell that before the morning is over, I will be climbing under a blistering sun. Once in a while, I overtake another pilgrim; once in a while, another pilgrim overtakes me. Like yesterday, we pass cows, sheep and horses with tinkling bells. They look peaceful. I try not to think they will be meat. I wish I could be fully vegetarian. Paradise would have to be vegetarian, would it not?

I walk alone for long stretches, enjoying the solitude, the silence only occasionally broken by the click-click of hiking poles or the chit-chat of excited pilgrims.

Paolo Belliciari 03/07/1963 – 24/02/2019

Along the path, someone has erected a shrine for Paolo Belliciari. Against a large stone slab is a picture of a man wearing a baseball cap. He looks healthy and friendly. The picture is recent. Although tall ferns have elbowed their way between the mound of large pebbles, the rain and humidity have not destroyed it. Beside the photo, someone has placed a painting of a shell and written in Italian: 'con noi per sempre'. (You will always be with us.) This is not a good place to be in the middle of winter. I pay my respects, but I must keep going. When I was here in May, I wore scarf, hat and gloves. Today, not long after the bracken, some of it already turning pink, it is not even mid-morning, and I am shedding layers.

The emerald-green pastures are picture-perfect like last spring. Further, more large expanses of ferns make way gradually for pretty yellow gorse blossom and grey prickly thistles which give the next village its name: Roncesvalles: The Valley of Thorns. When I pass large amounts of stones strewn over the tall, lush grass or piled high, it is like going from Scotland to Ireland. And the sheep are grazing peacefully, oblivious to the humongous birds soaring above them, casting their menacing shadows over the lea: the famous griffon vultures. Roland could blow his horn with all his might, these would not fall out of the sky! They remind me of the vultures at the *dakhma*, the Tower of Silence in Malabar Hill in Mumbai where the corpses of Zoroastrians are placed for them to devour thus preventing the pollution of earth, water and fire, at the same time ensuring the survival of vultures. *Dakhmas* are the ultimate environmental way to dispose of bodies.

Breakfast en route

Today, I am selfishly wallowing in solitude. In Orisson, breakfast was included, mostly gluten, so I only had juice. After the arrow pointing to Arneguy on route Valcarlos, the one to take in case of extreme weather, I am happy to see, at the top of the hill, the providential roadside vendor with his food van where Janine, Vicki and I stopped last May while Chloë, Randall and Joanna shot ahead.

A few steps back, there was a sign in several languages, including what looked like Korean: this is the only stamp before Roncesvalles. I pick up a couple of boiled eggs, some local cheese, a banana, a drink. The grass is littered with backpacks. I hope they're not collecting fleas. Nearby, there is even a hidden area behind which pilgrims can relieve themselves. I'll pass!

As some pilgrims disappear ahead into the distance, more surface up the hill. The man with the van is doing brisk business. Few pilgrims go by without stopping. I see many fresh faces. Where do they all come from? If four hundred left Saint-Jean-Pied-de-Port yesterday morning, I assume the same number left again today. Where do they all sleep? The Camino is mysterious in more ways than one. I recognize some faces, hang around for a while and then, satiated, after stamping my *credencial* with the contours of a cross (we are near a tall memorial cross), I go on at my own pace on the same beaten path. Soon I will be on the Basque territory's Spanish side.

The Enchanted Forest

Yesterday I was warned at the pilgrim's office and by Joe at my *gîte*, not to take the more scenic, more challenging, and slightly shorter path at the

Col de Lepoeder. That path leads steeply downhill through the forest. "It's closed," they all said, in Saint-Jean and at Orisson.

Last May, unaware of the danger, I inadvertently plunged into the steep forest. It was the most beautiful part of my whole hike. For a few hours, I went down a steep slope in the heart of a stunningly unreal beech forest, its trees twisted into tortuous shapes, their trunks covered in thick green or white moss. Expecting any minute to see gnomes and trolls poking their heads out from behind the trees, I understood the meaning of the word 'enchanted'. Tolkien must have walked through such a forest. Soon, I found myself totally alone. Chloë, Joanna and Randall had disappeared a while before. Where were Janine and Vicki? Since the food van, I had been walking ahead of them. I stopped and waited. Once in a while, a hiker with long legs and tall poles would zip past me, but still no Janine, no Vicki in sight. I started getting worried. Fortunately there were frequent, well-defined large yellow arrows painted on trees, but for long stretches, I was completely alone. Where were all the pilgrims? What had happened to my two companions? A sprained ankle, perhaps? I started feeling nervous, and debated about turning back, but although I could easily manage the trail downhill, it was much too steep and slippery to climb back up. Eventually, I convinced myself that if one of them was hurt, some other pilgrim would be helping. The best was for me to continue on.

Only in Roncesvalles did I realize my mistake. Such a serendipitous mistake. Janine, Vicki and the others had arrived before me on the longer, but easier and safer path. Of course, all the time, I had Brierley's book in my bag. Blame it on jet lag. Had I looked, I would have clearly seen the two options from the Col de Lepoeder to Roncesvalles.

Weeks later, I was pleasantly surprised to find two of my pictures from the beech forest, printed, framed, and hanging on a wall in our home. Neil would have enjoyed the scenery, but he likes his creature comforts, and he would never want to prevent me from going on my own adventures. He was quite happy at home cultivating his garden, munching on home-cooked meals from our freezer, and walking the Camino vicariously through the photos I sent home from my iPod.

This time I must be wiser than last May. I have not forgotten Joe's warning. Since I've come alone, no one might know if anything happened to me. I see many pilgrims disregarding the warnings, disappearing down the 'forbidden' path. I don't know why the beech forest is dangerous today. Maybe it rained a lot recently and it is too slippery from all the dead leaves. I would probably need hiking sticks. A fall down the extremely steep side of the path could mean death. I hesitate because I was so looking forward to that part. With extreme reluctance, I take the safer path.

Ironically, I am alone for what seems like hours. I am thinking about Charlemagne. Where exactly did the brave, legendary Roland and the rest of the rearguard draw their last breaths under his command? What about Napoleon's troops? They also were around here. Hard to imagine an entire army on these passes. They were brave warriors, hardy, if also pugnacious. They liked a good fight. Nothing would deter them. The history of Spain and of Europe is bloody and riddled with wars between territories, between Romans, Visigoths, Muslims, Christians, you name it (and that is just recent history)... Even Hannibal and his elephants are said to have passed through Spain. And had the Moors won the battle of Tours on October 10, 732, our pilgrim direction might be different. We might all be flying into Santiago or even Finistere, squinting at the morning sun, our long shadows in tow, greeting each other with "*Salam Aleikum.*" No matter; it's all the same God.

Now, it is Basques, Catalans, Galicians, and others who sometimes make it seem to the outside world as though Spaniards have an inability to compromise, an aversion to peace. Yet, when we meet individual Basques and Spaniards in general, they are a warm, friendly, generous, peace-loving, and courteous people.

The safer path is along a quiet, winding country road. Strangely enough, today most pilgrims have disregarded the warning and taken the other trail. Mine is a long and difficult hike because of the burning sun and no shade until the last kilometre to Roncesvalles. The beech forest would have been much cooler.

In early afternoon, my energy is waning. Having seen no other pilgrim for at least an hour, when a motorcyclist drives by, I signal to him to please stop. I want to make sure I am still on the Camino. "*El Camino?*" he asks, shrugging, perplexed. He does not know what I am talking about. He must be from Mars. I can only go on and hope I am where I should be. It would be just like me to have missed a fork in the road.

An hour later, at the top of a hill looking down onto an observation point for migrating birds, at last, I spot a yellow arrow. Down below, the trail will take me through a flat part of my beloved beech forest. Alas, in a park between the observation area and the forest, I see no one except a lone man at a picnic table. I hope he is not one of those perverts who would follow a woman into the woods. There have been incidents on the Camino. Now I wish I had followed the others on the steeper path. I wish I hadn't read Bryson's book. I wish I knew nothing about the psychopaths on the Appalachian Trail. Safety in numbers. Maybe I can follow the narrow, paved road instead of going through the forest. It also leads to Roncesvalles. But who knows how wide the shoulders are. It might be too dangerous on the curves. After debating a few minutes, I decide to bravely cross the park, past the man at the picnic table. I plunge into the forest, throwing quick glances behind me all along the path. No other pilgrim is coming. Where are they all? I hurry, hurry. Of course, it's all in my imagination. Like when I was a child in boarding school, and the nun sent me on an errand four floors up the narrow staircase. I thought the devil was hiding somewhere waiting to catch me. That was after she had told us the story of a saint whose dog turned into the devil under his bed at night. Was it Saint Ignatius? I only recall the vision, not the saint. These stories impress a child; they leave a lifelong imprint.

I was not attacked in the forest. My man at the picnic table was only a nature lover, a birdwatcher. There is nothing like a bout of paranoia to hasten one's step. When I reach Roncesvalles after a half-hour of walking alone and at speed, past the distant sound of barking dogs, the old monastery is a welcome sight. Will I run into yesterday's friends?

Saint Ignatius

Later, I am flabbergasted to learn that Saint Ignatius was a Basque. Born in a well-to-do family, near San-Sebastian between the Camino Francés and the Camino del Norte, orphaned of both parents at a young age, he spent years amongst royalty before serving in the army and fighting against the French at the Battle of Pamplona. Severely wounded, after enduring a couple of botched-up operations, too handicapped to contemplate staying in the army, he stumbled upon spiritual literature. Eventually, he would dedicate his life to converting Muslims to Catholicism in the Holy Land. On his way to Jerusalem, while spending time at the Monastery in Montserrat in the north-east of Spain, he shed his military uniform and weapons, and donned the rough robe of the hermit. Conditions not being propitious for travel, he lived for a while in a cave near Manresa, a day's walk north of Montserrat. By the time he finally reached the Holy Land, his conversion from soldier to evangelist was complete. However, not appreciated by the Franciscans in Jerusalem, his pilgrimage was not as successful as he had hoped. Back to his homeland, rejected in the Spanish intellectual milieu, suspected of being a heretic, beaten and even imprisoned, he went to study in Paris, but it was a tumultuous time. Ignatius ended up in Italy where, with disciples gathered in France, he formed the Order of Jesuits. Considering all this took place five centuries ago, don't his peregrinations make the Camino pilgrimage seem like a pleasant summer outing?

I still have not figured out who the saint was whose dog turned into the devil at night. I'm sure it's not something the nuns invented. There were enough gory tales about saints for them to pick from in order to impress us. Maybe it was one of the martyred Jesuit missionaries in Canada during the early years of colonization.

Albergue Colegiata

At the Colegiata in Roncesvalles, pilgrims step into the twelfth century. With its arched doorways and cobblestone floors, although the monastery has been modernized, it has retained much of its charm. Its large, enclosed courtyard supplies shade or sun as desired. Spotless, comfortable and well-run by an army of cheerful Dutch volunteers, it is a welcome sight after the long hike. Many of the volunteers look of retirement age. Apparently, all of them have been pilgrims.

Last May, there was a huge line-up when I arrived. Not enough beds for all six of us. Only Janine and Vicki spent the night here. As luck would have it, for the relatively modest sum of €25 each, Chloë, and I shared a luxurious six-person, two-bathroom apartment near the Colegiata with Joanna and Randall and with two Italian cyclists, father and son, we picked up in the hotel lobby. This time, my bed is reserved at the hostel. The efficient volunteers stamp my pilgrim's passport, dole out my chit for dinner, assign me a bed. I have not paid for breakfast as I am not a coffee drinker, and breakfast is synonymous with gluten. After exploring the sprawling building, poking my nose with amazed curiosity into the large boxes of discarded clothing and equipment already abandoned by overloaded pilgrims, I locate my backpack with a dozen others near the entrance, and climb upstairs to an immense dorm. (The number of backpacks delivered to hostels will grow daily along the Camino.)

The dorm is divided into cubicles, each with two sets of bunks. On the way to my assigned bunk, I pass a man having an afternoon nap. He must have walked all the way from Saint-Jean today. His snoring can be heard from one end of the dorm to the other. Six cubicles away, I can still hear him. I feel sorry for those who will occupy the beds near him, but also for snorers who are often treated like pariahs. I have learnt to listen to the rhythmical sound of snorers rather than try to block it out. It is a trick I learnt while in Varanasi, where I had a room with a view on the Ganges. Early morning, before sunrise, chanting rose from the banks of the sacred river. I listened to it and was lulled back to sleep. Admittedly, chanting is more conducive to sleep than snoring, but I miraculously managed the transition from one to the other.

Dinner tonight is served in a nearby restaurant. At my table are a young Korean woman who does not speak English and two women from Maryland who sat across from me in Orisson last night. Victoria and Hilary have been friends for a long time. "One day," says Victoria, "I announce to Hilary that I will be walking the Camino, something I have wanted to do for a long time." "Are you kidding?" replies Hilary. "It has been my secret dream for years." So, here they are, enjoying this adventure together. They are planning on walking together to Zubiri tomorrow where I have also reserved a bed. I will probably bump into them along the way.

The service is efficient, perhaps a bit too efficient. Overworked servers scoot around in the narrow spaces between tables, taking orders from the *menu del peregrino*. There are a few choices, but no time to deliberate over them. We have just been served when another group of pilgrims starts gathering outside, eagerly waiting for us to swallow our last bite, gulp down our last sip of wine. We pay with our chit so no money needs to change hands. Dinner tonight lacks the conviviality of the smaller hostels where there is time for conversation and where we hang around for a while after our meal, taking time to get to know each other a bit, indulging a little too much in the wine. No reason to complain. The staff are doing their amazing best with the daily invasion of pilgrims in this village of less than a hundred inhabitants. We are happy to have a bed for the night and not to go hungry.

Ghosts of the Camino

In my lower bunk, I go over my day's photos. One is of a stone slab inscribed in French and Basque:

1940-1944 Orion. Brett Morton
Réseaux d'évasion et de Renseignements
ihardok, sarekoen, orhoitzapenez
Horietan: Jean Baptiste Arretche
Jean Pierre Arretche
Jean Baptiste Cristeix
Aleman Nazian torturapean hil ziren.
Horieri esker zenbait mila jende
Salbatuak izan zuren
En mémoire des membres des 2 réseaux
Dont certains sont morts sous la torture
des nazis allemands. Grâce à eux des
milliers de personnes ont été sauvées

There will be more commemorative monuments along the path. One doesn't need to know Basque or French to understand. The dates, the names, obviously Basque (were two of them brothers?) and three words: *Aleman Nazian torturapean*, any pilgrim can translate this. What some might not decipher is that thanks to these three men, thousands of people were saved. It is sobering to think I have been walking in peace and serenity along paths where so much good and so much evil have been done.

Does a Shroud Have Pockets?

Last May, while Joanna and Chloë scooted ahead from Roncesvalles in the morning, Randall, Janine, Vicki, and I brought up the rear. We were still getting to know each other. Soon, another woman about our age who was walking alone ahead of us slowed her pace and joined our group until Zubiri. Recently widowed, she was in a talkative mood. Mesmerized by her incredible life story, I must have been blind to our surroundings. I think none of us paid much attention to anything but the woman's story as she related how, forty years before, in her twenties, she had met a mysterious, charming man, very attractive, although he looked a bit old for his age. He was funny, smart, debonair, and full of great business ideas. Soon they were dating. Soon they were married. Soon they were having children.

One day, the husband confessed he was ten years older than he had told her. "Had you never looked at his birth certificate?" asked Janine. It had never occurred to her. Janine was surprised. I wasn't. I don't think I have ever seen my husband's birth certificate. I thought nothing of it. "I had never felt the need to question his age," said our impromptu companion. A clever man, her husband took care of all business, filed the income tax papers and any form requiring a date of birth. They were married for over forty years. Even after he confessed about his age, she never saw proof of it, never looked for one. Life went on as before. He was a sharp entrepreneur and a good provider. He went from one eccentric venture to another, some successful, some not so. At least that is what she guessed. He kept his business details to himself, and talked about his successes, but only by accident did she stumble upon hints of occasional failures. Once, she had inadvertently come upon a warehouse of his, filled with dusty, unsold, obsolete merchandise. And there were business trips whose purposes were never discussed. "You would be bored," he would say. I could imagine him dismissing her inquiry with a casual wave of his hand, and refilling her wineglass, until one day she understood that his business was none of her business. He was also a gambler. Big time. At least, that is what she suspected. Although they lived in Britain, she often saw wads of American dollars in his pocket. Somehow, he always seemed to come out on top. As long as there was food on the table, money for clothes, pleasant holidays, as long as all the bills got paid, she learned not to ask questions. We could tell, between the lines, that it had not always been easy. Is sharing a life with another person ever easy? But he was a loving husband and father. "I had a good life," she said. She had accepted her role, and instinctively known not to venture out of that role.

At a restaurant, she showed us pictures of him in his last months. An attractive old gentleman, smiling, surrounded by their three sons. They seemed a genuinely united family. She and the children obviously loved him. And he loved them. "He died three months ago today," said the woman.

She had a Mona Lisa smile. I wondered who amongst us doesn't have a secret, a skeleton in the closet? What had loosened her tongue? Was it the fleeting moment of intimacy amongst strangers who would likely never meet again? Was the Camino a good place to bare one's soul? Oh, there was nothing on her conscience, perhaps not even a slight embarrassment at having been duped for so long by her most intimate companion. I had the feeling that back home, while tending the rose garden he had planted years ago and she seemed so proud of, more dreams of adventure would dance in her head.

Randal and Vicki were mostly quiet during the entire conversation. I sensed Janine was not given to intrigues. I have never liked intrigues, but I didn't think too much of this since I could easily imagine many others subtracting ten years from their age if they could get away with it.

"After his death," said the woman, laughing, "I found out he was not ten years older than he had said." She paused and gave us a quirky smile. "He was twenty-five years older! He was ninety-three."

My eyes nearly popped out of my head. I don't know how long we stood there. Although it is not unusual for couples to have a vast age difference, the strange thing was it had never occurred to her, even after his initial pseudo-confession, that she was being hoodwinked. How many people carry secrets all their lives? I wondered. How many carry secrets into their graves? They say a shroud has no pockets. I believe it does. And they are full of lies.

We knew little about the woman or her husband. All that stood out now was the lie. A monumental lie. She didn't seem half as perturbed as we were. I suppose she had had time in the months since his death to get over her shock. She meant to fully enjoy the rest of her life. She would be meeting two of her granddaughters in Santiago, and they would travel around Spain and Portugal for another month. Like a bird whose cage door has been left open, I don't think she planned on settling down too soon. Marriages and partnerships need an enormous amount of compromising. I could easily see her dedication to a man she loved. In his last years, he had suffered from paranoid schizophrenia. Did I detect a slight sense of relief that she was now free, and still young enough for adventure? There was no bitterness.

Blackberries

Today, since I plan to walk alone at least part of the way, there will probably be no amazing tales to gather. But each pilgrim is a book. I have an entire month to collect their stories while enjoying the scenery.

At the entrance to the pristine little town of Burguete, I am treated to a visual feast. One balcony straddles the front of a house, red from one end to the other with large potted geraniums. I love the white houses of Basque architecture. Here, some have attention-getting scarlet doors and shutters. Others have the more typical, thick, soft-cornered brown slabs of stone inset around windows and doors. Not an inch of peeling paint anywhere, nor a weed in front gardens. Tidy four-foot high stacks of firewood line the sides of houses. Winter must be cold around here.

Hemingway stayed at Hostal Burguete a hundred years ago, but there is more to this village than its claim to fame for having hosted a famous writer. In past centuries, women accused of witchcraft were burnt at the stake here and in many other villages in this area. I would like to know what exactly constituted witchcraft. Was it a midwife saving the mother instead of the baby? Was it a barren woman? I wonder if some women with my mother's determination had found occult ways of preventing pregnancy. Decades ago, while raising six girls, our parish priest vehemently chastised Mom for practising birth-control. In ancient times, would she have been burnt at the stake? At confession, the priest told her not to return to church until she had 'stopped that'. She never went to church again, except for weddings and funerals. That was then. The Church is different now. She didn't stop us from going. She even encouraged us to go to High Mass because it lasted longer and gave her more time to indulge in her latest Buck, Agatha Christie or Nabokov. I didn't mind church, especially if I happened to sit behind a woman with a fur animal dangling from her shoulder, its beady eyes staring at me. And I was already seduced by foreign sounds. I loved reciting Greek and Latin. *Kyrie eleison. Christe eleison. Mea culpa, mea culpa, mea maxima culpa.* I hit my chest three times and repented before even being old enough to sin. Show me a kid who doesn't like rituals.

At a table outside a restaurant in Burguete, Betty with brown hair from Calgary, who turned sixty-seven two days ago, invites me to join her. She has also been walking alone. We are both ready for a bit of company. "There is even a library here," I point out, amazed because of the small population. I should not be so surprised. Spanish tradition was, on the first of May, men gave women a rose, and women gave men a book. I hope it is still observed although I suppose now some feminists might object. I hope not. Where is the frontier between gallantry and sexism? I would gladly accept the rose and borrow the book later. After all, it is the woman who chooses the book.

When it starts to spit a little, Betty and I gulp down our drinks and get back on the path. From home, my husband continues monitoring our weather. I have a weather app on my iPod, but internet is not always reliable, and I know he enjoys checking it. He follows my itinerary in my old Brierley copy, and messaged me last night to expect rain. Already I can tell it's going to be hot, and my poncho would create more heat. No need for it yet. I'll take a chance. In this area, it is often hard to tell the difference between fog and rain. A prediction of rain could easily turn out to be no more than a Scottish mist. Besides, it can rain in one valley and not the next.

Whistling Randall

Blackberries for breakfast

On the outskirts of the village, a couple of pilgrims we met in Orisson are resting on a bench, one of the many that kind Spaniards have placed along the Camino for us. We stop a minute, comment on the strenuous hike, and continue on our way, but not before another "*Buen Camino*".

My inkling was right: after less than half an hour, the fog dissipates, the weather clears. Blackberry bushes beckon. Betty and I stop to pick some. They are small but sweet and plentiful this year. The bushes are prickly and sometimes the berries are hard to reach. The prickles catch on our clothing. It doesn't matter, they are irresistible. Last September, on my first autumn Camino, after Pamplona, Andrea and I passed many patches with appetizing berries. We dared not touch them until we were sure they were edible. I know there is another tiny village a few kilometres ahead, so I empty my wide-necked water bottle and fill it with berries.

When Betty and I can pick no more, we continue along a path lined on one side with large conifers and more of the sinuous birches like yesterday. Each tree has its own well-defined personality. Only in their bark and leaves is there uniformity. It is exhilarating to be back on such an enchanting stretch. Although I had planned to walk alone, I am glad to have Betty's company. In the pastures, the cacophony of bells dangling from the animals' necks fill our ears with cheerful notes. The dozen cows and their calves look well cared for. From their emerald-green fields, they stare at us. I hope they enjoy watching us as much as we enjoy them. "How now brown cow?" I ask. There is no reply.

At a shallow stream, narrow, two-feet high cement blocks serve as stepping stones. When I hop from one to the other, I'm ten years old again. Light and liberated. I wish the stream were wider and I could hop a little longer. Today, the water is only a few inches deep. I suppose it rises higher. We often forget how much work communities and volunteers do to accommodate pilgrims. I would not like to have to wade through water early in the day and walk for hours in soaking wet shoes.

Further ahead, sitting on the grass, their backpacks beside them, are Carolyn and Karen. Carolyn has taken off her socks. She is nursing her blistered feet. Oh, my! And it is only Day 3. By some incredible luck, in my previous three hikes, I have never suffered from blisters and this time I will still be blister-free all the way to Santiago. I suspect the heavy backpacks are partly to blame. But there are others who don't carry theirs and still get blisters. I count my blessings.

In Espinal, Betty and I stop at the bakery. Of course, there is nothing for me there. I still enjoy looking. Luckily, I have never been a pastry lover. I don't feel deprived. This is the bakery where Janine, Randal, Vicki and I caught up with Joanna and Chloë on our way to Viskarret last May. I was still dizzy from the British widow's story about her husband.

Serendipity

To send our bags with the transport company, we place €5 in a special envelope with our name and destination. The bags are collected during the morning. Last May, after Roncesvalles where some of us shared the six-bed apartment with the two cyclists picked up in the lobby, we tried to book six beds at Albergue Corazon Puro listed in Brierley's guidebook in the tiny village of Viskarret, but could reach no one. We sent our bags there, anyway. If it did not exist, the delivery man would leave them at a nearby hostel.

Sometimes, if your bag arrives somewhere and they have room, they will assume you are planning on staying there. We hoped that would be the case. Otherwise we would look around the community. It should not be a problem since we weren't walking far. We would probably arrive there around noon. If there were no beds in the village, we could carry our bags to the next one.

Randal, Janine, Vicki and I should have been paying attention to the yellow arrows and getting off the road after Burguete. We missed a turn and were late meeting Joanna and Chloë in Espinal as planned. The two of them were resting on a bench, munching on baked goodies while waiting for us. Randal, Vicki and Janine went into the bakery. "I'm going to mosey on ahead," I announced. "Don't forget to look for the arrows, Grannie Dannie," shouted Chloë as I disappeared down the street.

Espinal is a long, narrow village with all its houses spread out on either side of the Camino. Before the end of the village, the yellow arrow points left past an opulent-looking area of Basque houses. I put my daypack on top of a stone gatepost while waiting for my companions. A van pulled into the driveway. A woman and her young son came out of the car towards the house, and I commented on the elegance of their property. With my French accent and my daypack, it did not require a genius to guess I was walking the Camino. "How far are you going?" she asked. "Viskarret." "Do you have accommodation there? I have a place in Viskarret." "We are six." I replied. "I can give you six beds in three separate bedrooms and a modern bathroom just for the six of you. Dinner and breakfast available if you wish."

Who says flattery will get you nowhere? When the others arrived, they were more than a little pleased at her offer. At €20 each, her price was relatively steep, but €20 for a bed can hardly be called extravagant. None of us were on a tight budget. By the time her groceries were unloaded, we had all agreed it would be the cat's meow. Her business card in hand, off we went, happy some of us had taken the wrong path that morning.

Randall and Joanna

We walked, all six of us scattered, more or less in sight of each other. Occasionally, when we regrouped, Randall, our crooner and Cordon bleu chef, entertained us with descriptions of some of his favourite meals or jazzed up our hike singing gently, "If I could reach the stars and pull one down for you…" and whatever else came to his mind. When he wasn't singing Clapton and company, he was whistling. From Espinal, we climbed many hills. I was amazed at how he could hike up a hill while whistling a tune without ever being out of breath. The only challenging parts for him were downhill. Later, he said he was born with clubbed feet. "In order to fix them, they had to put me in a pair of Forrest Gump braces in high-top brown shoes and the whole deal." I looked at his feet. There was no sign of it. They had done a good repair job, but he had to walk five whole years with the braces. "I remember hearing the doctors at the Cripple Children's Hospital tell my mom, 'He's gona be fine. If he has any trouble at all, it won't be until he's an old man.' Well, here I am, an old man on the Camino. And I'm not doing too bad."

I had a feeling he and Joanna had not been together all that long, but they were obviously a solid pair, a couple where neither dominated. Almost always on the same wavelength, yet both strong people in their own ways, they were thoroughly enjoying every minute of their adventure. Joanna took the obstacles in stride. The oldest of our group, she out-walked Janine and me. Her only difficulty was the cold. She was just skin and bones. Being Hawaiian did not help. I often lent her my rain cape against the icy breeze. With her piercing brown eyes and her easy smile, she was a joy to be with. She and Randall told us about their restaurant in Hawaii. It sounded so appealing with Randall in the kitchen when not at the piano, we all wanted to fly there and enjoy a gourmet meal in their company after we got back home. Sadly, Hawaii is a bit far for dinner out.

Chloë and I would only have enough time to walk with them up to Terradillos, a few stages before León. Later, from home, when I connected with them, Randall was proud of his accomplishment. "Made it through the Camino. Had a wonderful time. Saw two specialists when I got back. One in Hawaii and one in Oregon. They both concurred surgery wouldn't give me enough of an improvement. Basically, they both said it was just wearing out. So I got a nice American-made brace and high-top hiking shoes and I think I'm cool..." I'm sure he is. He and Joanna are hoping to hike the Camino Portugués someday.

No pasa nada

Cultivated lands and wooded areas hide in the folds of hills from Espinal to Viskarret, another well-manicured hamlet that still exists perhaps because of pilgrims. Much restoration work has taken place in this village of less than a hundred people. My pleasure at walking the Camino is magnified by the knowledge that perhaps, as pilgrims, although some Spaniards might see us as nuisances, at least, our meagre Euros help to pay for the upkeep or restoration of some of these superb homes. It was a stroke of luck for the six of us to land in the quiet and comfortable Posada Nueva. The tiny village was impeccably clean and harmonious. All its houses were white, often with wide arched doorways, shutters, and balconies.

We enquired about recovering our six bags at Corazón Puro. It did not exist anymore. A man directed us to the nearby Pension El-La. When I rang the doorbell and saw our bags sitting there in the large entrance, suddenly

I realized this *hospitalera* was also expecting us. There was a brief look of disappointment on her face. I was extremely embarrassed. Corazón Puro had changed hands; she was the new owner with the new name and a new telephone number. I apologized profusely for the confusion we had caused.

"*No pasa nada.*" she graciously replied, although her hope of six rented beds, dinners and breakfasts had vanished. I took her card and promised I would stay here if I stopped next time.

"What does "*no pasa nada*" mean?" asked Vicki. "Literally" I told her, "it means 'nothing happens', but it really means 'don't worry about it, it's nothing'; It's a friendly and conciliatory *passe-partout* expression."

If visitors in any Spanish-speaking country would learn four words or expressions, *no pasa nada* should be one of them. The other three: *Gracias* (thank you); *Buenos Días* (Hello or Good Day) and *Discúlpe* (Pardon me) if one must interrupt a conversation to ask for directions, etc... For some, even those four expressions are not easy to learn, but in Spain, as in most Spanish-speaking countries, courtesy is extremely important. It is rude to approach a stranger and blurt out a question such as "Where is the hostel?" without first saying "*Buenos Días.*" Pilgrims will be forgiven for wishing someone a good day even if it is afternoon or evening. And, one can always say "*Hola*".

Poor Vicki, sharp as a whistle when it comes to giving a quick repartee, was definitely not gifted with languages. We had a lot of banter when I tried to teach her a few words. Her tongue refused to obey. In the end, we both gave up. As for Joanna, she was no linguist either; we would have a good laugh weeks later, when Chloë and I prepared to leave the group, and Joanna realized they would be without a translator. (Janine would have had to leave our group by then.) Their panic was hilarious.

Dinner at La Posada Nueva was served at a large table: thick soup dished out of a gigantic china tureen, (the kind handed down from our grand-mothers and stored safely wrapped in old newspapers in our basements), chicken risotto, salad, bread, red wine, and dessert. Joanna, our vegetarian, was offered a large tuna salad. Vicki was missing her butter. It would take her a few days to understand that in Mediterranean countries, olive oil prevails over butter. Eventually she found some in a grocery store and kept a small container of it in our larder. (I had brought, instead of a backpack, a carry-on suitcase. The extendable part ended up serving as larder for our gang of six).

Breakfast was €5 (usually €3 in most places). Dinner also cost a little more than I was used to. Before committing to breakfast the night before, I asked for the menu. "Coffee, tea, fruit, bread and butter, jam, and boiled egg." "Orange juice?" Our hostess hesitated and, perhaps not wanting to lose the opportunity of six breakfasts, replied, "Yes, orange juice."

The next morning, we noticed guests at the next table drinking fresh orange juice, and enquired about ours. "No, no orange juice," said our hostess. As the words flew out of her mouth, she must have remembered she had promised us some. She quickly corrected herself, "Sí, sí," whereupon she disappeared into the kitchen to return with the dreadful liquid from wax-coated cardboard boxes. It was not worth making a fuss. Obviously, she had run out of oranges. Later, a cursory look in my guidebook told me she might have lowered her price to attract us to her posada. Brierley lists her accommodation at €25. Had she inflated dinner and breakfast prices to make up for it? Perhaps she had honestly agreed to orange juice for fear of missing out on the sale of six breakfasts. We had slept well in impeccable rooms with crisp clean sheets and warm blankets, enjoyed hot showers and fluffy towels in a bathroom better than mine at home... more than our money's worth. I could just imagine what that would have cost at a hotel in Barcelona.

This morning, when Betty and I pass by Pension El-La where the six of us had sent our bags in May, I wish I were staying there, but I want to walk further today. Maybe next time?

A Sad Story

No matter how many times you walk the Camino, each time is a fresh experience. Not only do you meet new people, but you never have to stay twice at the same place. The trick is to not stick to Brierley's stages. It is, of course, instinctive to do so. He has set it up so logically with each day a reasonable length, but he never meant to be dictatorial about it. In my four hikes, I have stayed in different villages, often between official stages.

Tonight will be my fourth night this September and, except for Orisson, I have not yet slept in the same dorm as last year. Maybe next time, if the weather cooperates, I will stay in Burguete, less than an hour after Ronces-valles. Or in Espinal, also called Aurizberri, a bit further.

About names of places in the Basque Country: on his topographical sketch of Phase 2, Brierley refers to the small village half-way through as Viskarreta. On his detailed map, Viskarreta loses its final 'a' and is accompanied by its other name: Guerendiain. In his accommodation section, it trades its 'k' for a 'c' and regains its 'a' to become Viscarreta. This is no fault of Brierley. In Wikipedia, I read 'Viscarret/Guerendiain (Bizkarret-Gerendiain in Euskera and officially)'. Euskera is the Basque word for 'Basque'. Google Maps uses the Viscarret/Guerendiain combination. Oh, my! Every tiny village in the Basque country and in Galicia and perhaps in many other parts of Spain seems to have gone through the same battle over its spelling if not over its actual name. If anyone asks if you have been to Iruña, the answer is yes if you were in Pamplona.

Some people don't easily concede defeat. I think of all the feuds there must have been because of a 'k', a 'c', an 'a'... To top it all, a glance at my stamp reveals a grey shell under a grey roof with the words Bizkarreta-Gerendiain. Go figure! Since Saint-Jean-Pied-De-Port, we have passed Roncesvalles/Orreaga, Burguete/Auritz, Espinal/Aurizberri... It is no different on the other side of the border: Saint-Jean-Pied-de-Port is Donibane Garazi in Basque and San Juan Pie de Puerto in Spanish. Vestiges of past feuds live on all along the Camino. I will say no more.

This is my first time sleeping in Zubiri. Before the sturdy-looking Medi-eval bridge into the village, the path veers left. That is unusual because most of the Camino Francés takes us through villages rather than bypass them. This way, pilgrims can drop a few Euros in the local pub or in the tiny grocery store.

It is easy to miss Zubiri and see only its huge, prosperous-looking and hopefully job-producing industry half a kilometre further along the path. Inside the noisy buildings, magnesium is processed into products for the aeronautical industry, the car industry, and many more. Only tomorrow morning, when I go by the refinery, will I remember passing here last May.

Betty, with whom I have been walking and picking blackberries today, has reserved a bed in Larrasoaña, the next village. Before the bridge, we wish each other *"Buen Camino"* hoping to see each other again. I have enjoyed her company, but am ready for a refreshing shower. With the sun not far past its zenith in a cloudless sky, I don't envy her carrying her backpack. She still has an hour and a half to go. Afternoon hiking is the most brutal. She has my admiration.

At my hostel on the other side of the bridge, María, my *hospitalera*, doesn't fit the mold. With her high heels and dyed hair, she seems too much of a city woman. But she has all the right qualities. She respectfully goes outside to smoke an occasional cigarette, and when a young Korean woman arrives with a humongous backpack she has incredibly lugged since Saint-Jean, María, who speaks English well, tells her to smarten up. She says it in gentle terms, but in terms the young woman will take seriously. Incredibly, the young woman's bag weighs over twenty kilos, which is why the transport service would not take it! "I am going to be travelling around Europe for a whole year," she explains. María instructs her to make a parcel and ship it to Santiago where, for a small fee, it will wait for her.

Soon, all beds are taken. In the albergue, there is no offer of a meal. At the nearby restaurant, I will get decent grub and fodder for my book. Indeed, after dinner, before settling in for the night, while the story is still fresh in my mind, I fill many pages in my notebook.

All the tables were occupied by locals and pilgrims, a couple of whom invited me and a young man to their table. On the Camino, there is often a kind of immediate intimacy I have rarely experienced since pre-internet travel. Pilgrims who, an hour before, did not know each other, bare their soul to pure strangers. The conversation skipped from one subject to another while we waited for our meals. The man and woman were not a couple. She was from Boston. Her husband had died last summer, eight years after being diagnosed in his late fifties, with premature Alzheimer's. She took care of him in their home until his dying day. "Dreaming about the Camino helped me keep my sanity," she said.

After a while, the boy joined in. He spoke softly. His blue eyes had a sadness most certainly accentuated by what he was about to tell us. Maybe he was indulging a bit too much in the wine. He wasn't drunk, but without the wine to loosen his tongue, he might not have revealed so much to three strangers. Maybe it was easier for him to unload his story on people he would likely not meet again. It was as if he had carried it all the way here, and the sooner he got rid of it, the better.

"I've never told anyone about this," he started when asked why he was on the Camino. He was an only child. His natural father had died before he was born. His mother taught pottery-making two nights a week, and his step-father had been an executive. "My father was a jerk and a hypocrite," he said, and he recounted how, on his way to a movie with friends, he had seen the man approaching prostitutes in his car. It was dark. The boy wasn't sure if his step-father had seen him. One day, soon after, the man showed him a Swiss knife, flicked one blade open and said, "This is what I would use if anyone did anything bad to me." The boy understood rightly or wrongly that he was being threatened. Meanwhile, the step-father continued finding excuses to be out in the evening while his wife was teaching. He loved to carry large sums of cash on him, and boasted that restaurant staff loved him. He always paid in cash, and always got the best table.

Every day after work, when his wife was home, he emptied his pockets of keys and wallet and placed them in a small tray on a shelf between the entrance hall and the living-room, by the stairs to the bedrooms. In the morning, he stuffed them back into his pockets.

The boy started planning to run away. What depressed him so much was everyone seemed to respect the man. At parties, he was the entertainer, the one guests elbowed their way to. "Believe me, I really understand the meaning of two-faced," he said. Running away from home became an obsession. Where to go? He didn't want to live on the street. At night, when his parents were in the TV room at the back of the house, he would tiptoe down the carpeted stairs and pull a ten or a twenty-dollar bill out of the man's wallet. He laughed shyly as he recounted this. "Even though it made no difference to him, it was the only way I could get back at him without him killing me." He hid the money in their garage. Its side door was kept unlocked; if ever it was discovered, he figured they would not know whose it was or where it had come from. Every morning, when he took out his bicycle, he placed his take in a rusty ammunition box. By the time he graduated, he had amassed more than $3,000. "It was quite a stash," said the boy, with a sad laugh, and demonstrating with his finger and thumb. "They were all tens and twenties." He worked at odd jobs during the summer. He wanted to go to university, but didn't know what he wanted to study.

"You're young," said the Dane, "don't rush if you're not ready." "That is what my mother says." An avid reader, he had always been keen on history and geography, so in July, when his step-father died following a massive heart attack, one thing led to another and he made it to the Camino. He was torn between telling his mother and trying to forget. Would she believe him? And why hurt her?

From my bed, as I scribble his story in my diary, I can still picture him, elbows on the table, his head in his hands. Suddenly, he looked so sad. I thought he was going to burst into tears. I wished the woman or the man on either side of him would put an arm around him. "Maybe by spending time alone, by the time I get to the end, I'll have decided what's best," he said. That is something I have heard and will hear countless times along the Camino.

"How does your mother feel about you being here?" the woman asked. "She is OK with it. The funny thing is she gave me the money for the flight and for the whole Camino. I don't even need to use my stash," he said, laughing shyly.

The Danish man was for him keeping his secret from his mother, and the woman for him telling her. The debate went on a bit. I said nothing. When the wine was gone, on my way out, I went to the boy, put my hand on his shoulder and wished him good luck and "*Buen Camino.*"

My Korean Escorts

The weather forecast is worrisome: searing heat by early afternoon every day for the entire week. At five o'clock, I am wide awake. I get dressed and wait for other pilgrims by the bridge. A dark curtain hangs over the town. The sky is pitch black except for the fleeting, occasional appearance of a gibbous moon playing hide-and-seek among pregnant clouds. My hike today starts through a dark area. Even with my small light, I won't venture alone.

Shortly after six o'clock, the headlamps of two Korean girls pierce the darkness. "Do you mind if I hike with you until daylight?" I ask. "Of course not," they reply in unison without further introductions. We hear menacing rumble in the distance. Thunder and occasional lightning streaks presage an interesting if challenging day, but we can only progress slowly over the less than perfect terrain out of Zubiri. I expect to arrive early afternoon in Pamplona. My poncho and folding umbrella are in my day-pack, very near the top. I love rain, so I am not worried. In fact, I much prefer rain to heat. In Pamplona, I will be able to dry my clothes if need be.

Soon, the magnesium plant looms incongruously in the distance. It is the first industrial area since Saint-Jean. Danger signs warn of heavy trucks. In the darkness, it feels eerie. We are careful to stay on the right track.

Before Larrasoaña, we stop to take photos of a large mural on an abandoned building as it slowly emerges through the dawn: green mountains with blue sky, a large coat-of-arms, a young woman and a young man in traditional costumes holding a flag between them. In the foreground, another young man plays a drum and, simultaneously, a sort of flute. The boy and the young man are wearing Basque berets. On the side, with the scenic painting as background, are friendly words: *Welcome to the Basque Country. Kultura sentitu. Feel the culture. Siente la cultura. la culture sientir.* It takes a lot of paint to welcome pilgrims in the Basque country! Below the word *Basque*, some angry person has scribbled *Spain*. Oh, the perils of multiculturalism! And there is more graffiti: *Euskonazis Kampora* and *Fuera* (Go away). And, finally, painted by a friendlier person: *"leer mas, matar menos"* (read more, kill less). No need to understand Basque to know that *Euskonazis* is not a friendly word. Has there ever been a time and place in history where all people could get along?

At Zuriáin, the sky is still heavy with clouds, but the thunder and lightning have stopped. We have escaped the rain. I stop for bacon and eggs and *zumo de naranja*, the real, freshly squeezed orange juice. We were walking in Indian file on a narrow path, almost in total silence, but the Korean girls each give me a hug before continuing without breakfast. I suppose they regarded me as a venerable elder.

The restaurant is full of young Asian pilgrims. They are a cheerful, friendly, and hardy bunch. They are almost always the first out in the morning, always carrying their backpacks and they often walk further than one Brierley stage a day.

After breakfast, I stop to decipher a blurb in Spanish and Basque by Puente Irotz across the Río Arga: some years ago, the women who had no access to the fountain in the village washed their clothes downstream. For that reason, the place was called Iturgaiz (Big, bad fountain).

Larrasoaña

Larrasoaña will not be one of my stops today. I have fond memories of the six of us here last spring. I don't remember the small hamlet itself as anything special. At least, what I saw of it: a long and narrow strip with a modest church (I didn't go inside) and not much else.

To go into Larrasoaña we crossed the Medieval Puente de los Bandidos (Bandits' Bridge) over the Arga. Hostels have proliferated there since the Camino has been revitalized. The small hamlet has survived and perhaps even prospered. It is the kind of miracle one is more likely to encounter today, not so much virgins appearing, nor saints on horses wielding swords at bad guys.

I remember well a blistering hot day last May. The San Nicolás, where all six of us slept, had a great backyard. Janine and I enjoyed an icy beer while our laundry dried in the sun. Some Koreans were concocting an enormous meal of spicy noodles, soup, and other dishes. They carried spice and condiments from South Korea. And they ate like horses. It's no wonder even the small Korean girls carry their heavy backpacks. They take their food seriously. None of this bread, cheese and *chorizzo* for supper. Not that they don't enjoy those as well. They offered Janine and me some of their food, which we gratefully accepted. Chloë and our three other companions had gone to a local pub for dinner.

Beside the San Nicolás, in the small store where I went to pick up provisions for the next day, *You ain't Nothin' but a Hound Dog* was blaring. The owner, dark and handsome, and four pilgrims busy picking up groceries broke into rock-and-roll, so I joined them. A minute before, I was drained. Where had my energy come from?

Serendipity dwells along the Camino. When we asked our *hospitalero* to recommend a good place for the six of us the next night in Pamplona, for €20 each, he suggested his friend Jesús' modern four-bedroom, two-bathroom apartment right on the Camino. Full laundry facilities, television, internet... the whole shebang. Jesús (pronounced *Hey-Zeus* with the accent on the God of Thunder) would pick up our bags in the morning. We could get there at our convenience. Jackpot! We ended up staying in Pamplona two nights, dining on home-cooked meals. It's amazing how much fun grocery shopping and cooking can be when you are hankering for familiar food. Especially when you are wise enough to hike with a Hawaiian chef.

Alfonso The Quarrelsome

Our apartment was on Calle Alfonso El Batallador. *Batailleur* in French brings to mind someone aggressive, quarrelsome. In English history, the name translates to a more honourable title: Alfonso the Brave. A friend of El Cid, Alfonso lived a thousand years ago. I suspect that legend must have found some inroads into history. If some details are to be taken with a bit of suspicion, one thing we can be certain of is he was hungry for territory. He spent his life fighting to acquire more. Conquest, sometimes followed by defeat and reconquest, characterized his reign, assuring him of a place in posterity. Fight, fight, fight was what he did. Of pugnacious temperament, he spent most of his life on the battlefront.

Alfonso also fought against his two brothers, going as far as imprisoning one who died in prison. The history of Spain is bloody and full of twists. For three hundred years, Moors and Christians had been dividing territories among themselves, and the country would remain divided for another four centuries. Couldn't God in his infinite wisdom have given us each just one little acre? At different times and in different provinces, it is said Catholics, Muslims and Jews lived in harmony, but I am not sure peace was ever the preponderate way of life for too long on the Peninsula.

The Dirty Half-Dozen

Our Alfonso is buried in Sahagún, a small town with a distinct Templar flavour a few days' walk before León. How good it is to be in Spain in more peaceful times!

Three Nuns

I wonder what awaits me in Pamplona this time. The heat is rising fast. I open my small umbrella for shade. I have only seen one other pilgrim using one on a previous hike. From the occasional positive reactions I get, I wouldn't be surprised if they started proliferating. People are funny. Perhaps if they realized that umbrella means shade-provider, instead of rain-protector, they wouldn't be so embarrassed using one. We, French-speakers, know we can use a *parapluie* against the rain and a *parasol* also called *ombrelle* (shade-provider) against the sun.

After Larrasoaña, I tread lightly along the ankle-twisting, uneven, stone-and-tree-root-encrusted path. I am enjoying the time on my own. I even pick a few acorns; they are such perfect treasures. I enjoy having them in the tip of my pocket. I do the same with tiny smooth pebbles. I can't help it. (And I have seen many others doing it.) There must still be something of the child in us.

During times of near-famine, Spaniards in this area must have been thankful for the abundance of nuts, berries, figs, mushrooms and all other gifts of nature. Depending on the season, there are snails, birds, deer, wild boars. There are also wild herbs. I run my closed fist along the tall fennel to extract its perfume. I stand there, talking to myself, one of the things age allows me to do. "Ooh, that smells nice." And I do it repeatedly until the herb patch is behind me. I hate leaving it behind. Imagine! Picking wild herbs! There is a paradise after all. And it is no wonder Spaniards are such meat eaters. Around these parts, as witnessed by the *Caza* signs, the hunting areas are vast and frequent. I hope no wild boar runs out to meet me. Andrea and I did meet one last September. It was a very dead one. But more on that later.

There seem to be more pilgrims on the Camino today than yesterday. Is it because of the topography? Our path is a long ribbon with few twists and turns, so I often can see far ahead and far behind. Except for the humid hot air which is getting heavier by the minute, it is a relatively easy trek although not without an occasional short but steep hill. The hotter the sun, the steeper the hill, it seems. While I was nonchalantly listening to the birds, admiring nature, picking acorns, smelling the herbs, the wind completely swept away the clouds; the only thing left in the sky apart from the blazing sun are the crisp, almost parallel jet trails all heading west.

The heat is now cruelly punishing me for loitering. Is it obligatory to suffer in order to be a good pilgrim? As I near Pamplona, the red line in my minuscule travel thermometer (a gift from a travel companion twenty years ago) is climbing way too high. I know I am a wimp. It's not the heat itself I find difficult, it's the humidity. Besides, I am Canadian. No one hears me complain in winter. My pace is slowing down. The temperature will go up too many more degrees before I reach Pamplona. Oh, how I long for a cool shower, a cold beer.

On a bench, in the shade, sit three old ladies. Tall and slim all three, they look serene in their patterned mid-calf skirts, pastel coloured blouses buttoned up to the neck and thin sweaters. Their white hair is short. No jewellery. Three nuns, I think. They don't wear crosses anymore? I smile at them and wish them a good day. "*Buen Camino*," they reply in unison. "May I take your photo?" I ask. "Yes. We are three nuns."

Pamplona Fourth Time Around

After the suburbs, I pop into a shop to replace my nail clipper which I have managed to lose. I was in here with Randall and Janine last May. We had arranged to meet our three companions at the Plaza del Castillo. They were already there, on a bench, waiting patiently for us. The store is huge, like a Dollar Store full of merchandise that looks great but is often of dubious quality. Older Spaniards often call these Chinese Shops. I bought my umbrella here last May. It is pink and corny. The cornier the better. Less chance of anyone lifting it. Janine, who has more aesthetic sense than I do, gently tried to steer me towards a more subdued one. "Too much uniformity on the Camino," I told her.

The air conditioning in the store feels sooo good! Since I am alone and my bed is reserved for tonight, I can spend a long time looking at every attractive gizmo that of course I don't want to buy. Like a kid in a candy store, I pick up the pretty notebooks, pens, clips, kitchen gadgets, dozens of items people rarely need but often can't resist. I examine them and put them back in their place, wondering who in the world invents all that stuff we didn't know existed yesterday, think we need today and will end up pitching tomorrow. After a while, I figure I should go back out and face the heat before the clerk thinks my loitering means I intend to filch something. My daypack, water bottle, and dirty sneakers, obvious signs I am a pilgrim, will not reassure her. I pride myself at coming out of there having bought only the nail clipper.

A few doors down, at a small grocery store, I grab a frozen treat. Oh, how good it feels sliding down my throat after this long hike. It detracts from the heat for the next fifteen minutes when, after one last hill, I check into comfortable and friendly Albergue Plaza Cathedral but not before I have pulled out a sheet Andrea and I found last year: a short list of words in Spanish, English and Basque some patriotic soul had placed in a small pile inside a shelter along the way.

Kaixo

Chloë and I stayed at Albergue Plaza Cathedral before our flight back home last spring. The young man in charge was Basque. He was tickled when he greeted us with "*Hola*" and we replied, "*Kaixo.*" I know the x is pronounced more or less like ch, so it is not difficult. I have taught myself to remember the word as a muffled sneeze (kachoo). I check to make sure. I hope it will be the same young man. Indeed, it is. It is amazing how much light can shine in a person's eyes just at the mention of one word. *Kaixo.* I suppose the use of the word by a foreign pilgrim validates who they are, what they fought so hard for. They want to preserve their identity. Who can blame them?

I dump my belongings in a locker, shower, and go for a bit of real food gathering in the nearby shops with windows like art galleries. The assortment of cured hams is to die for. One butcher shop serves the cured meat thinly shaved in tiny, environmentally friendly paper cones like the ones by the water dispensers on my childhood trains. The meat beats an energy bar. Of course, not for vegans. Once in a while, I need my fix of pork. I could never be a full vegetarian. If God didn't want us to eat meat, why did He make it taste so good?

I must admit I was disgusted in May when Randall, Janine and I walked past some attractive, sturdy-looking, spotted horses. Randall was pretty sure they were headed for the butcher shop. I hope he was wrong. Why we discriminate between one animal and another is a mystery. "Maybe because horses are often pets," said Randall. "They are very intelligent." I cannot imagine horse meat on my plate. We are evolving, and if some of us 'need' our meat, we are at least finding ways of eating less of it. Will there be a day when sheep graze for the pure pleasure of filling us with wonder at their sight? A day when horses are only pets, when cows have large expanses of grass to raise their young and share their milk with us? In a vegetarian world, might there be pigs in heaven?

Familiar Faces

At Plaza del Castillo, I am thrilled to spot some friends from Orisson. Kate Elliott, the writer from Seattle, Betty from Calgary, with whom I walked yesterday, Carolyn also from Alberta, and Veronika, a beautiful Dutch woman, are enjoying a beer under a canopy at a restaurant patio. "Danielle! Come and join us," shouts Kate.

We compare our experiences so far. It's not long before the subject veers to books and movies. We talk about *Saint-Jacques La Mecque*, the French comedy about sibling rivalry and the Camino. I love its artistry and its Fellini-like scenes of the characters' dreams. It's going on my new friends' 'movies to watch' list. Then, inevitably, we start discussing *The Way*, which I saw only after my first Camino hike. Kate, Carolyn and Veronika liked it. I loved the German and the Irish characters but felt that the mood of the movie

Cizur Menor

Zariquiegui

Uterga
Muruzábal

Puente la Reina

Lorca

Villatuerta

Estella

N

did not reflect that of the Camino. Betty did not enjoy the movie. She had a son, an only son, Stephen, a handsome young man, the picture of health, who died in a work accident in Australia. She felt the director of *The Way* did not understand the pain of losing a child. How can anyone who has not been through it fully understand? It is the ultimate tragedy for a parent.

Later, I bump into Betty again. She is staying an extra day in Pamplona. I had hoped to walk with her tomorrow. Chances are we will not meet again. I have no idea whether she would have enjoyed my company, and I know once back home, plunged back into our regular lives, it will be impossible to cultivate all these new friendships. I have her contact details, so I plan on being in touch, if only to ask how the rest of her Camino went.

Travels with Grannie Dannie

The thought of my first time in Pamplona with my granddaughter makes me laugh at myself. Chloë knew my ways. We had travelled together before. Across Canada when she was fifteen, to Norway and other European countries the next summer, to Ireland the next. For my first bout on the Camino, I was fortunate to have her along. When I asked her to accompany me, she was ecstatic. We would fly out right after her second year of university once she had finished helping her mother scrub the stoves, fridges and toilets in our student rentals. We would have time for Pamplona to Burgos. If we really liked it, we would return another year.

We had packed the minimum. At least, I had. Chloë has the strength of youth. She had proven her endurance more than once already. Five years before, she had backpacked, canoed and portaged with a group for two weeks in Algonquin National Park. The next summer, she did a week of mountain hiking in the Adirondacks where I had hiked with my own mother thirty years before. She is strong. She is also clever: on both treks, she carried the food for the entire group. Every day her load got lighter. For our first adventure on the Camino, unbeknownst to me, (and probably in cahoots with her mother) she had left some space in her backpack in case she had to carry some of my belongings.

I had studied the Pamplona map carefully before leaving home. We had a few choices. Spain is six hours ahead of us in Ontario. Usually, after an overseas flight, I check into my hotel, shower, spend an hour or two exploring, have an early dinner, take a sleeping pill and head off to bed for around-the-clock sleep. This takes care of my jet lag.

Cizur Menor, where we had reserved for our first night, was at the most a couple of hours' walk from downtown Pamplona. "We can get our first stamp in Pamplona," I told Chloë. It would be a shame to miss such a historical town." I was far from knowing then that I would be returning time and again. They say some people take one dose of a drug and become addicted. How could I know my granddaughter and I would become Camino addicts, that I would have plenty of chances to see Pamplona, that I would return in September, and that she would be with me again the next May?

Even though she should have known some of my ideas are sometimes a little hare-brained, Chloë politely kept her comments to herself. Tolerant, easy-going, she is always open to suggestions. And sometimes, perhaps too trusting of me. Although I assume with time she will learn to be less so.

When we landed in Pamplona after a change of plane in Frankfùrt and a five-hour early-morning stopover in an inhospitable area of the Madrid airport, we had been up around the clock and more. We caught a bus to downtown. Our plan (my plan!) was to have a leisurely walk to Cizur Menor. The friendly bus driver pointed us in the direction of the Ciudadella along the Camino.

I suppose a septuagenarian can be forgiven for being forgetful. The problem was I had forgotten a few things when I planned on walking to Cizur Menor: I had forgotten that as usual, after a night of pre-flight insomnia, I might be flying across the Atlantic and all the way to Madrid all bright-eyed and bushy-tailed; I had forgotten I would be carrying a heavy backpack; I had forgotten I was not twenty, I had not trained for this. And I had forgotten it might be hotter than hell in Pamplona.

It was hotter than hell in Pamplona; in a few days, I would be crossing the threshold into my seventh decade; I had not slept a wink the night before we left home, nor had I had forty winks on the flight; my backpack was heavy; I was, well... exhausted.

At least, we weren't starting in Saint-Jean-Pied-de-Port. I had read too many scary anecdotes and heard too many rumours about the horrible difficulties of that stretch. I had no intention of throwing myself into the lion's den. There would be enough difficulties between Pamplona and Burgos, I assumed. Let the braver ones hike through the mountains!

The Ciudadella is a large green park with, as its name indicates, an ancient citadel. We started walking south. Typically, in no time, Chloë had spotted our first Camino arrow. Our destination was Albergue Maribel Roncal, run by mother and son. On the website, it looked inviting. And I loved the name Maribel. It sounded like a name some French composer would use in a love song, or that of a princess in a fairy tale.

The Long Walk

After two nights of insomnia, six kilometres under a sizzling sun is a long way for an exhausted, starving, dehydrated senior carrying a full backpack. After twenty minutes in the humid air, I secretly wondered if we shouldn't just abandon this insane idea, stay in Pamplona and get a train to my beloved Andalucia the next day. How could I suggest that to my granddaughter without losing face? That was the question.

My shirt was soaked, the weight of my backpack had doubled, my eyes were scanning the area for trees with large, leafy branches that might spread over the path. There were none. I slowed my step at each of the rare and stingy little patches of shade. After what seemed like an eternity, we came upon a green open space with noble buildings of pale limestone in the distance. A sign and an arrow indicated we had reached the renowned University of Navarra. It stood a good hundred metres off the actual path. I had read about it while preparing for our adventure. Supposedly the best private university in Spain with strong ties to the Vatican, its students are mostly children of the elite from around the world. I am a curious woman. Chloë and I stopped and looked at each other. Did we really want to add steps to our already insane start? I have been accused of masochism. "Let's get our first stamp," I said. A large, crisp white shell on sky blue background, and the date bear witness to our flighty presence on the famous campus. It had added what seemed like a thousand laborious steps to our day, but I would cherish the stamp, our very first one, a reminder of my insane plans.

Now we were true pilgrims. After Calle Universidad, we crossed a short bridge over the Río Sadar. I was really dragging my feet by then. Although I refrained from complaining, Chloë knew I was already in distress. She was kind enough to say nothing. Streaks of sweat dripped over my face. I had forgotten to refill my water bottle at the airport, and there was no fountain in sight. We had probably passed one without noticing it. Any minute now, I might faint or worse. My shirt was stuck to my back. Although I had packed less than half the recommended necessities, my bag might as well have been full of melons. I knew Chloë was hot and tired too, but she was being her usual stoic self. Soon after the bridge, she suggested I give her some of my heavier items (my rain cape, sandals, toiletry bag...).

"What is that?" she asked suspiciously when I pulled out my sleeping-bag liner: a thin, white cotton envelope. "It's grandpa's liner." "What do you mean, Grandpa's liner?" "You know, when he used to stay in youth hostels." "When was that?" she asked, rather abruptly, I thought. "Well, he bought it when he was a teenager." She refrained from commenting. It was true. As an airplane spotter, when he first travelled on his bicycle across Scotland and England and on the continent, that was what he used. It had not served since 1968. "I never throw anything away."

Chloë is very polite; she just smiled. I could swear it was a little like the kind of smile I might receive down the road in a long-term care home, accompanied by 'dear'. It was already obvious that my idea of walking from Pamplona after our overnight flight with the four-hour long stopover in Madrid was plain stupid although I refrained from acknowledging it out loud. I knew what Chloë must be thinking, and I preferred not to hear it. I am not the kind to browbeat myself for my mistakes. Pinned to a bulletin board beside my desk at home is a folded, yellowed newspaper article. Only the title is visible: *Why regret is a waste of time*, by Nancy Collier. I have only read it once. The title is enough to remind me there is no use gnawing at past mistakes. I already knew this was one I would not repeat. Anyway, isn't the road to success paved with failures?

I managed another half-hour before plopping myself down on a bench. Or perhaps it was a low wall. I don't remember. Oh, how long a mere five or six kilometres can be! By now, I was sure I was about to meet my maker; my face was beet red and burning; my hair was stuck to my forehead. I could tell in Chloë's eyes she too was horrified, afraid I was about to bite the Spanish dust. I was dehydrated not only from the walk but from the last two nights. Oh, how I regretted having succumbed to too many free glasses of wine on the flight.

After we had rested awhile, Chloë generously picked up my backpack and carried it in front of her. I plodded along beside her under a cruel mid-afternoon sun. I needed more than a coolie; I needed a stretcher and bearers. My baseball cap shielding my face was acting like a hothouse on my head. And with my hair in a ponytail, my ear on the sunny side was being turned into crisp pork rind. Not a metre of shade anywhere now.

After an eternity, a welcome sign: Cizur Menor. For two hours now, I had dragged myself along interminable sidewalks, up what seemed like steep hills but probably weren't, on to the suburbs of Pamplona, and finally into the bedroom community of Cizur Menor and oh, deliverance... to Albergue Maribel Roncal!

And to think we could have sat in a pub in Pamplona, grabbed some lunch and a nice long, cold drink, and taken a bus or a taxi to Cizur Menor once we knew the hostel was open! But no, I had had the hare-brained idea it would feel good to have a few Camino kilometres behind us.

Of course, the Maribel Roncal would have to be on top of a cruel hill! Incredibly enough, Chloë, who must have also been exhausted, managed to pop a smile.

I am a person of many ideas. My father was an inventor. My sisters all have inventive minds. My children have inventive minds. An online test told me I was a visionary philosopher. I am still wondering whether this is a compliment or an insult. I often have great ideas. I often have incredibly stupid ideas. What kind of stupid idea had I had to head to the Camino? And without training! Would I meet the Grim Reaper? *Mierda!* I had mentioned over and over to Chloë and to all my family that if ever I dropped dead, it would be the best thing that could happen to me because, like most people,

I think living too long and surreptitiously slipping into dementia is a fate worse than death. Oh well, I thought, Chloë is resourceful. If anything happens, she will cope. It will give her a story to recount when she is older. And should she become a writer, *Travels with Grannie Dannie*, that should sell.

Unlike on my previous trips to foreign countries, I had wisely taken insurance. My family knows wherever my soul takes leave of me, they can have my ashes scattered there. In my notebook, I had noted the contact information for my Spanish friends. Just in case. But having to jump to Chloë's rescue was not the best way to thank them for all their wonderful hospitality during my past visits to Spain.

Maribel Roncal

The XVIII Century home of Maribel Roncal stands at the top of a hill. A hill much steeper than it would be on my next Camino hikes. Inside the hostel, dwarfed by the Northern-Europeans in line at the check-in area, Maribel and her son were busy jotting down names, stamping *credencials*, allocating beds, taking money. Hoping I would not embarrass myself or Chloë by dropping dead in front of all these people, I waited on the welcoming bench until our turn. By the end of my journey, the forest green stamp, our second, would rank amongst my favourites: two pilgrims with capes and walking sticks, a small church in the background and the attractive stone-detailed corner of Maribel's house, a proud hint of its Basque architecture.

Chloë and I were shown to our ten-bed dorm. Maribel indicated we must leave our hiking shoes under a shelf outside, along the wall. It is a good thing footwear stays outside. Not only do floors stay clean, but I would, some days later, almost be knocked out by the stench of stinky feet in one dorm.

Maribel is an energetic woman of few smiles, a no-nonsense businesswoman. Short and stocky like her son, there is a determined way about her. Later, I heard a pilgrim say, not too generously: "She must have piles of money stacked up in a room at the back." If she seemed to lack charisma, it was perhaps because the line-up of tired and anxious pilgrims didn't give her time for smiles between each registration; she did not deserve the unfair remark. She handed us each a sheet and pillowcase in sealed plastic bags. I explained that we had just flown in, that we had our own sheets, that they were spotless. She insisted we must use hers; she did not want bedbugs. She used a more delicate word. I opened the plastic bag and felt the jay cloth sheets. I waited until all the beds were rented and Maribel was out of sight, and I spread my own sheet on my bed. No way was I going to sleep on jay cloth. I assumed these were destined for the bin after one use; it seemed contrary to the spirit of the Camino. Eventually I would learn to use the jay cloth sheets, to grin and bear it!

At the end of the garden, rows of clotheslines sagged with pilgrims' merino wool and Gore-Tex. The sun was moving towards the back of the building. Soon the laundry would be in the shade. A tall, imposing, older Dutchman spread his washing neatly to dry on the large expanse of lawn in the area where the sun still shone and might cast its last rays for a while yet. By then, Chloë and I were relaxing, enjoying a bit of shade. The scarlet colour had drained from my face. Some of my energy was back. I knew by then I was going to make it. At the office, the inflow of pilgrims had stopped. Maribel and her son looked more relaxed, but suddenly, Maribel erupted into the courtyard and, pointing at the clothes on the lawn, she looked at each one of us in turn, shrieking: "Who is this? Who is this?" She was frantic, going from dorm to dorm now, pointing from each doorway to the lawn, "Who is this?" The bearded Dutchman came out of his dorm and said they were his clothes. "Take it off," she said. "Put it on the clothesline." "The clothesline is full," he replied. "Are you blind?" Maribel walked over to the clothesline and re-arranged the clothes, taking off the ones already dry. "What is the matter with you?" asked the man. "Are you my mother?" He retrieved his wet clothes, hung them on the line and, shaking his head, walked back to his dorm. All the other pilgrims in the garden looked at each other and chuckled without really waiting for Maribel or the man to be out of sight. It was our first day, but Chloë and I already knew pilgrims were no saints.

We investigated the kitchen. With its toaster, kettle, microwave, and coffee machine, it seemed a work in progress. We decided to ignore it; we would eat later across the street.

Tadeus

At the large but cozy restaurant, we shared a table with Eugenia, a gentle, middle-aged Italian who had once walked from the north of Italy to Rome. She was not ultra-religious, but enjoyed getting away for long periods of meditation. She assured us only good things would come to us on the Camino no matter our reasons for being here.

After dinner, the three of us sat in Maribel's garden and listened to a chatty Polish Tadeus with his thin, greying Dali-like moustache (Dali's stuck up, his drooped). One side of his moustache kept his fingers occupied, twirling it during our entire conversation. His head was bald, his cheeks hollow, his teeth crooked, and his complexion sallow. He chain-smoked, holding his hand-rolled cigarette inwards in his bony, yellowed hand like men used to do when I was a child. All the while he downed one beer after another, entertaining us with stories about his travels in India. We compared his journeys there with mine. It was fun to reminisce about places with magical names. Khajuraho and Orchha, Ajanta, Jaisalmer, Pushkar... He was a good person, but I was glad I had not met him on the Poorva Express on my fourteen-hour journey from Delhi to Kolkata. I can be quite chatty, but he..., he definitely had come back from his Indian peregrinations with the verbal Delhi Belly.

The temperature dropped. It started to drizzle. We headed inside to our separate dorms. Chloë and I briefly made the acquaintance of some of our roommates: four women, friends from university who had not seen each other for twenty years. They were walking together for a couple of weeks. We only whispered polite conversation for a minute or two because the others were already asleep.

Hiking Amongst Ghosts

Maps can be misleading. Half-way between Pamplona and Puente La Reina, Brierley shows an abrupt climb to Alto del Perdón. If I leave Pamplona early, before the sun is out in full strength, take my time and use my 50 step, stop, 50 step, stop technique up the hill, I should reach it mid-morning.

Since this is my fourth time on this stretch, I know what to expect. From Pamplona I will pass the tiny hamlets of Cizur Menor, Zariquiegui, and Uterga where the six of us stayed last May, and where I inadvertently went into the men's bathroom, bumping into a fellow standing outside the shower stall in his birthday suit. It was all Chloë's fault. "There is only one bathroom here," she had announced as we were dumping our bags beside our beds. I had taken her at her word, barging into the bathroom, not realizing it had a *Men's* sign on the door. "I meant only one *women's* bathroom," said Chloë in stitches when I recounted my adventure. Fortunately, the fellow was German. No big deal for him. I had muttered an apology and slipped past him into the toilet cubicle.

Today, I will sleep on the other side of Uterga, at El Jardín de Muruzábal. Despite my good intention of leaving Pamplona early, at breakfast, I chat a bit too long with Marie-Cécile and André, a French couple. I will not be early enough to hike up the hill before the heat is upon me. So be it. I only have myself to blame.

The beeline of pilgrims out of Pamplona makes it unnecessary to look for the yellow arrows or the shiny metal shells incrusted in the sidewalks, but ever since we followed half a dozen pilgrims on the wrong trail last year, I am more careful. Like lemmings, we all added a good kilometre to our hike that day before the 'leader' realized he was on the wrong path and we had to retrace our steps.

The trimmed plane trees look eerie in the darkness. With their camou-flage-patterned skins, their powerful arms and gnarly fists reaching towards a low, steely morning sky, as if shouting angry words at the gods for all the woes the Spanish people have endured, they remind me of Renaissance paintings with illustrations of hell.

After Cizur Menor, there is the occasional bench or low wall to rest on. I am bursting with energy this morning so I plod on ahead. The path is strewn with six or seven-inch stones. One soon gets used to it. And to be honest, I prefer that. Smooth paths can be boring.

Soon, it's up, up, up. My lungs are crying out for me to take it easy, the result of ten years of chain smoking from the age of thirteen. Everyone smoked in those days. My mother, my father, four of my five sisters. We put beautifully wrapped cartons of cigarettes under the Christmas tree. Our clothes reeked. Our house reeked. We reeked. The town reeked.

The Camino is a time machine for me. Today, as I ponder the history of this trail, a pilgrim resting, eyes closed, under a tree takes me back twenty years when I sat in the shade of an olive tree in Athens and closed my eyes to see Socrates and his disciples in their long white togas and thin leather sandals, debating about life, death, love, governance... For a fleeting moment, the old philosophers had come to life for me. When I opened my eyes, young mothers were irreverently licking ice cream cones while pushing modern baby carriages in Socrates' and Pericles' steps.

Here, if I close my eyes, I see a procession of armoured soldiers, conquerors, valiant or perhaps cruel souls who had nothing better to do than pick a fight, conquer land, hoping to keep a piece for themselves. I hear the clip-clop of horseshoes on large stones, the loud, panicked neighing as some brave knight in his suit of armour frantically pulls the reins of his horse to evade an opponent's lance. I imagine Christians and Moors fighting for domination following the Moorish invasion of the Iberian peninsula. That was over a millennium ago, but it will live forever in history books. It lives in names of people and places. It lives in the most refined architecture of Spain, especially in Andalucía. I even heard it said some Jews and Muslims in Morocco still have the key to their ancestors' homes in Spain. Those ancestors were chased out of the peninsula over five centuries ago. There has continued to be a string of conflicts since then. Never a dull moment in Spain. Or anywhere, it seems. Ancient and not so ancient ghosts line my path. On the Camino, I never forget I am walking in an area that has seen many atrocities as recently as during Franco's reign. With its hills and valleys, one can easily see how propitious the terrain would have been for ambush and battle. Europe is like that, full to the brim with a continuum of bloody history. Savage conquests and defeats. So, what have we learnt? Nothing. Will we ever learn? Probably not. Does travelling to another country, learning about other people, their wisdom, their mistakes, help us become wiser? I don't know. I dare hope so. At least on this trail, our invasion is a peaceful one.

This morning, in the penumbra, pilgrims from Europe and from far-away continents pass me. With their multi-European, American and far-Eastern languages, state-of-the-art backpacks, hiking boots and walking sticks, they seem more rooted in the present than in history. The windmills they will capture with their iPhones are the tall, white, imposing metal structures on hill crests. Far from most minds Don Quixote's rustic wooden windmills.

Sacred Images

Until night completely vanishes from the fields, the thousands of giant, robust sunflowers look ghostly. Their leaves have withered. The stems still stand proud, their heads, black and heavy with seeds, bent like those of penitents. Then, at the top of a gentle hill, Zariquiegui welcomes the pilgrim with its XIII Century San Andrés church, a rather nondescript brownstone building with a squat tower and a pretty Romanesque doorway. This is where grumpy Martin Sheen meets grumpy Deborah Kara Unger in *The Way*. Many pilgrims don't bother to go around the low stone wall and into the church unless they learn they can get a stamp in exchange for a coin or two, not obligatory. Donations are used towards upkeep of the church. It is a pretty stamp: a crisp, blue oval with an image of San Andrés.

Pilgrims surround the fountain at the far end of the church grounds. Time to refill my bottle. The church is not open yet. Last year, inside, one woman was horrified at the bas-relief artwork depicting scenes of torture. "What is that all about?" she asked me. "Everything in a church has history or symbolism," I told her, "but to the average Catholic, much of the meaning has been lost."

The art in the San Andrés church is definitely not going to attract anyone to the Catholic faith. In one of four main scenes of the remarkable retable, while one man, in a loin-cloth, is stretched spread-eagle on an x-shaped cross, others are busy at their task, nonchalantly tying him at the ankles and wrists with the calm demeanour of anyone intent on a job well done. Not the slightest sign of horror depicted in their gestures. In another scene, we see much wielding of weapons in the form of a hatchet, a lance, and a long knife that would pierce a man's body through his entrails and emerge gorily through his back; at the bottom, one man is being crushed under another man's foot... Looking at the artwork which, one has to admit, is beautifully created, not to say 'executed', I have to wonder. Who says the Quran is full of violence?

Around the corner from the church is the San Andrés where Chloë and I had our double room during our first hike. Sharing a wall with the hostel's restaurant, a tiny shop offers coffee, fresh baguette, fruit, sausages, cheeses... A few shelves are stocked with canned goods, olives, jams... and pharmacy supplies. Yes, some unfortunate pilgrims already have blisters.

Chloë and I had plopped ourselves down with our baguette, cheese and cured sausage at a table outside the restaurant only to be informed, along with a few others, but not unkindly, that the tables were for the restaurant patrons. It explained why a dozen pilgrims were sitting on the ground by the stone wall across the quiet street, munching on baguettes. We had erroneously assumed the shop and restaurant were all the same business.

I had gone inside and ordered hot chocolates. "Cola Cao?" asked the woman behind the counter. I had no idea what that was. She pointed to a small yellow envelope on a shelf behind her. I was presented with two cups of hot milk, two spoons, and two envelopes of Cola Cao (Nestlé Quick in our part of the world). I guessed the thick-as-pudding hot chocolate I had enjoyed in Barcelona and Madrid was not to be had here, but we could now sit legitimately at a table.

Chloë was not interested in any of the cured sausage, and I did not want to keep the rest of it in my bag, so I offered it to the pilgrims across the narrow street. One young man with shoulder-length, dishevelled hair keenly reached for it. "Thank you," he said, "I'm famished." It was then I noticed the pilgrims clad in fashionable clothing, with expensive hiking gear, were sitting at the tables; the younger ones and a few older ones who were roughing it in old clothes and sneakers had dropped their backpacks against the stone wall and were resting on the ground, filling themselves with baguette, the cheapest nourishment available. Class division accompanies us wherever we go. Of course, the iconoclast I am was not wearing state-of-the-art hiking clothes, but that was by choice, and I was glad I could afford to sit at a table.

Chloë didn't say whether she approved of my passing on the food to someone else. She knows I don't like waste. I even take my wrapped, untouched airplane food to give to street people. And yes, since airlines have to throw away everything even unopened from our trays, I save all the little salt and pepper envelopes and sometimes even the tiny butter or jam squares. I once collected a dozen yogurts on a morning flight to Mexico City. In my book, wasting food is a humanitarian crime.

Zariquiegui was where Chloë and I realized my lame itinerary was not going to work. Although I had carried my bag that morning, which might have slowed me down a little, I was still full of energy (or farting bullets, to say it in French) and wishing we had not reserved a room here. We could not have a regimen of hiking eight or ten kilometres and doing nothing the rest of the day. We had reserved in the tiny hamlet, and in the next for the next night, so we were stuck. Both restless and raring to go, we had gone to explore a bit. Chloë did not reproach me for my lack of vision. Brierley's depiction of the hill from here to Alto del Perdón had discouraged me from planning a longer hike for our first real day of hiking.

"There can't be more than two hundred people living here," said Chloë, "including all cats and dogs." Probably the only residents who spent the day close to home were those who ran the hostel and the hole-in-the-wall store. The hamlet is one of many set high amongst verdant hills and valleys all along the Camino. In the spring a profusion of red poppies colour the slopes along with other bright orange wildflowers. I could understand why people would want to retire here after a day's work. Beyond the two or three dozen centuries-old houses hugging each other, further up and around a small hill, a playground serves the children from about a dozen almost identical modern houses all in a row and with high gates. Chloë was right. By 2010, the population of Zariquiegui had almost quadrupled from less than fifty a decade earlier. The new houses were all the same style, a single developer must have built them. Close to Pamplona by car, the modern houses would have been an easy sell to someone looking for a high-quality, quiet place to retire after a day's work. A couple of bored, barking dogs were the only sign that owners would return at night. These modern houses have a splendid view of the valley. Walking back through the old part of the village we had found a similar cluster of another dozen new houses. Not a child or adult in sight. With the long mid-afternoon break, a Spaniard's working day stretches into the early evening. We didn't see any of the inhabitants in the afternoon (do they all eat lunch in town?) Before any came back from work, Chloë and I would be fast asleep. The next morning, we would leave the village having seen only other pilgrims and the people who catered to us.

At the hostel, a woman had showed us to our room, past a dormitory. We were to share a bathroom with the occupants of one other double room. We had the choice of a cramped room with two single beds, no bedside table, no lamp, but with a door. Or we could opt for the one where we could actually swing a cat or two should we be so inclined. Instead of a door, an opening the width of two doors gave anyone a view into the room on forays to the bathroom. It was easy to make our choice. The early bird... I asked for the key. Our door did not lock.

It would be no time before we realized that each hostel has its own character. Five-star seekers, better abstain. Of course, we felt rather selfish when the couple for the door-less room arrived. They were old, perhaps older than me, and the woman had knee problems. I could see they were exhausted. Their walk had been much too difficult for her. The caring husband massaged her knee at length with ointment while we compared our experiences so far. They had also started their pilgrimage (theirs was indeed a pilgrimage) in Pamplona. Going up and downstairs was torture for her. The next day must have been quite challenging up to Alto del Perdón and then down on the other side. We might have graciously exchanged our room for theirs, alas we had already unpacked and scattered our belongings everywhere.

Chloë and I wrote in our diaries and, before going for dinner, I sent a message to my husband to let him know we were still alive. I said nothing about our walk from Pamplona the day before when I was sure it would be my first and last day on the Camino.

By six o'clock, in the dining-room, all tables were occupied. We joined two other pilgrims at a table for four. Dominique, a handsome Frenchman about my age reminded me of my father. I figured he must be of the same genetic stock. Blue eyes, white-haired now, probably blond in his youth, square shoulders, tall... Most likely a descendant of Normans. He was hiking alone and was in touch daily with his wife. Across from him, Hailey, a cheerful, thirty-year-old Canadian from Edmonton, was travelling around the world for a year.

"You remind me of my father," I said to Dominique. I didn't mean to offend him. "I hope I don't look as old as him," he said. I quickly added, "Oh no, you look like my dad in a photo I have of him in his forties." That pleased him. We had a friendly conversation over dinner.

Patricia *und* Rita

I have learnt my lesson about distances. Today, when I come up the hill to Zariquiegui, I am happy to be heading to Muruzábal a few hours away, and downhill after Alto del Perdón. I have been hiking alone since Pamplona. It felt like a long climb, but since it was familiar ground, I knew what to expect and I enjoyed it. I need to catch my breath before Alto del Perdón on the sometimes challenging narrow path along the steep precipice. After the church, when I turn the corner into Zariquiegui, at one of the restaurant's outside tables, a blond-haired, rosy-cheeked middle-aged man catches my attention. "Danielle!" he greets me as though we have known each other for years, and removes his backpack from a chair next to his. I have no idea who he is.

"Come and join us, Danielle." Embarrassed, I confess I don't remember him although, with his German accent, he does sound familiar. Where in the world have I met this fellow before? "Patricia *und* Rita," he says, slightly rolling the r of Rita and pointing to his friend across from him. The penny drops. "The airport taxi!" I never cease to be amazed at how quickly bonds form between people on the Camino. Fifteen minutes in a taxi from the airport to downtown. Of course, once I leave the table and continue on to Alto del Perdón, I will probably never see them again, but how sweet it is to be greeted by my name. I feel like I own a little part of the Camino.

'Patricia' is suffering from gastroenteritis, so he is staying put for an extra day in Zariquiegui. Oh yes, he and his friend were spending time in Pamplona before hitting the trail. Did they indulge a little too much in Estrella Galicia? I hope he has a good book with him or a deck of cards because if I remember well, internet was not great here. And if these two have been together since Pamplona, what is there left to talk about?

Ars longa, vita brevis

From Zariquiegui to Alto del Perdón, in front and behind me, is a long procession of pilgrims laboriously climbing, many burdened by backpacks and perhaps the *desiderata* so many bring to the Camino. I hope their wishes will be fulfilled. After Alto del Perdón, for those of us with good knees, downhill will be a cinch, especially since it is not wet and slippery today. I had forgotten how much of an obstacle course the uphill part could be. The trail is often only wide enough for one person. Many cyclists are walking beside their bicycle. They would need a mountain bike to ride up the often deeply rutted hill, and might not even be on this stretch were it not for the famous sculpture at the top, one of the most iconic spots of the Camino.

Our way is strewn with stones of all shapes and sizes. Most are too small to serve as stepping stones, yet too large and uneven to step on them absentmindedly without danger of injury. The devil must surely lie in wait somewhere on this path if not at the bottom of its precipice. I walk gingerly. I don't want to sprain an ankle. My tensor bandage is in my daypack; it is the one 'just-in-case' that always accompanies me.

Under a blaring sun, my parasol is put to good use. Our first time, Chloë and I climbed in cold, damp weather. Long, fat, black slugs lay across the path. I don't see them today. They must be sun-shy. At first, I thought they were animal droppings, but they shone like silk. After I noticed their small antennae, we watched our steps even more so as not to crush them. I don't think Chloë appreciated the idea that some locals might find them a delicacy. I bet they once did. Later, I would come across an old woman gathering some little creatures from the path for dinner. I had once heard of a Catalan who had escaped poverty and misery, and had prospered in France, but still had a secret craving for paella with the tender and tasty flesh of rice-eating rats.

If Spaniards suffered during the Civil War, it was not the first time they did in the twentieth century. Large groups of peasants exploited by rich landowners and industrialists had been living a life of destitution for a long time before the Civil War. Some say the Second Republic which immediately preceded the Civil War was the expected reaction of an oppressed people aspiring to a more just society. Once in power, though, some leaders unfortunately made the mistake of being too reactionary, trying to eliminate all the clergy's power, forbidding the teaching of religion in schools, insisting on civil rather than religious weddings, allowing divorce, and worse, forbidding church funerals. These new laws were not going to win all hearts. Had the Second Republic been less radical, Franco might never have risen to power.

Fortunately, Spain has had more moderate governments since the Caudillo's death. It does not mean all is quiet. There always seems to be a bit of discontent simmering in different regions. Hopefully, they have learnt from the past; hopefully they will continue to fight with words rather than swords, and will never again have to suffer the cruelty of war like their parents and grandparents did.

Closer to Alto del Perdón, although many Spaniards resent them, I do enjoy the panorama of large windmills on the crests of surrounding mountains. They have a certain elegance in their movement. I also sympathize with those who find fault with them. They are an intrusion on the scenery. What is the alternative? And, to be honest, not in my garden!

From the famous peak with Vicente Galbete's tall and airy metal sculpture, the windmills are also visible. But here, the star is Galbete's art. Against the sky, on this hill crest, are depicted ten pilgrims across centuries, accompanied by donkeys and horses, even a dog. Our modern pilgrims are taking pictures, incorporating themselves into the life-size icon.

Auden asked, "Who can bear to feel himself forgotten?" *Ars longa, vita brevis*, said Hippocrates. There is probably enough vanity in each of us to want to live on in posterity. Surely posterity is a bit of compensation for mortality. At Alto del Perdón, I think how rewarding it must be for Galbete to know his labour of love will travel the world in people's photo albums, and live on long after he is gone. His sculpture has been adorning the hill since 1996 and I suspect will welcome pilgrims for centuries to come.

Revisiting Mom

The first time Chloë and I reached Alto del Perdón, we stopped to catch our breath, take pictures, enjoy the view over the valley. We met people who had walked from as far away as Germany and France. We were struck by how many were carrying what looked like overloaded backpacks. Some appeared in a hurry, as though part of a competition. A few didn't seem to be having much fun.

Little did I know then that with Andrea, I would be spreading some of Mom's ashes on this very site the next September. Mom had been an avid walker and would have loved the Camino. Sadly, the occasion never presented itself. Well, here I am, under a pitiless sun. Thinking of her. And how could I have guessed that today, on my fourth time here, I would pose with Ms DeGeneres?

Everyone is looking for shade, a rare commodity up here except at the base of the large monument across from the sculpture. And here is Ms DeGeneres. Alma unties her from her back, and stands her by her side. Soon, all the pilgrims want their picture taken with the two of them. We manage to squeeze eighteen of us in one photo. Cameras switch hands, photographers run to be photographed. Pilgrims take out their money. Alma refuses to take their donations, invites them to sign their names and directs them to the website. She has been hiking alone today, and has not stopped since Pamplona. She must have left earlier than I because I did not see her pass through Zariquiegui when I was at the German fellows' table. She looks pretty hip in her short black skirt, sleeveless top, and big brown hiking boots. Built of solid stock, not much taller than five feet, with her tanned skin, if she weren't so attractive, she would remind me of a hardy woman from an old Communist country. She is one tough cookie. No €5 backpack transfer for her. She will be meeting some of her new Camino friends at an albergue later this afternoon.

Alto del Perdón is as good a place as any to pause for lunch. I have been picking and eating more blackberries today, but I had no container to fill. I need to be careful with my water. You can never guarantee there will be a fountain where there should be one. Or that the water will be safe. In Zariquiegui, I only had a drink, but the berries have taken care of some of my appetite. In my daypack, I have an apple, corn cakes and foil-wrapped triangles of the soft cheese La Vaca Que Rie. This cow, it seems, laughs all around the world. At home, she is The Laughing Cow or La Vache Qui Rit. Alma has fruit and trail bars. We share our food with each other.

More pilgrims have arrived, so I explain again, in the languages available to me, and to whoever wants to hear it (they all do) the purpose of Ellen on the Camino. More cell phones and cameras come out. More pictures are captured. More offers of funds and signing of names on Ellen's cardboard cutout. I am amazed at how Ellen is known in Europe and even in South America and Korea. Alma can't believe I have never watched her show. To be honest, I once did watch ten minutes of it. Those talk shows must be engaging and wonderful for lonely people, bringing life into their otherwise silent living-room.

Before Alma, Ellen and I leave Alto del Perdón, I want to spend some time with Mom. She had a good run for her money. She had hoped to beat her aunt to 100. The aunt died at 99. Mom still had less than seven years to go, was living in her own home, still devouring books, not hurting from anywhere. One minute she was doing her crosswords, the next she was gone. What more can one wish for? But it does not stop me from missing her.

The descent is dangerously steep and again strewn with slippery stones. I wouldn't want to be here when rain rushes down the hill. Along with the trail through the forest to Roncesvalles, it is one of the rare occasions when I could use hiking poles. I am a head taller than Alma, and I have long legs, so my stride is longer than hers. Soon, I catch up to her. Alma doesn't use hiking poles either. We tread gingerly, squinting in the sun. We progressively strip down to the bare necessities all the while trying to remain decent. It takes us the better part of two hours to reach Uterga. On flat land, we would have been there in less than an hour. Exhausted, soaked in perspiration, we enter the village together.

Neusta and Inmaculada

At the village fountain, in the company of other pilgrims, we refill our bottles and splash ice cold water on our burning faces, necks, arms, legs. We don't care that our clothes are getting wet. In minutes, they will dry. We both have reservations not too far ahead for tonight so we rest awhile on a bench in the shade at the front of a house. Soon, a woman arrives by car with her eight-year-old daughter Neusta just picked up from school. The girl runs into the house and comes out with gifts of mandarins and small boxes of apple juice for Alma and me.

Having spent time in California, Inmaculada, the mother, speaks English well. She says the water at the fountain with the *agua non tratada* sign is better than at the one where the water is treated. Her family gets water from the *non tratada*, which is checked regularly. I assume the reason for the sign is the authorities don't want to be blamed if ever there was anything wrong with it. Last year, at a fountain with the same warning, upon spotting a villager filling a large jar, I asked him about it. He told me that yes, it was drinkable. It always seems to be. And I once saw a man in a van from a Health Unit collecting a sample from a fountain. I always ask first.

Inmaculada works with a group called *Semillas de Luz de Amor* (Seeds of light of love). It sounds very Zen. She explains its principles: live in the present; do something good every day; accept what comes to you... She is living what she preaches.

I pull a tiny Canadian flag pin from my bag for Neusta who, with her mother, wishes us a "*Buen Camino.*" We thank them for their presents and their good wishes before pouring out the water from our bottles into the nearest flower pot and refilling them at the *non tratada* fountain. Shielded from the sun with my parasol, it's time to march on again.

Buddha in the Garden of Eden

My bed tonight will be at El Jardín de Muruzábal, less than an hour's walk from here. Alma is meeting other pilgrims at a different hostel. El Jardín de Muruzábal is, well, El Jardín de Eden! the *Crème de la Crème*, the Cat's Meow. For the meagre sum of €10, I not only get a place to sleep, but I can swim in a large, well-kept pool, stretch my weary body in a comfortable lawn chair surrounded by an orchard of pear, apple, orange, peach, olive, almond, and other nut trees. Where are Adam and Eve hiding today? Oh yes, I forgot. They were chased out.

"This house was built by my grandfather; it became our *casa de vacaciones*, now it is our *casa de trabajo*," says Alicia, laughing when I ask her how she came to run this place. From vacation home to workhouse. I can see she loves her work. She is not complaining. One needs to be smart, enterprising and hard-working to stay in this business. And one needs to have the right attitude. When the Camino is quiet, at Christmas or during school holidays, (like many other albergue owners) she rents the entire place to large groups and families.

The house is large, modern, bright and airy. It doesn't cater only to pilgrims. Tonight, a few private or semi-private rooms are taken by a group of middle-aged motorcyclists. They have their own bathroom at the end of their corridor.

My lower bed is in a spacious dorm with thirteen others. Not all of them will be occupied tonight. Downstairs, we have modern bathrooms. We can also use laundry facilities and a ping pong table. Alicia tells us, dorm occupants, to use the bathroom on our floor during the night. It's normally only for the bedrooms. I imagine she doesn't want anyone fumbling for light switches and falling down the stairs in the dark.

When her husband Carlos comes home from work, he helps her prepare a generous and attractive meal for nine of us: a huge salad with fleshy tomatoes and other local vegetables, boiled eggs for protein, and *tortilla de patatas* for the vegetarians. There are also tasty pork chops, and later, ice cream. They will not get rich with the pittance they charge for such generous fare.

At the table, we are a mixture of nationalities: Koreans as always, Marie-Cécile and André, the French couple with whom I ate breakfast in Pamplona this morning, and one Irish, one American and two Spanish pilgrims I have not met before.

In the night, in semi-darkness, on my way to the bathroom, I bump head to head, or rather, flat tummy to beer belly, with a towering Buddha in the briefest of briefs I have ever laid eyes upon. Not even enough fabric in the little triangle at the bottom of his enormous paunch to wipe a runny nose. His jewels must be inversely proportional to his belly; otherwise, they surely would not fit in the tiny scrap of Spandex. The paunch alone must weigh at least fifty kilos. Is there a sheep or a grandmother in there? I have not seen him before. I would have noticed him in our dorm. He must have one of the private bedrooms. "Vere eez daz badroom?" he asks. When I get over my shock, I point to the end of the corridor and quickly avert my eyes. Not for me Buddha's G-string. Some sights are better forgotten, but hard to forget.

Christians and Moors

Puente La Reina is one of the prettiest villages between Muruzábal and Villatuerta, my destination for today. I will have some climbing to do after the famous bridge. I leave early and take it easy. Maybe I will heed Kipling's advice today: 'He travels fastest who travels alone.' If I happen to fall into step with anyone, it will be fine, but I will neither slow nor hasten my pace in exchange for conversation.

On my first hike with Chloë, I had sent my bag from Zariquiegui to Muruzábal. Nearing our destination, we both realized it was a big mistake. I had grossly underestimated my capacity for hiking, and foolishly reserved rooms before leaving home. Blame it on the dietician. Asked about my activities, I told her I walked an hour or two a day. "That is probably more than fifty times what most people your age walk," she said, so I figured three or four hours a day would be pushing it. Chloë and I had reached Muruzábal mid-morning. The climb to and descent from Alto del Perdón had taken a lot out of me, but nothing that half an hour's rest and a filling breakfast would not restore. I could tell Chloë was keen to keep going. So was I. "Perfect day for hiking," I said. She agreed. What to do then?

"Let's see if the owner would let us cancel our reservation," I suggested. My bag had not yet arrived. If we could catch the delivery man and ask him to drop it off at the next village, we could hike further after breakfast. The owner was disappointed, but since it was early in the day, she agreed to let us cancel. To make up for her potential loss, I purchased shell trinkets as presents for my other granddaughters. The transport company arrived with my bag; the driver agreed to deliver it to the Jakue at the entrance to Puente La Reina and reserve beds for us.

Early afternoon we reached the Jakue. By then, I realized I could easily walk five or six hours a day as long as we stopped for breaks. (I would eventually walk up to 27 km (17 miles)). Though I might not do well on steamy hot days, there was no doubt in my mind that it had been a bad idea to believe the naysayers who warned that one needed to train before embarking on this adventure, or that we should reserve rooms before setting out from home. Of course, if one intended to walk a whole Brierley stage daily no matter what, with a backpack, that was another story. Since this little adventure of mine was neither an endurance test nor an act of self-mortification, I could decide each day at my own whim. Fortunately, I had only reserved for the first few days.

At the entrance to Puente La Reina, the Jakue had put us in a comfortable six-bed dorm. Before exploring the small town with the famous bridge, we met our dorm companions, German sisters in their early fifties, one living in San Francisco, the other in Rome. They had not seen each other since their father's funeral two years before, and had originally planned to meet at an all-inclusive in Greece, until a friend told one of them about the Camino. "I am so happy we changed our plans," said both of them at the same time. The other two, sisters from Poland on a religious pilgrimage, would arrive late afternoon. They were going all the way to Compostela, praying for their forty-year-old brother's recovery from a degenerative disease.

On our blue stamp from the Jakue, two horsemen face each other. One looks as though he is blowing a horn. I cannot decipher the background. Its composition looks like a coat-of-arms and, superimposed on it: 1990, perhaps the year our refuge and the hotel next door opened. Is the horseman Emperor Charlemagne announcing his victory? He supposedly stayed in Puente La Reina after a victorious battle. Or maybe the stamp is of a Templar. We will be on Templar grounds all the way. There is no getting away from it: we are following in the wake of convoluted history.

The Templars were not only involved in battle. They belonged to a wealthy and powerful fraternity that built churches, hospitals and hostels for the thousands of pilgrims who came from all parts of Europe. They patrolled the Camino, and even established a kind of banking system so pilgrims would run less risk of being robbed. It is hard to imagine how it was done now that we only need to enter a code for money to pour out of a machine. They amassed extreme wealth, which would eventually cause their demise. Was there an early banking fee for their service? Or perhaps enough pilgrims succumbed to disease, bandits or the elements along the way, and the Templars' coffers grew with unclaimed gold? Did wealthy pilgrims offer gifts to their order? The banking system was just one of their many enterprises. Imbued as it is with myth, the real story of the Templars might never fully come to light, but they will continue to intrigue thousands of history aficionados. One thing is certain: we are not only on their beaten path but also on the path of millions of pilgrims straddling more than a millennium.

This morning, entering Puente La Reina for the fourth time in two years, aware that armies confronted each other in this area, I cannot help but think how sad it is that Christians, Moors, and Basques could not get along like the Christians and Moors on our dinner plates. Today's Spaniards have gained enormously from the Moors in the fields of architecture, philosophy, science, mathematics, arts, hospitality. All over Andalucía especially, the Moor's touch still lingers in the art, gardens, and architecture. Even the language is full of Arabic words.... *albergue, alfombra, alberca, alameda...* and not only words starting with *al*, the Arabic article. *Ojalá* (God willing) is derived from *Inshallah*. Throughout the centuries, the language of the Iberian peninsula has been enriched by hordes of Greeks, Romans, and Arabs, amongst others.

Oliver Schroer 1956–2008 RIP

Puente La Reina, the biggest town since Pamplona, grew by about thirty percent between 2009 and 2019 to a whopping three thousand people. On Calle Mayor (Main Street) Chloë and I found a small grocery store. Half a dozen pilgrims were busy getting provisions. Everything we wanted was available at a fair price. In fact, except for one place in Galicia, at no time would I feel gouged on the Camino. Quite the opposite. With a baguette for Chloë, corn cakes for me, cheese, apples and nuts, and something to drink, since our walking day was over, we joined the beeline to the bridge. Down below, on a stretch of grassy shore, we enjoyed a picnic lunch in the company of a dozen pilgrims.

One young hiker was strumming his guitar. Between tunes, he said he was taking a year off between high school and university. At first, his parents, both janitors, were less than happy, but he kept daily contact with them and they were coming around to the idea, even starting to encourage him. The boy looked hungry. We shared some of our food with him. Other pilgrims offered olives and nuts. One woman went back to the store and returned with a couples of apples, a stack of nutritious bars, and drinks that she offered all around. Before climbing back up to the bridge, she said to the young pilgrim, "Here, take these. I don't think I'll need them. I don't know why I bought so much." "Thank you," he said shyly as she placed the extra food and drinks beside him.

The boy was not the only one playing his music on the Camino. In 2004, Canadian musician Oliver Schroer lugged his violin along a thousand kilometres from Le Puy-en-Velay to Santiago. He 'fiddled' in churches and fields along the way. (He called himself a fiddler.) His music is divine. Occasionally one hears the church, cow, sheep, or horse's bells in the background of his recordings. Incredibly enough, at a presentation about his pilgrimage, at Queen's University in Kingston, I learnt that he was occasionally kicked out of a church for playing his violin. But most churches welcomed him. Sadly, four years after his pilgrimage, two weeks after his fifty-second birthday, cancer took the talented musician away. His music often comes alive in our home.

Breakfast at the Bidean

There was no musician under the bridge when Andrea and I walked across it last September nor when the six of us went by one early morning last May, nor will there be one there this morning. Not at this early hour. Not in this cold. Even less when the skies open up. I am salivating at the thought of a hearty breakfast at the Bidean on Calle Mayor. Now that I know its name means 'On The Way', thanks to Joe in Saint-Jean, it seems even more fitting to get breakfast there today. I only discovered it last May. I knew it would be a required port of call for me from then on.

At 6:15, in darkness, I was already on the road, leaving Buddha, my Garden of Eden, and Muruzábal behind. Although I am walking on my own, I have my headlamp, and we are a procession of pilgrims all at a reasonable distance from each other. Much of the path is along a quiet road. It is smooth sailing all the way to Puente La Reina.

The sky is behaving but looks belligerent. At the entrance, when I pass Iglesia del Crucifijo, I pause only to oblige two women pilgrims by taking their photo. The church basks in a mysterious, artificial, golden glow. Its doors are closed. The main thing pilgrims can gaze at is its arched entryway with the familiar decorative shells.

The more I dally, the more I will have to endure the mid-day heat, but I am determined not to miss a good breakfast at the Bidean. I want to revisit this art temple with its hearty fare, even if it means getting soaked later. Surrounded by a rich collection of paintings, sculptures, and art of all sorts, I almost feel as though I should be dressed for the occasion. This morning, amid the cacophony of excited pilrims, it is a pleasure to revisit the Art Nouveau stone carving of Venus with her lover, a cherub and doves at her side. In a carved, gilded frame, it caught my attention last May and again today. I remember Janine posing beside it.

Vases with fresh flowers, tapestries, antique tools complete the decor on a background of stone-incrusted walls, arched ceilings, precious wood. Even the bathroom is like an art gallery. Seeing that I hesitate to occupy a large table by myself, an Alaskan couple invites me to theirs. I am grateful for the invitation. They are finishing the last bites of their breakfast so we won't connect much. The service is swift, and my stick-to-the-ribs breakfast comes with real orange juice and real, thick-as-pudding hot chocolate.

From my seat at the back of the restaurant, I can't see outside. Soon, more pilgrims file in, dripping wet. In no time, the rumbling of thunder reaches all the way to our table. The Alaskans slept here last night. They are planning on walking more than one stage today. Pulling out their plastic capes, they cover each other's backpack with waterproof shields and, with a *"Buen Camino"* bravely walk out into the storm.

In Puente la Reina, not only the restaurant appeals to me. The thousand-year old Roman bridge over Rio Arga with its six wide arches, where a generous woman had given the young boy some of her extra food, confirms that I am walking in the steps of ancient pilgrims. Not one of us on the Camino today could measure up to their bravery. The river is wide here.

It must have been perilous in days before the queen had the famous bridge built. There would have been, I suppose, boat owners ferrying passengers across. I would not have liked to go across in a flimsy boat at times of year when it might be fast flowing. Occasionally, crossing the various rivers of the Camino, pilgrims must have wondered if they were crossing the River Styx at the hands of Charon.

My platter licked clean and belly full, I hang around a while, waiting for the rain to ease. After what seems like a good half hour, it is still pelting down. I forgot to bring my rain poncho this morning. Fortunately, I have my umbrella, and after fifteen minutes back on the path, the rain abates. The soil is drenched. In some areas, I must straddle large puddles sometimes the width of the path. I hop scotch over mud holes, careful not to slip. Sometimes all I can do is tread through them. My granny mobiles are a disaster by the time I come to gravel again. (One granddaughter gave them to me because her sister had given them that moniker the first time she wore them.) Even the laces are caked with mud now. Fortunately, by the time I get to Villatuerta, the sun will have dried them, so I can flick off the mud. One of my more elegant friends once called me a vagabond. I wonder where she got that idea.

Land Without Bread

After Puente La Reina, I have about four hours to go. Despite its many hills, this is a relatively easy stretch. Before Mañeru, the rain stops. I walk for a while with Leila and Carol from Ireland. Funny how conversations have lives of their own. By the time we part, about an hour later, I know Carol's husband chased her in grade school. I know much about Leila, and I am amazed at how much I have talked about myself. Can our lives be summed up in an hour? Well, perhaps not. We get the outlines. Fill in the blanks. We are not, as my husband would say, just hatches, matches and dispatches.

The olive trees, bamboo, grapes and large flat beans on the other side of a high fence are still heavy with large droplets. There is incessant thunder and lightning now, all noise and flashes. The rain is somewhere else in the distance. *Deo gracias.*

In Mañeru, a door is ajar. I hear a radio. I poke my head in. An old man sits on a low makeshift seat in front of a large expanse of almonds over a tiled floor. "*Buenos días*," I say. He smiles. "*Pase.*" I was hoping he would invite me in. There are almonds *ad infinitum*, enough to fill a small swimming-pool. Armed with a sharp knife, like a fisherman shucking oysters, the man is shelling the nuts and placing them into large black rubber buckets with handles. "This is your work?" I ask. "I do it because I like it. Man is not made to be idle." I am curious to know what he thinks of pilgrims. "They are welcome." He did the pilgrimage some years ago. He lets me take his picture and, after polite salutations, I'm on my way again. Without these brief connections, these vignettes of life, the Camino would have little appeal for me.

Last September, around here, Andrea and I were greeted by the slim, silky, black slugs and pretty snails with variegated brown shells, and even a praying mantis. If any of them are around today, they are hiding. I hope I haven't been squashing them under my shoes. Further is an infestation of tiny snails in white shells clinging to tall herbs. Miraculously, the blades are not bending under their weight. On some of them, I count dozens of shells. I wonder if people ever used these in soups. Too bad they don't grow on the wild dill; the locals would have their protein and seasoning all at once.

When I come upon wild edibles on the Camino, I think of Luis Buñuel's heart-wrenching 1932 documentary *Land Without Bread*. Buñuel exposed to the world a harsh reality about the poorest of the poor who survived only on what a harsh climate and hostile land could offer. Much of their diet was based on walnuts, cherries, a few other products from the soil, and perhaps a wild goat that accidentally lost its foothold and tumbled down an escarpment.

Buñuel and his crew spent two months filming in small villages in the mountains of Extremadura which translates to 'extremely harsh', and well does it deserve its name. Far to the south of where I am walking, near the border with Portugal, it is one of the most inhospitable areas of the Iberian Peninsula. Buñuel's documentary was filmed in the twentieth century, yet the unfathomable misery it depicted seems medieval.

Filth, disease, starvation, excruciating pain, were the lot of those people isolated in hostile mountains. Men and women in their thirties looking

Shelling nuts

Near Cirauqui

decades older, dying of dysentery or malaria, disfigured by goitre. Men and their mules literally devoured live by bees. Children dying in front of the camera. The families who were better off were those who received 15 pesetas a month for 'taking care' of an orphan from Ciudad Rodrigo, two days' walk away. These people were barefoot. They make the Camino from Orisson to Roncesvalles look like an afternoon outing.

Buñuel did not give statistics on longevity. From his images, one can easily deduce life expectancy would have been about thirty. Here and there stand half-ruined, abandoned hermitages. The villages are unreachable by road. Amidst this unimaginable destitution, luxurious church steeples reach up to heaven. Buñuel had a remarkable surrealist talent, yet he only depicted reality. His films convey more about life than history books ever could.

Extremadura lived up to its name then and, to a much lesser extent, still does today with its high unemployment figures. Yet, that is where the most prized *jamón ibérico* is produced from Black pigs fed on acorns. Thanks to Buñuel, the sufferings of those people will never be forgotten. One can only hope his documentary gave awareness to more fortunate people and government, and moved them to action. Part of the reason for the political currents that swept through Spain then would have been a desire to alleviate this kind of cruel, unjust poverty.

I wonder if the misery depicted in Buñuel's documentary existed also in the areas I am passing today. Here, the mountains seem less rugged, the climate less harsh. Nature seems much more generous, but when I read of peasants of old severely punished for gleaning some meagre windfall, I have to wonder. The rich shall inherit the earth?

Cirauqui and Mañeru's Festival Days

Half an hour before Cirauqui, at the end of a sinuous path, I spot the beige cluster of houses huddling together on the slope of a hill. In my memory, Cirauqui is a place with good vibes. Passing through the first arches, I understand why. Here, on a scorching hot day last September, Andrea and I landed in the middle of a week-long festival. It was Women's Day. Musicians, flutists and drummers with their traditional black Basque berets had just arrived.

Most of the women wore white, and sported red neckerchiefs. Many of the men also wore white with red sashes and red neckerchiefs. Cirauqui and the next village, Mañeru were celebrating together. Some celebrants asked to have their pictures taken with us. The women invited us to a church service, and we joined them. Later, Andrea and a young man, also a pilgrim, danced in the square while I kept watch over our belongings. Not that it was necessary, but I wanted to capture the moment on film. Singing, everyone joined hands and moved around in a circle. They then invited us to share their meal. By then the sun was high and scorching above our heads. We knew the day would not get any cooler, so we thanked them and moved on. What a delightful interlude.

Ivan and Bea's Oasis

Today, like almost every day, is full of surprises: tall, fat cacti and a palm tree seem out of place around here, but the sunflower field is a common sight. Images of the giant flowers still dance in my head from last year. I find it strange though, that despite this being my fourth time in this area, I don't remember at all the cacti or the palm tree.

Sometimes when walking with a companion, absorbed in conversation, I notice little of the surroundings. It is a good reason for walking at least some stretches alone, but the people and their stories will vanish, the scenery will remain. I remember though, further along, the series of steps. The hill is too steep to climb and would be impossible after heavy rain. Who are the kind people who built these steps for us?

The terrain in these parts can be sneaky. Of course, it doesn't seem quite so bad the fourth time around. One has a fair idea what to expect. The first time you are on the Camino, you climb a small hill, its top hidden behind deceiving clumps of trees. Forgetting you are still in the Pyrenees, you picture it flat at the top, and think within a hundred steps, there will be a long flat stretch to give your lungs a break. At the top, past the trees that were hiding the view, there is a change of direction with another climb of another hundred steps. Then, at that top, hidden behind some bushes, another turn, and it starts again, sometimes for ten or twelve consecutive turns. Patience.

Take your time. Breathe. Count fifty steps. Stop. Breathe. Onward soldier. *Carpe diem.*

At a wooden cross in memory of a Danish man, as I always do, I calculate his age. I can't help it; it's automatic. Arne Skov Schmidt from Odense died four days after his 76th birthday. Pia Vi Schmidt mourns his loss. The Camino can be a dangerous place. Life is a dangerous venture. There are plenty of opportunities on the way for someone my age to reflect on the brevity of life. There are also probably plenty of opportunities for someone like me to meet her maker... *Carpe diem* indeed.

Not long after the overpass over the busy highway, is a welcoming oasis Ivan and Bea, a laid-back young couple, have set up amid a large olive orchard. Thoughtfully, they have placed reclining chairs and logs here and there, inviting pilgrims to rest. On a couple of rough wooden tables is a generous display of fruit, snacks, bottles of water, cool drinks, and a thermos of coffee. And, semi-discretely displayed, the usual sign hoping pilgrims will be fair: *La Voluntad.* Large, bright red ceramic ladybugs decorate the base of some trees. Ivan and Bea's stamp is one of my favourites: the words Olive, Gard, and Zen, a massive tree with roots deep underground and large powerful branches reaching out at the sides and up into the sky, two pilgrims resting under it. At the bottom, a long curved snake holds the scene together. I forgot to ask what Gard means. Ivan does look Zen with his waist-length ponytail. Somehow, I cannot imagine that couple having an argument. They are too laid-back for pettiness. After stamping my passport, enjoying a refreshing slice of watermelon, I'm off. But not before they wish me "*Buen Camino*".

In the early afternoon, I manage to take the wrong path. Fortunately, this is after I spotted a couple of pilgrims having their lunch on top of a large haystack, a most bucolic scene. I shouted to them, "Hand down your camera. I'll take your picture." After, seeing me go in the wrong direction, the husband whistled a loud warning, and saved me who knows how many steps.

The hike to Lorca is easy this time around, doubtless because of the cooler weather. Last September, Andrea and I stayed in Lorca although I had mistakenly sent our bag to the wrong village. We scored a semi-private room above the restaurant. Towels were not supplied. After our shower, we used our bedsheets for towels. Thankfully, they dried before night time.

It had been a searing hot day. Under the short medieval bridge near Lorca, we had soaked our burning feet in the babbling Rio Salado and, like children, splashed each other with the glacial water. Our clothes were dripping wet. Fifteen minutes after the bridge, they were completely dry. Andrea and I were wearing only thin cotton dresses. After the bridge, her knickers had snapped on one side, and fallen to her knees. Fortunately, there was no one else around when it happened. She managed to tie a knot in them and to keep them on until destination, but not before I took a few pictures so I could use them to blackmail her should she misbehave.

Mad Dogs, Pilgrims and Englishmen

If I have reserved a bed at the Casa Mágica in Villatuerta today, it is for a good reason. Neither Chloë nor I will forget the first time we were in that little town. That morning, without bothering to reserve, I had sent my bag to Lorca a good hour's walk before Villatuerta. We had relaxed a long time in the shade of the olive trees in the Zen garden. Alas, in Lorca, it was 'no room at the inn'. We had no choice but to grab my bag and carry it to Villatuerta. Without my asking her, Chloë had kindly taken out some of my heavy items and moved them to her bag, so with my lightened backpack, after a lunch of paella, we left Lorca remarkably cheerful, sure to find accommodation in Villatuerta. I had read about The Casa Mágica. It sounded perfect. "Let's hope there's room for us there."

Maybe without our backpacks, it would have been bearable under the cloudless sky, but with our loads, and on the shadeless path without even the hint of a gentle Zephyr, it soon felt brutally hot. After a long hour, my step got slower and slower. My shirt was drenched under my backpack. It was mid-afternoon when we dragged ourselves into Villatuerta with its quiet streets. Only mad dogs, pilgrims, and Englishmen go out in the noonday sun. In fact, it was way past noon but the sun peaks later in Spain because the country is on the wrong time zone. Logically, it belongs on the British time zone, but to please Hitler and to make communications easier, Franco kept Spain on the same time zone as Germany. And now, I assume, with the European Union, it must be easier for trade. The result is late sunrises and sunsets. And two o'clock noonday sun.

A sign at the entrance to Villatuerta says 'Albergue Casa Mágica 500 metres'. We already knew that in Spain 500 metres meant anything but 500 metres; it is only there to give you hope. We could not find the next arrow. Chloë was tired. Her feet were blistered. Carrying much more than her load, she too was drenched in perspiration. Fortunately, a nearby park offered shade. "Sit on this bench," I told her, "I will enquire." Armed with my parasol, my Spanish, and my optimism, I found a pub where a man gave me vague directions to Casa Mágica. They always make it sound so easy, but how could anyone give precise directions to a maze of buildings? I found the bridge. A child directed me to the famous Casa Mágica. No way it was only five hundred metres from the sign at the entrance. I mean, has anyone ever seen a sign that says 'Albergue 585 meters'? They paint a sign saying '500 metres', and find a spot somewhere, anywhere, to post it. Or do metres grow longer at the end of a day of hiking up and down hills under a beastly sun? There must be a law of physics, a formula accounting for packages getting heavier and metres getting longer as the day progresses, including a factor for weather.

In the inviting, spacious entrance to the Casa Mágica with its cushy armchairs, a dozen backpacks awaited their owners. After a long wait, a woman showed up at the desk. "*Buenas tardes*. Do you have two available beds?" I asked in my best Spanish and with my friendliest smile. "Sorry, we are all booked." The gavel came down hard. Guilty of not reserving! To the Guillotine!

She turned and walked back to where she had come from without a word of courtesy. I felt like Elizabeth Smart in Grand Central Station. I just wanted to sit down in one of the armchairs and cry. If only she had said it in a compassionate tone, it might have made a difference. Or would it?

I was standing there, debating what to do when three pilgrims came in to the Casa Mágica (Magic for them maybe. Not for me). The woman came back to the desk. I let her register her guests who had been smart enough to reserve, and reluctantly, asked if she would kindly call and reserve two beds for us in Estella, an hour away. She suggested one in Ayegui at the exit from Estella, and secured a reservation for us at the San Cypriano. I forgave her initial curt answer to my request. Looking back now, I imagine she must have been busy and overworked in the kitchen, getting dozens of pilgrims' dinners ready. It would not be easy with the constant interruptions from arriving pilgrims. And she had probably already turned away many other disappointed hopefuls. *Hospitaleros* and *hospitaleras* have to multitask. They are usually amazingly patient and obliging. Like everyone else, I suppose they have their moments. I must learn to be more tolerant.

This time, I am not worried. I have a reservation. It will be my second time staying here because last May, the six of us had wisely reserved at Casa Mágica. In the airy lobby today, pilgrims are welcomed with a huge container of icy water and large glass tumblers. Ensconced in a posh leather armchair, I enjoy every drop of the water sliding down my throat while the *hospitalera* registers pilgrims ahead of me, stamps their *credencials* and disappears upstairs with them. They will be my roommates tonight.

Surely this only happens to me: I have the same bed as last May. And it's the best one in the best dorm. Six beds, no bunks. This is my lucky day. The Casa Mágica ranks amongst my favourite places to stay on the Camino. The natural stone walls, beamed ceilings and ceramic tile floors give it its magic feeling. The lobby floor is embedded with smooth, oval stones (beautiful, but a killer of bare feet). Many antiques adorn the walls. Whoever transformed this building into a hostel has combined the atmosphere of the old with modern amenities without sacrificing history. It carries its name well.

The Casa Mágica seems to serve two clienteles: at the front, up the stairs, are spacious dorms on two floors. Mine is on the first floor, which of course we, Canadians, would call the second floor. The bathrooms are bright and spotless and have lots of shower stalls. Downstairs, at the back, past the laundry area and the clotheslines, I discover the pool. Although it is small and above-ground, one could certainly have a refreshing dip in it. Above, on a long balcony, a couple of hammocks are strung between pillars. The area reminds me of hostels in Central America. Maybe it is designed to cater to the younger clientele? When the six of us were here in May, I must have been exhausted because I didn't see any of that.

My dorm companions, a couple from Western Canada, an Australian couple and the husband's sister, are all retirees. Each couple sleeps in an alcove while the sister-in-law has a bed in a more spacious area with mine. Although we only exchange a word or two, I immediately sense a collision of atoms with the Canadian couple. It happens. I can't help it. I feel more tired than I should be. Maybe that explains it.

I stow my belongings on my large shelf, hand-wash my clothes, and while they dry on our balcony, I curl up in bed for a short nap only to wake two hours later with a sore throat. Drat! I never get sick at home. On the Camino, I must have less resistance. I was sick on my first and third time. Only when I came with Andrea did I stay well the whole time, while she suffered with a stomach ailment and bug bites. Oh well, it will pass. After dinner, I stretch out on my bed and read for a while before falling asleep for the night.

In the morning, my sore throat has vanished. I leave in darkness with the Australians who are fast-walkers. I don't mind. I have lots of energy. In Estella, I stop for breakfast at the restaurant-cum-gift shop where Janine and I ate last May. She knew my 71st birthday was coming. While I wasn't looking, she purchased a beautiful diary for my Camino notes, which she would produce three days later.

As I approach the counter, two women are tying on their aprons; they are still getting things ready when more pilgrims walk in. We are seven or eight at the counter now. The women run from one customer to the other at a frenzied pace, never complaining, always managing a smile. Sadly, more often than not, pilgrims leave no gratuity because they have read it is not required in Spain. All the more reason for foreigners to leave a few coins.

Estella is a picturesque mid-sized town. Our first time through, after finding ourselves homeless in Villatuerta, Chloë and I had caught the last bus to Ayegui, which had taken us through a modern, uninteresting part of Estella. We had returned home convinced Estella was an unsightly town, better skipped. Last September, with Andrea, although we had erred from the main path, we arrived at the historical area with its narrow streets and old stone facades. This morning, knowing how easily I miss an arrow, not wishing to find myself alone on the wrong path in darkness, I am grateful for having started out with the Australians.

Ayegui

Monjardín
Luquín

Los Arcos

Torres

N

Fellini and Mastroianni

After breakfast, I continue alone until Irache, much of it steeply uphill, bypassing Ayegui, where the *hospitalera* from the Casa Mágica had kindly reserved a room for Chloë and me and where we had been entertained with some quite bizarre, perhaps even tall tales. Down the hill, at a large grocery store, we had met a Korean woman and agreed to combine our purchases. When I asked her name, she hesitated one moment and then blurted out, "Maria." We all three burst out laughing. *Maria* was obviously tired of being asked her name, then asked to repeat and spell it, which doesn't help Westerners to pronounce it. Maria it would be.

Together, we had bought too much food. At a table next to ours were two old fellows (in fact, they were much younger than I). We invited them to join us. They had already eaten, but with a bit of overindulging and some wine to make the food go down, betwixt the five of us, we licked our platters clean.

Our improvised dinner companions were Italian. They had met on the Camino, where they had both been *hospitaleros*. As so often happens, their friendship had sprouted during one encounter. A year later, they walked the Camino together. They entertained us with what later in my bed, I suspected might have been tall pilgrims' tales. Following Nietzsche's advice, instead of summoning sleep which every insomniac knows doesn't obey orders, I reviewed my day, not quite step by step but almost. Only then did it occur to me that the men had told us their names were Federico and Marcello. Really? Was there not a twinkle in Federico's eye? I couldn't remember. Had they been pulling my leg all along?

Because we meet so many people on the Camino, I usually try to make an association with each name. There would be Catherine the Great; Ivan the Terrible; Georges Pompidou.... Chloë is the Chloë of Daphnis and Chloë; Andrea, of course, was a female Botticelli; I get people to remember me as Daniel in the Lion's Den. That evening, I had forgotten to do that. Only in reviewing my day did I realize we had shared our meal with Fellini and Mastroianni... Our two dining companions had enough material to make a Camino movie. I had mentioned I was planning on writing a book of vignettes about the Camino someday, and they had entertained us with amusing tales about pilgrims they had hosted as volunteers.

There was the couple who slept in the same bed for warmth. Nothing too new on the Camino. There was a heavy man who had crashed through the bed, and an eighty-year-old Hungarian who went back to the wrong bed after a nocturnal trip to the loo. The legitimate occupant (a woman) had also gotten up and was in the women's bathroom. Upon her return, only when she tried to slip under the blanket did she feel the lump in her bed. In shock, she jumped out screaming, banging her head on the metal frame above, waking the whole lot of pilgrims. The dear old man, not realizing he was in the wrong bed, seemed not to understand what the fuss was about. The problem was he only had a few words of English, and she spoke only French. Eventually, with multilingual pilgrims to the rescue, the woman accepted the old man's apology and there had been no need to call in the Guardia Civil.

There was also the cocky pilgrim who had arrived wearing someone's jacket. She swore it was hers until the rightful owner pointed out her initials were on the label on the inside seam.

There was a pilgrim who went to put on her boots, only to realize they were a size too small. Someone must have accidentally left with hers. How she managed that day, God only knows. (In Burgos, at the Casa del Cubo, I would witness a pilgrim desperately looking for his hiking boots which had vanished.)

Marcello and Federico's best tale (their tallest?) was about two couples in their fifties who decided to divorce two-thirds of the way to Santiago. I bet that happens a lot. They had met in Orisson on their first day, and had been walking as a foursome since then. The wife of one couple, a philosophy professor, and the husband of the other, also a philosophy professor, were rather slow hikers while their mates, two lawyers, were fast and energetic. The slow hikers had been more or less dragged to the Camino by their partners. From Orisson to Roncesvalles, they climbed and descended along the challenging path as a foursome. Annoyingly fast for our philosophers, annoyingly slow for their mates. The next day, it was hard going again for the philosophers. Lagging behind, they agreed to meet their partners at a particular hotel.

From then on, all four of them left together in the morning until their paces set them apart and the one picked up the pace of the other's mate. At the end of each day, they met at a hotel. Soon, the wife of one walking with the husband of the other became routine. "The rest is history," said Marcello, laughing. The irony is both couples had come on the pilgrimage hoping to fix their marriage. They celebrated their plans for divorce and new unions with a dinner in Santiago, with other pilgrims as their guests. That is where Marcello had learnt their tale. "I'll drink to that!" I said.

Later, I wondered if the tales were true. In retrospect, they did seem rather tall. The two friends had entertained us for a while. Their yarn would have been long enough to knit a couple of scarves for wintry mornings. As my Italian friend would say, *se non e vero e ben trovato* (it might not be true, but it's a good find). I would never know their veracity. Did it really matter?

The next morning, as Chloë and I walked out into a chilly morning, *Maria* came running after us. "Wait, wait," she shouted, and produced two colourful dolls smaller than my baby toe, handmade of twisted and knotted thread. Chloë attached one to her pack. I tied mine to my bag where it still hangs today. We hugged, and each went on at our different paces. Soon, *Maria* left us in the dust, or to be more truthful, on the large pebbles covering our path. Sadly, we did not come across her again. With her photo and her gifts, we will never forget the beautiful stranger from the other side of the world.

Jesús the Blacksmith

After Estella, I will have the long, flat-topped mesa on my right, the vines on my left. If I am lucky, there will be figs. The grapes are plump and plentiful, ready for harvest. I stop at La Forja de Ayegui, the large open blacksmith's shop in Irache, to say hello to Jesús, the owner and artisan. As usual, he wears his wide smile, his blacksmith's thick leather apron folded down at the waist to expose a t-shirt with the shop's logo. His smile is of a man who enjoys life. One might expect a blacksmith to be a giant with big muscles. Jesús' arms remind me of my father's, strong and sinuous, but he is not a big man. Like him, Dad enjoyed his manual work. As long as it presents problems to solve, manual work is often more satisfying than desk work.

Jesús the Blacksmith

Without the distraction of obstacles, life can be a long, interminable wait in the doldrums. Jesús, the blacksmith, produces art. That means a constant solving of problems. No wonder he wears a permanent smile.

The shop is immense, its front wall open. Pilgrims, out of breath from this morning's climb, float in and out. Tourists who visit the wine bodega next door must be his best customers for the large art pieces. Jesús is not working as much at his art these days. He produces most of it in the winter when the Camino is quiet. A fine balance.

I love a workshop. This one reminds me of my grandfather's where one after the other, my sisters and I would stand on the imposing scales. He would move the weights into the notches along the arms until the verdict was given. "Growing like weeds!" the aunts and uncles would say, as though it was not the most ordinary thing for a child to grow. In Jesús' workshop, piles of wood are stacked near a hearth and two stone fonts in the centre of the forge where he heats, shapes, and quenches the iron. A dozen long-handled tongs hang with old horseshoes on a bar by the fire pit. Tools from his father, his grandfather, his great-great-grandfather? They might be the same ones, unchanged. In the pit, a fire is burning, its smoke escaping up a conical chimney made from an inverted metal pail decorated with a half-metre iron sunflower with yellow centre. Its petals, long, sharp, irregular pieces of black metal jut out in all directions. His work is playful. His shelves are stacked with dozens of six-inch high, twisted iron pilgrims with walking sticks, each one different. Some are like the Pillsbury man. A foursome displayed around a miniature table with chairs reminds me of my kids' plasticine days. Snails, shells, candle-holders, locks, whatever his imagination fancies, they are all here. Outside the wide entrance to the shop, within reach of passing pilgrims, is a display of his forged pendants. No two are the same. Everything is handmade. Business is brisk. Inside, a large bowl of plump figs beckons us to help ourselves. And of course, I avail myself of the shop's stamp.

It used to be if your father was a blacksmith, you apprenticed as a blacksmith. If he was a shoemaker, you became a shoemaker. That system still lives on in parts of India with the Caste system, but our Western world has changed. Now, a *Zapatero* (shoemaker) can be prime minister of Spain, and an *Obrador* (a workman) president of Mexico. This blacksmith is happy in his ancestral trade. Lucky are they who can blend work with fancy. Jesús belongs to the fortunate few who earn a living doing what they love most. For him, this is play, not work.

Next door, the sign by the free wine fountain says (in English): 'Bodega de Irache invites the pilgrim to have a swig of the wine and thus continue the tradition of the Benedictine monks... Bodega Irache implores for a reasonable consumption of wine... daily wine provision for the fountain is a hundred litres... please let the ones after you enjoy their swig.' Sadly, many pilgrims abuse the generosity of the winery, filling large bottles while others wait. Later, I find a half-bottle of wine discarded on the side of the path. Each time I have stopped at the fountain, I have witnessed such behaviour.

Two Old Ladies

On my first two Camino hikes, I stayed at Albergue Villamayor de Monjardín in a hamlet of the same name halfway between Estella and Los Arcos. With Chloë, by the time we got to Villamayor, I had caught some sort of bug. Alas, today, by the time I pass the wine fountain, the beast that reared its ugly head last night at Casa Mágica, and that I thought had vanished this morning, has just returned. My throat is sore. My cough is just starting. Drat!

Last May, Chloë, Vicki, Randall and Joanna had secured four beds in the nearby dorm run by Dutch volunteers. When Janine and I arrived, it was 'no room at the inn' anywhere in Villamayor. It had been an arduous hike. Like two stubborn brats, hoping for a miracle, we refused to budge. Not one to be defeated so easily, while Janine sat at the nearby pub, I investigated around the village to see if anyone might rent us a room. A local girl directed me to a private house with rooms for rent. The owner was expecting a group of four pilgrims. If they had not called to confirm or arrived by five o'clock, she would let us have two beds. At five minutes to five, her guests arrived. Perhaps sensing our despair, the kind Dutch volunteer, a man our age, offered to call the *hospitalero* in Luquín, a couple of kilometres away. "I have two old ladies here who need beds for tonight," he said without a hint of humour. When Janine and I, and all the pilgrims who were relaxing outside finished shaking with laughter, he kindly drove us to the pretty village of Luquín on an alternate path.

Going Hungry in Luquín

In Luquín, Janine and I filled in time exploring the church by the albergue. Upstairs, on the organist's seat, a large threadbare cushion was propped up by a couple of thick books. Curious, we lifted the cushion. One ancient, decrepit volume had beautiful illustrations, elegant calligraphy and golden-edged pages. The inscription on the inside was dated 1923. Alas, it had been unceremoniously demoted to a mere practical bottom prop, its disintegration exacerbated each time an organist plopped their behind down on it.

In the hostel was a tiny kitchen which a couple of gargantuan pilgrims commandeered while preparing an elaborate meal for themselves only. They were in front of the stove for almost two hours. It never occurred to them to invite the rest of us to throw in an extra potato or two and to share with us who were being deprived of the possibility of cooking. I had to make do with corn cakes and cheese from my backpack while Janine ate nuts and dry fruit. At least we could look forward to filling up on breakfast since we had signed up for it and it promised to be plentiful: fresh fruit, coffee, hot chocolate, juice, bread, jams, the whole shebang. There was a coffee machine, kettle, toaster and microwave. Our *hospitalero* had set the breakfast table before going home at ten o'clock. He would only be back the next day, after we had all left, to clean and get ready for the next horde.

In the grand breakfast room the next morning, Janine and I were met by total darkness. A pilgrim had dropped water in the toaster, causing a short-circuit. We searched in vain for a fuse box. Adieu coffee machine. Adieu kettle. Adieu toaster and microwave. At least we had fruit and juice, and those who could eat bread left with a full belly. There was even a variety of the little cakes individually wrapped, often part of a pilgrim's breakfast. The table had been set with tablecloth, china, and silverware. There would have been lively conversation stimulated by the elegant table and generous fare. Janine and I looked at each other, shrugged, grabbed some fruit, and went our way.

Pair'o'Gringos and Perrogrinos

Many pilgrims stop for a break in Villamayor. The small grocery store stocks a good variety of foods. As witnessed by the already overflowing large garbage and recycling containers near it, it is doing brisk business with pilgrims today.

This time, I have smartly reserved at the Villamayor de Monjardín. When I arrive, it is still closed, so I have plenty of time to relax on the bench by the church. It is hard to forget that church, not only because of its beauty but because its bells seem to ring on the hour and half-hour around the clock.

Frank and Sonya, a Florida couple resting on the bench, will go on to another village. "Would you like me to take a photo of you?" I offer. "We are not *peregrinos*," says Frank, with a cheeky smile. "Really? You could have fooled me." "We are a *pair'o'gringos*," he says, laughing, with his exaggerated accent. "That's nothing," I tell him, "I met a *perrogrino* this morning." He obviously understands Spanish because he immediately knows I mean the dog (*perro*) accompanying a pilgrim. They too talked to the dog's owner. I wonder if she gets tired of everyone who passes her, commenting on her small friend. I would find it tiresome. She walks at a gentle pace. The terrier's short legs are going like mad to keep in step with her. I hope she carries it sometimes. I'm sure she does. He's not ten inches high. Everyone can tell how much she loves her companion and how much it enjoys being with her.

On the bench in the shade with the *pair'o'gringos* is a heavy, amorphous young Danish woman hiking alone. She is finding it much harder than expected. "I am in love with the Camino, but am not in great shape," she says, shrugging sadly. "I hope I'll make it to Santiago," she adds, clearly not convinced, between two puffs of her cigarette. Another woman, Holly, is from Ohio. She turned forty-five three days ago, but looks a decade younger. Quite overweight also, she is not used to hiking either. Her pack looks heavy. Crushed by the heat, she worries she will not get a bed in Los Arcos, her destination today. "You can call and reserve," I tell her. Just then, the delivery van arrives with my bag. "What is he doing?" asks the Danish woman. Neither she nor the other woman knew about the bag transfer service. Quickly,

Pair o' Gringos

they run to the driver who kindly takes theirs. A call to Los Arcos to reserve beds, and the two of them tackle the rest of today's hike together.

Others have seen me take the *pair'o'gringos'* picture. Now I am solicited to take shots of them by the picturesque church portal. The San Andrés is nearly a thousand years old. It is closed today. I remember its humble yet beautiful interior. When I was inside last year, a ray of light perhaps from a side window illuminated the agonizing Christ on the crucifix. It is the kind of event a believer might interpret as divine intervention. Today, the church is closed so I can't go in and see if the same phenomenon would happen again. It was probably caused by an artificial light from within the church. Some miracles are better not scrutinized. Meanwhile, a small queue is forming at the door of my albergue. A young Korean woman is at the front of the line. Since I have a reservation, I don't bother to line up. I don't really care whether I have an upper or a lower bunk. Instead, I decide to investigate the Dutch albergue at the top of the hill where last May, the volunteer referred to Janine and me as old ladies. Kim, an Australian woman about my age, is waiting for it to open. When I mention that not only is my iPod dead, but I have lost my cord, she spots a socket on the wall and lets me use her own cord. Later, her husband Karim arrives. On his face, he wears the scars of a terrible accident, a fire perhaps. It has not obliterated kindness from his eyes. Kim and Karim have been enjoying the Camino. I will bump into them again tomorrow morning in Los Arcos.

Karim is not the first one I meet with a scar, but most pilgrims' scars are invisible. Two women I met on previous hikes told me about the sexual abuse they had suffered from their father starting in early childhood. I suspect many pilgrims have suffered such fates. "I loved you so much," said one father in his defence. He had died in old age after four years of incarceration. Decades later, she still wore the scar. "You never get over it," she told me. Her entire family had turned against her for denouncing him. They had even turned her sons against her. "I'll take my pain to my grave," she told me, "because I can't bring myself to forgive him." She hoped her pilgrimage would help her heal. She desperately wanted to forgive. Some-times pilgrims remind me of a procession of Fellini's characters with hiking sticks click-clicking in cadence along the stony path. Everyone looks quite normal, but the burdens some carry would sink a ship faster than a stone coffin containing the bones of Jesus' disciple.

Back down the hill, when Leticia, our *hospitalera* arrives, we are eight or nine ready to check in. We plop our bottoms on the couches while she gets her ledger ready. When she asks who was first in line, we point to the Korean woman but, seeing we are all older, the girl insists on letting us all go before her. This is not the first nor the last time I find this kind of courtesy from young Koreans.

Leticia only speaks Spanish and English, so I can help with a group of French pilgrims on the telephone. Worried, they are calling to say they will arrive late. She promises to hold their beds, thanks them for calling. So many pilgrims reserve beds, don't show up and don't bother to cancel. Don't they realize this means a loss of income and perhaps another pilgrim turned away? Now, most places will ask for confirmation if we have not arrived by a certain time. Reservations not honoured are the bane of *hospitaleros*.

A Good Samaritan

Once settled in, I go downstairs to use the kitchen. Peter, from Devon, has just arrived. He reminds me of Michael Moore but in a tamer and tidier version. Sweating profusely, visibly exhausted, with a sigh of relief, he drops a bulging, old-fashioned backpack near the entrance, plops himself down on a sofa and, with a wrinkled handkerchief, wipes the sweat from his forehead. While Leticia is showing pilgrims to their dorm upstairs, he tells me about the kindness he encountered last night.

"It was nearly ten o'clock. I was coming into Estella. A Spaniard pulled beside me in his car and asked if I would like a ride. I was exhausted by then and more than happy to accept. In the car, he asked if I had eaten. I told him I had, but he insisted. He thought maybe I was just being polite. When he was convinced I was telling the truth, he drove me to the hostel. It was after ten o'clock. The *hospitalero* was standing outside, smoking a cigarette. He said the place was closed."

The Spaniard insisted, and after an animated argument, the man relented and accepted to let the pilgrim in. Since all the dorms were full, Peter slept in a large room by himself. This morning, when he stepped outside, the good Samaritan was waiting for him. He had done the pilgrimage to Compostela. He knew that for some pilgrims, it is important to walk every step. He asked Peter if he wanted to start from there or would he like a drive back to where he had picked him up, which Peter accepted. "I'll never forget," said Peter, moved by the Spaniard's kindness.

The Bells of Villamayor

I am in a six-person dorm. In the other bunks are two retired Swedish couples hiking as a foursome. Men above, women below. A young Korean woman (not the same who let us go first at reception) will sleep in the bunk above mine. Around 9 p.m., as she is rummaging through her backpack, one of the Swedish men jokes that our room looks like a seniors' home. Already tucked into our beds, we all burst out laughing. "And we have our cute little nurse," I say, perhaps politically incorrectly. Now we are all roaring with laughter, including our 'nurse' who, after rearranging her bag, goes out to explore the village with the other Korean pilgrim. At San Andrés' ten strokes of its bell, downstairs, our *hospitalera* leaves the premises, locking the door behind her. Ten minutes after, I hear a faint voice outside my window, gentler than a cat's meow, hardly louder than someone trying to blow out a candle, but supplicant. "Hello. Hello," the voice calls, rising up to the dorm, hoping to attract the attention of someone still awake (you can count on me for that!) but not wanting to wake anyone. At first I don't register the plea. When I finally do, I come to our little balcony, see the two girls standing there, distressed, and signal I am coming down. When I open the door, they are literally hopping with joy. "Thank you, thank you, thank you," they keep whispering excitedly. For a few panicky minutes, they had thought they would be spending the night outside. Now, they can't stop giggling. "Thank you, thank you." I have no doubt their little escapade will make it into *their* diary. Sleeping under the stars is not a great prospect in an area where the temperature plunges drastically during the night. These girls are natural gigglers. In the afternoon, when my drying underwear flew off our balcony and got stuck in the upper branches of a tree, I had to borrow a pilgrim's hiking pole to fetch it. That got one of them giggling away. It's nice to see such great spirits.

Our dorm is on the second floor, across from the belfry. Every half hour, I am reminded that *tempus fugit*. I use Nietzsche's trick again (revisiting all my actions today; did I make a positive contribution?) Sleep is never fooled. The last time I hear the bell, it tolls twelve strokes. In the morning, I wake at one peal; half-an-hour later, it is five peals or is it six? I lie there, hoping without success to catch another forty winks. Eventually, defeated, I drag myself out of bed, feverish.

I was not well my first time here either. A well-meaning British woman had insisted on nursing me and hovered over me until I had to feign sleep. "Have you had enough liquids? Do you have a fever? Have you such-and-such medication with you?" "Yes" I said, lying. My Florence Nightingale was a generous soul who could not understand the meaning of "I am fine." I could see her husband rolling his eyes in the background. It was obviously not the first time she thrust her unsolicited help upon an innocent victim. God bless her generous soul.

I must have been in the same room because I remember the superb view towards the church and over the hills. And I remember the bells. Oh, how I remember the bells! Despite feeling rotten again this morning, I am glad there is no Florence around.

I force myself to eat breakfast, swallow some aspirin, and off I go. I should be able to pick up some cough syrup at a pharmacy. I will walk five or six hours to Torres del Río today. I know that is more than I should, but except for the last stretch before Torres, the terrain is not too taxing. I hope for the best. Deep down, I wish I could stay curled up in bed. There won't be much spring in my step today. Am I being punished for being so unkind in my thoughts to Miss Nightingale last year?

Orion

I slept at Casa Mariela in Torres del Río on each of my previous three hikes. Today I will try a new place, the Pata de Oca (the Goose's foot). There is plenty of manna on the way to supplement my breakfast: soft, ripe figs and big, juicy blackberries are there for the picking; it's still dark, but I can see enough to stop and stuff my face. Orion watches over me, up there, over my left shoulder, assiduously every autumn morning when the sky is clear. I loved walking here at daybreak in the spring with our long slim iconic shadows leading the way. At this time of year, the sun will rise much later. We get a double-treat with the starry morning sky and the sunrise.

I always carry a thin cloth bag. This morning, I fill it with fresh, plump figs from a wild tree. I don't know it yet, but they will be my supper tonight. Lined with wild herbs, vines, olive and fruit orchards, not to mention all the nut trees, this is one of my favourite legs of the Camino. I run my closed fist along a bunch of wild herbs and inhale the perfume. Aroma therapy. It is easy walking this morning and, despite my rough night, while the aspirin is having an effect, I'm on a little stretch of paradise.

Field Workers

One thing is missing: on our first hike, Chloë and I passed field-workers. In the distance, men and women, each wielding some tool which I could not identify, bent over high mounds of brown soil. They wore gloves and heavy jackets. Bandanas held back the women's hair as they toiled in the middle of an immense, undulating field, the land beyond them still covered by large plastic tarpaulins. We stopped and stared, wondering what they might be harvesting. Or were they planting something? From the distance, there was no sign of vegetation. It was only May; what was ready to be harvested in May? I shouted in Spanish to see if one of them would answer. Only one gloomy-faced woman turned around; she looked at me as if to say, "Go away, mind your own business," and went back to work. "Maybe she doesn't understand Spanish," I told Chloë. "They must be migrant workers. From Morocco, perhaps. Or more likely from Eastern Europe." No other pilgrim showed any semblance of curiosity. Am I nuts or what?

On closer inspection, I saw the workers slicing through the plastic with sharp knives and pulling out long white stems. Then it occurred to me that in early May in Germany, I had feasted on tasty, fat, white asparagus and boiled potatoes with melted butter, served with thin slices of smoked ham.

Harvesting white asparagus

It was everywhere on the menu at that time of year in Berlin, in Dresden...
The main midday fare almost always seemed between it and the traditional
huge pork hock. In France, the white asparagus is even deemed a noble vegetable. Strangely enough, in Spain, only once did I see it in a grocery store
and once, on a menu. Are they mostly for export? It would not be the only
time a country grows delicious produce its people don't eat because they
can't afford it or simply because it didn't use to be cultivated on their land,
and they have never acquired a taste for it.

It was a damp and grey morning. Chloë and I were shivering, but it was
still beautiful. The poppies' petals were closed like tantalizing ladies-of-
the-night wrapping their scarlet cloaks around themselves. We wondered
what it must be like for the workers in the field watching us, a bunch of lazy,
privileged people whiling life away. I could not imagine the kind of work
where I would have to do the same repetitive movement all day long. My
back ached just thinking about it. Once in a while, it is good to remember
our privileged life; it helps to loosen up the purse strings when solicited.

The path is stony now. In some areas, instead of large vineyards and
homogeneous yellow fields, the occasional olive tree stretches its crooked
old limbs erratically in all directions while birds sing happily.

Los Arcos

A bit more than half-way to Torres, Los Arcos boasts about a thousand inhabitants and lots of accommodation. It is the end of a stage for pilgrims who
do it by the book. At the entrance is a small yard with goats and chickens.
On the high wire fence, a hand-written sign asks for donations to help feed
the menagerie. When tired pilgrims pass the farm animals, their mind is on
finding a place to stay, shedding their hiking boots, showering and taking
care of their blistered feet. Most ignore the sign. They step around the lazy
dogs sleeping on the path without even attracting each other's attention.

It was quiet when Chloë and I arrived early afternoon. I would not have
guessed I would pass through here three more times. Each time, I might see
one or two old people in their dark coats walking out of a stone row house,
but it was hard to imagine the streets really coming to life except for the

constant passage of pilgrims. Unfortunately for the people who live here, their day must be filled with the click-clicking of hiking sticks against the hard stone path. Too many pilgrims don't bother to muffle their poles with rubber tips. Uninterrupted from April to November, how irritating it must be for the residents. I find it hard to imagine how a pilgrim can hike almost eight hundred kilometres, accompanied by that sound.

That first time with Chloë, a glacial wind swept down Calle Mayor, chilling us to the bone. It was almost mid-May, yet I was wearing hat and gloves, and this, in a country tourists imagine sunny and warm. The Camino is not the Costa del Sol. The weather at the foot of the Pyrenees can be harsh, and the temperature curve very steep during the day. Some mornings, we start dressed for winter, but there is always room in our backpack for the clothes we will be shedding under the brutal mid-day sun with its clear sky and perhaps, if we are lucky, a couple of floating puffy white clouds for an occasional respite. Only Magritte's bowler hat is missing in those moments. The heat will then linger for five or six hours, and as fast as it had come, we will be plunged into a frigid night with starry sky. That day with Chloë, the weather curve was flat. Flat and cold.

The people who live in these small villages are from hardy stock. There is a sense of continuity here, and I find it strange to think some might be descendents of ten, twenty, or more generations who dwelt in the same villages, perhaps in the same houses, trod the same cobblestones, worked the same fields, and at least until relatively recently, followed in their father's footsteps. They became farmer, butcher, baker, candlestick maker until a new society did not need those trades anymore, until the goods on offer at the weekly outdoor market at Plaza Santa María were mostly imports come by ship from China, Bangladesh, Vietnam or other far-away countries, loaded onto large trucks, and downloaded into warehouses, trickling down eventually to the weekly stalls of the market vendors.

There might still be a village baker or a butcher. With the developing awareness of the need for food we can trust, hopefully their days are not numbered. The fruit and vegetable produce at the market might be local, but there is no guarantee of that either. The redundancy of ancient trades is responsible for the decline in population of the villages and towns we pass.

Let sleeping dogs lie

A hundred years ago, about 2,200 people lived in Los Arcos. Now, they are less than half that. Although we pilgrims are not big spenders, I hope we contribute to some stability of population.

Los Arcos lives up to its name: *arcos* means arches. There must be a hundred arches fronting the buildings all around this town, charming and gloomy, depending on the weather. However, *arcos* also means bows. Some say the town is named Los Arcos because of the master archers who, centuries ago, won it for the king of Navarre against the kings of Aragon and of Castille. I find this quite an interesting coincidence, if it is true, because although there are many buildings with arches in the villages we pass, Los Arcos boasts more than its share.

La Casa de Austria

In a shop window along the main street, a mouth-watering display of pizzas calls to the pilgrim. Each one is a work of art. Inside, the pizza lady and I had a minor altercation because she falsely assumed I was taking photos of her fare. I said to Chloë, "Let's get out of here. We're not getting any of her pizza. I'm sure there are friendlier places in this village."

It took us a while to find our hostel, the Casa de Austria. There were signs for Casa de la Abuela (Grandma's house), Mesón de Gargantua, Hostal Ezequiel, and many others. Everything but Casa de Austria. We walked up to Plaza Santa María, the village square with its arcades and namesake church. The narrow restaurants were overflowing. While a procession of restroom-users slipped in and out, at tables outside, shivering pilgrims warmed their hands around their hot cups while hardy servers filled orders and stamped *credencials*. Few pilgrims pass through Los Arcos without stopping.

In the plaza, the open market was wrapping up. Vendors seemed eager to go home and warm their frozen fingers. I have seen the same market in one town one day and in another the next. For the locals, it beats having to drive to the next village. At a table nearby, a waiter was berating a French customer. Hammering the table with his index finger, he tried to explain without much success that it belonged to the restaurant in front of it, and since she was patronizing the other restaurant, she would have to move to

one of their tables. Eventually, after gesticulations galore, the pilgrim understood. Sighing loudly, she grabbed her backpack and poles, and moved to
another table. Chloë and I were lucky to find two empty chairs inside where
we ordered hot drinks. Later, searching for our night's abode, we were once
again whipped from all sides by the penetrating icy wind. Eventually, a local
gentleman pointed us in the right direction. Less than a block north of the
plaza, we had passed the side street where stood the Casa de Austria. A large
fountain at its entrance clearly marks the spot. Neither of us had thought to
glance sideways down the lane.

In the lobby with its peeling yellow wall and small plaster angels, antique
armchair, wooden bench, and modern coffee table, a pilgrim is welcomed
by a plethora of signs in different languages, a sculpture of the Virgin Mary,
and a two-foot wide plaster sculpture of two eyes. A low limestone wall pro-
trudes at the base of the modern wall with its typical blue and white tiles.
The miscellany of objects give the place a hippy aura. It had us wondering...
Would we be scratching like mad on leaving here? No, our room was lovely
and clean, with only four bunks. As usual, Chloë insisted I take the lower
one. In the other lower bunk, an old couple were having an afternoon nap,
the two of them snoring gently in cadence, snuggled inside one sleeping
bag for warmth. They never used the upper bed except for sorting out their
stuff. How can I forget that night? All night, he would snore. All night, I
would cough.

After some time under our blankets, wearing our coats, hats, socks, gloves
and I, leggings under my trousers, trying to stop our bones from rattling,
we had braved the cold once more in search of something to eat. Alas, it
was too unbearably cold out on the plaza and, inside the small restaurants,
not a seat was vacant. Neither did the menus appeal to us. Chloë, I figured,
still had visions of pizzas dancing in her head. Dragging my tail between
my legs, we headed back to the pizza lady... She had probably had hundreds
of pilgrims through since we had first come in. Her shelves were emptying
fast. Busy as she still was with a long line of hungry customers, she didn't
seem to remember our little altercation, nor did she refuse to serve us. Chloë
got a tasty pizza while I made do with cans of olives, tuna, corn cakes, and
a piece of humble pie.

Carmen and Günter

Later, tucked again under her warm blanket, Chloë read while in the kitchen
I met Carmen, another French-Canadian also living in Ontario. She was
hiking with her arthritic husband. His hip was acting up, so he had gone to
bed. There was also forty-year-old Günter, a machinist from Germany. He
had come here alone. He asked me if I believed in God. "You would first have
to define God for me," I told him. He looked downtrodden and confessed he
was sick of the Catholic church; he felt hostage to it. Haltingly, as though he
might burst into tears, in broken English he said he had to contribute to the
Church directly from his pay. "Why don't you tell them you want to stop?"
I asked. If he did, he said, he would be excommunicated. His English was
minimal and my German is quite rusty. I am not sure I understood correctly.
Did he really mean 'excommunicated'? It is a harsh word in the Catholic
Church. Perhaps 'shunning' was what he meant, but that is not either a word
one learns in German 101. What I understood was if he left the Church, his
family and friends would not talk to him anymore. He needed that money,
and it made him angry to have to give it to the Church.

I understood his dilemma, and I felt sad for him. "I am happy we don't
have such a system in our country anymore," pitched in Carmen. "The
Church has finally lost its grip on us." Like me, she had grown up in Quebec,
where our parents were even told who to vote for by the priest. Now the
Church has lost most of its adherents in Quebec. "They kept repeating to
our parents that we were made for a *'petit pain'*" (literally, for a small loaf
of bread), she said. I had also grown up hearing that we, French-Canadians,
were born to be the workers, the cogs in the industrial machine. We were
not to have outlandish ambitions. The English, (the Protestants), lived in
fancy houses with gardens; their children each had their own bed, even their
own bedroom; they had orthodontist appointments, took ballet and violin
lessons, went to the seaside in the summer, got university degrees. They
had the keys to power. They owned and managed the gold and silver mines.
They ate steak; We ate beans and pea soup. Though it seemed strange talk
on a pilgrimage road. It would not be the only time this kind of discussion
arose when French-Canadians of a certain vintage met.

This was Günter's fourth pilgrimage. He and his wife wanted children, but it had not happened. He feared she would leave him. Although he did not want to contribute anymore to the Catholic Church, he still believed in God and hoped by offering this sacrifice of a pilgrimage, his wish might be granted.

Mother and Son

We were sitting at a large table. A Californian asked if she and her son could join us. They were celebrating his university graduation. "The Camino is something I wanted to do for a long time," she said. "I am so lucky my son also wanted to do it." She was proud this kind of holiday appealed to him more than "gallivanting around European cities." They were both dedicated environmentalists. The son had not bought a new piece of clothing in three years. "Everything he is wearing is from second-hand stores, even his shoes." "Join the club," I said, laughing about my granny mobiles. We went on lauding the virtues of second-hand shopping. "It is so much more fun," I said. "You have all the different labels in one place. At a fraction of the price." We knew full well that if we did have all those fancy labels, we had them a couple of years later. "Who cares! At least, we are not using new materials," said the son, but we all had to admit we felt guilty at the frivolous way we pollute by flying. "The plane will cross the sea whether or not you're on it," pitched in a pragmatic Carmen. In a way she was right. It is a conversation I have had many times. There are always ways to justify our own behaviour.

We talked for a long time. Before I left the table, I went over to the other side and gave Günter a long, warm, motherly hug. I think he needed it. "Trust in God," I said. I had no idea why I said that. They were the only words of consolation I could find to say to a believer. Then, braving the glacial wind one last time, I went out to buy a box of cereal and a litre of milk so I could have my gluten-free breakfast. On the milk container, I wrote: Please do not take. *SVP ne pas toucher. Por favor, no tomar. Bitte, nich nehmen.* I stuck it on the bottom shelf at the back of the fridge. In the early morning, when I went for breakfast, it was gone! Grrr!

Leaving Los Arcos on our way to Torres del Río, the sky was dark grey. Like the day before, more bone-chilling wind swept the path. I think Chloë and I were both expecting to meet, around the corner, coming out from under an arch, one of Victor Hugo's miserable characters. I wouldn't have been surprised to see Quasimodo's face popping out of an upstairs window or, swaddled in grey, mended rags, his tortuous shape silently brushing against the walls of the Calle Mayor on his way to ring the church bells at the Plaza de Santa María.

The Camino, a metaphor for life itself, presents us with a series of obstacles interspersed with smooth sailing, or vice versa. I must have been feeling terribly sick then as now because usually, no kind of weather can dull my spirits. Except perhaps excessive heat. I love a storm: the more thunder and lightning, the better. In winter, I wrap up and walk out into polar weather, a smile on my face. But that day, I just wanted to leave that cold and damp place behind. I took with me the memories of all those lovely people I had met: the tenderness of the French couple snuggling in the bed next to ours; heavy-hearted Günter; feisty Carmen; the American woman and her environmental son, the cheerfulness of our volunteer *hospitaleras*, and the charm of the eclectic lobby. I left behind the frustrated waiter, the pizza lady. We all have our bad days.

Today, when I arrive in Los Arcos, it is time for a break. Outside the pizza place, the woman catches me looking in her window at her fancy fare. She smiles at me. I smile back, wish her a good day, and continue on my way. Around tables outside the restaurant are some friends from Orisson: Alma with Ms DeGeneres as always, Carole, Karen. At another table, there is also Jacob whom I met briefly in a tiny village on the way this morning. He greets me with a smile. At yet another table are Kim, the Australian woman who let me use her charger yesterday, and her husband Karmel.

"Wow"! says Carole jokingly as Jacob leaves the table next to ours and disappears past the church and back onto the Camino. "Was that Brad Pitt? How did you score that? Where did you meet him?" It is no wonder they want to know all about him. He is devastatingly handsome, and he does look a lot like Brad Pitt, although since he is closer in age to my grandchildren than even my children, I had not dwelt too much on his handsomeness.

Peril on the Camino?

I recount to Carole and the others an inconsequential incident that happened this morning to our Brad Pitt and me. In a small village, there was an old man with a long, untidy white beard sitting on a bench by the path. I think many old people like to kill their boredom by watching the parade of pilgrims. I have made it a habit to smile and say "Buenos días." When the old man saw me approaching on my own, he stood up with his tall, sturdy stick that served as his walking staff and offered to stamp my *credencial*.

I asked where he kept the stamp. "*Está en mi casa*" he replied. "And where is your house?" He motioned down a side street. He looked rather frail and innocent. He had to be close to ninety. I asked him if he had always lived in this village and if he had children here. Where did they live? Was he retired? I already knew the answer to that one. Did he often stamp pilgrims' *credencials*? Had he done the pilgrimage himself? After several long minutes, Brad Pitt appeared along the path and I asked the old man if he could come too. "Yes," said the old man without much enthusiasm, although I did not notice it at the time.

Only now when I relate the scene to the others, before I mention the appearance of Brad, and their response is unanimously if unexpectedly, "oh, oh!" do I understand that maybe it was wise to stall the old man with questions and not to go into his house by myself. In retrospect, I realize he did not look too happy after Jacob came on the scene. He stamped our *credencials* and unceremoniously showed us the door. It had not occurred to me to be suspicious. After all, at my age... at his age... But last September, Andrea and I did have an incident when invited into a house in a tiny hamlet between Burgos and León. But more on that juicy bit later.

I linger on in Los Arcos long after Alma, Ellen DeGeneres, and the others have left. I still have a long way to go today, but I feel awful. I wish I could just check into a private room here and go straight back to bed but my backpack has gone to Torres so I must go on. But first, I must eat something nourishing and drink lots of hot chocolate to prevent my cough and fever from developing into something more serious.

With Chloë – Somewhere under the rainbow

Bernard, Christine and Zebulon

In late afternoon under a punishing sun, at the bottom of today's steep hill of dry earth into the tiny village of Torres del Río on the other side of Rio Odrón, I am met by a biblical scene: a couple of pilgrims with a donkey. Have I landed in Palestine two thousand years ago? Or in Fez's medina last year? Bernard and Christine let me take their picture with Zebulon, the donkey. They have walked to Santiago from Compiègne in France, and are on their way back home, fund-raising for the Jean Vanier foundation. (This is before devastating revelations about Vanier will shock the world a few months later.) "Jean Vanier was a Canadian," I tell them. I am familiar with L'Arche, the organization this 'extraordinary', 'compassionate' Canadian founded in France. One of my university friends volunteered for L'Arche decades ago.

Bernard and his wife are raising funds for a home for mentally handicapped adults in Kolkata. I am blown over. "It's a small world," I say. "For almost fifteen years, I have been raising funds for Calcutta Rescue, an organization founded by Dr. Jack Preger, that provides schools, clinics and vocational training for the homeless in Kolkata." I love these coincidences. I take their card with their picture and blog, Le Chemin de Zébulon. The wimp that I am cannot help but think there are pilgrims, and then there are pilgrims.

A Room of My Own

In Torres, I feel like a traitor for not staying at Casa Mariela where Chloë and I had a warm welcome on our first hike, Andrea and I on my second, and the six of us last May. Andrea and I have especially fond memories of Casa Mariela. There we met Robin and Claudia, a young retired couple from Arizona walking the Camino as reward for having looked after Claudia's mother who suffered from Alzheimer's. Claudia had been the only one willing to take on the difficult task. It said a lot of Robin that he supported her throughout. "In the U.S., it is too expensive to have someone in a long-term care home," Claudia had explained when I asked if it would have been an alternative. Andrea and I would connect with them several times after Los Arcos. They were always a cheerful sight. When I asked if they were on

Facebook Claudia said they had gone off it. "There is too much hate on it," she said. I understood. They invited us to visit in Arizona. Who knows... When I connected with Claudia some months later, she and her husband had taken in his ailing sister.

Casa Mariela is a comfortable establishment run by Colombians. The dorms are cheerful with their palette of pastel-coloured sheets. The bright blankets look straight out of a box of smarties. With its look and smell of cleanliness, it is reassuring. To be fair, most dorms are spotless. Casa Mariela even has a small swimming pool with a cascade. Alas, it was bitter cold the first time, with Chloë. Like the day before, we had been shivering since Los Arcos. Bizarrely, the owner said, it was hot the day before. "People were enjoying the pool." Were they smoking opium?

At the entrance to the hotel area, past a wine bar, a large restaurant opens for a three-course pilgrims' dinner. The service is swift, the fare, good. Unfortunately, on my third stay there, after our meal, Janine and I, intent on getting more acquainted with others at our tables, were unceremoniously shooed out so they could serve the Spaniards who eat later than pilgrims. At the pittance we pay for our lodging and meals, I can tolerate a few flaws. At least that time, Janine and I had enjoyed a dip in the pool.

"You were here before, weren't you?" asks the owner when I poke my nose inside the San Andrés today on my way to the Pata de Oca. With the thousands of pilgrims they see, I am tickled to be recognized. But then I think maybe she remembers me as the loony grandmother who, on her first stay here, ordered calamaris and a hotdog, and when she had gobbled up an unexpectedly humongous plate of calamaris, could not touch the hotdog piled high with everything but the kitchen sink. Even Chloë, with her healthy appetite, could not give full honours to her hamburger. We are not used to finding a fried egg, all four of relish, ketchup, mustard and mayonnaise, tomatoes, pickles, and fries, sandwiched between the two halves of a bun on top of a fat sausage or thick meat patty... Embarrassed, I told the waiter I was happy to pay for the hotdog. "Please explain to the chef that it isn't that I don't like it." I'm sure he was thinking 'loca, loca'.

This time, a hundred steps further near the Templar church, at Pata de Oca, I land a room with four bunks. This place has seen better days but the

Laundry time

Claudia and Robin

owner is friendly. The place has a definite Templar flavour. Joy of joy, miracle of miracles, I have the room all to myself, a blessing because I could not find cough syrup today. I feel miserable. I know I have only myself to blame. No one forced me to come on the Camino. I wonder if, hearing me cough non-stop while signing in, the host thought it wise to isolate me. Pity anyone who would have had to share my dorm. I tuck myself in under two blankets, devour my dozens of figs and cough myself to sleep.

Next morning, I hop on the bus to Burgos. I will be early enough to get a lower bunk at Hostel Burgos by the bus station. There, some dorms are better than others. If I am lucky, I will get a bed in the one I like, and since it's privately owned, I can stay until I feel better.

Torres del Río is part of Stage 7. Burgos is at the end of Stage 12. At the bottom of the hill, we are a baker's dozen, all pilgrims, scanning the horizon for our bus. Some of us are ill, others injured or exhausted. Some are meeting friends or ending in Burgos. I am really sorry to miss this stretch. I am sorry to miss any area, but from the bus, each little hamlet it passes will bring back a memory. Each has its own personality and is like a friend to me now.

Most pilgrims at the bus stop are coming from the popular San Andrés. At Pata de Oca, they have taken good care of me by letting me have the dorm to myself. Intentional or not, it doesn't matter.

I wonder if the bus will pass by old Pepe in his Camino-blue sweater; I wonder if he still has his stall of fruit and drinks near here, offering something he calls coffee. Janine and I asked if he could earn a living from his tiny stall. "This is my hobby," he said. "I am retired. I used to be head of a medical clinic. Now I want to help pilgrims. I earn nothing from it." It seems easy to find a hobby if you are retired, enjoy fleetingly meeting strangers, and live near the Camino.

With a little help from our friend

Viana

Logroño

Navarette

Nájera

Santo Domingo

On the Bus

Felix the Philosopher

When our bus passes Viana, Felix the philosopher pops into my mind. Less than five feet tall, he looked very intellectual with his round eyeglasses, bushy white hair and nicely trimmed white beard. Under one arm, he carried an illustrated book whose cover piqued my curiosity: *Historietas - Museo del Prado*. Chloë and Randall had shot ahead. Janine, Vicki, Joanna and I, were having a morning break in a local pub. While I leafed through the book, Felix said he was researching centuries of women pilgrims. We would be quite surprised, he assured us, at the number of women on the Camino since its very beginning. He was enjoying imparting some of his knowledge. I could have listened to him for a long time, but since Janine and I were the only two who understood, we had to translate for Vicki and Joanna. I could tell they were getting antsy, so we cut it shorter than I would have liked. We still had a long way to go. I had hoped to bump into Felix today. I would have shown his picture around, found him, and asked him to tell me tales about the Camino that I would find nowhere else.

I knew I would have to skip several stages to make it to Santiago. Four weeks of hiking are definitely not enough from Saint-Jean. And I hope to get to Finistere either walking or by bus. I have not decided which part I should skip. After recovering in Burgos, I could take a bus to Léon, past the meseta. This should allow me to walk the rest of the way. *Ojalá*! I'll let Destiny decide. It always has the last word anyway.

We all spend so much time planning just to see our plans fall apart. Man plans; God laughs. Indeed. I am a vagabond. I have a vague outline of what I wish to do, but things have a habit of going awry. I have adopted the Muslim habit of never using the future tense without adding *Inshallah* (God willing), or *Ojalá,* its equivalent in Spanish, if only in my head. I even find it arrogant not to.

An Old-fashioned Grandpa

About Viana, I also recall one funny scene from last September. Andrea and I had helped a sweet young Brazilian teacher who strangely did not understand any Spanish at all. Having taken him under our wing and accompanied him to the bus stop, we waited with him for a good hour for the elusive bus which thankfully, eventually showed up. Later, at the plaza, we were entertained by a young grandfather having the time of his life teasing three four or five-year-old girls. Not much taller than the girls, he brandished a fat, grey plastic sword, pretending to attack them. They must have been his granddaughters, or perhaps one granddaughter and her friends. Several small groups of young people stood chatting in the square, ignoring the scene. Three women, the girls' mothers perhaps, chatted on the steps near us, occasionally glancing at the foursome and smiling. One of the girls, a feisty little thing, was furious when the grandfather grabbed her by the arm, playing the bad guy. You could already see in her a woman who will let no one step all over her. She punched him and tugged at the plastic sword. The others rallied to her defence, grabbed grandpa's trousers and tried to kick him in the legs. It was all in good fun. Andrea and I hung around for the denouement. Of course, it all ended with grandpa saying, "Enough now, girls. Time to go home," and the little ones begging for more. That is what I remember of Viana. Yet with a Borgia buried there, the place is replete with history. It is much more than just a small town with the lively teasing of a grandpa in its square, or a noble, white-bearded philosopher intent on celebrating the history of women pilgrims along the Camino.

César Borgia

Near here, César Borgia was killed. By the Iglesia de Santa María his body lies. He tried to conquer the city by starving the troops occupying the castle. Ironically for a man of so many exploits, when some citizens delivered food to the captives, Borgia pursued them, was ambushed, and met his Maker. Methinks it's a rather lacklustre end for such an accomplished warrior only in his thirties. The King of Navarre had Borgia's remains buried here under the church. They have since been moved a few times, but always near the church. Here, we are thrown back hundreds of years, to a time when in Italy, Machiavelli and Da Vinci, Borgia's friends, were also leaving their imprints on history.

César Borgia was a complex mixture of evil, audacity and heroism, a tangled web of virtue and vice. Much has been written about him and his father, Pope Alexander VI, and about César's sister, Lucrecia. Once again, legend blends with history. Their notoriety has given them immortality. By the church, a plaque commemorates César Borgia's death March 12, 1507. No living an extra couple of days until the Ides of March for *that* Caesar. Those are the ancient spirits who come to life as my bus bypasses Viana this morning.

Spaniards are proud of their medieval history. Every year, local history buffs stage a re-enactment of Borgia's demise. Men don suits of armour and tall leather boots, while women wear long, heavy dresses of rough cloth in earthy colours and go around carrying baskets of food. The men draw their swords to fight in mock battles. César is killed.

Most literature depicts the Borgia family as scoundrels, immoral, incestuous, power-hungry... yet César's father was a pope, a successor of Peter, the representative of God on earth, and César fought on the side of the Church. Like the Templars, they are heroes with a dark side. Was religion ever a peaceful enterprise?

I always get a strange feeling from being in a place with so much history. Is that what is meant by eternal life? Is our soul what we leave behind? Is it a dissemination of our teachings, our art, our music, our deeds, good and bad, our genes? Is it in paintings, in books, in philosophy, in scientific discoveries? In our children? Are we surrounded by the souls of those who came before us? Does César Borgia's soul roam around Viana? I find it strange for his resting place to be by a church. According to some historians, there were no taboos for him. In the Borgia family (as with Machiavelli) ambition justified the means. Killing his brother was only one of César's unscrupulous deeds. Inviting his enemies, unarmed, to a banquet to celebrate their reconciliation and, before the night was over, having them strangled, (something he did on the last day of the year 1502), that was in line with his way of governing. Happy New Year, Señor Borgia!

In Viana, first with Chloë, then with Andrea, and later with the others, it was thrilling to step into history. I took many photos of miniature sculptures of saints and pilgrims here and there above arched passageways. Near

Calle Fuente Vieja (Old Fountain street), in a niche high above a stone arch, wrapped in his grey, rough pilgrim's cape, only his walking stick for company, the quaint, dwarf-sized, mustachioed and bearded pilgrim looked lonely. I wonder how many thousands of pilgrims have gone by without a thought for him up there above the arch.

Some passageways in the old walls of Viana still have doors. Its street names keep the past alive. I can almost hear the old lady, the old man with humble past, but who has prospered in Madrid, revisiting the city of their birth and, passing Calle Fuente Vieja, saying nostalgically "When I was a child, we used to carry water from the fountain down there." Their grandchildren might be doctors and lawyers, university professors and leaders.

The Law of Historical Memory

History alters memories. The deeds and personalities of its subjects depend on who is telling the story... Historians can bleach or darken facts, skip over moral turpitude. Who was Cesare Borgia? And more recently, who was Franco? Until the law called *Ley de Memoria Historica* was passed in 2007 disallowing any kind of political demonstration at the Valle de los Caídos (Valley of the Fallen), a group of falangists would meet on the anniversary of Franco's death for a ceremony of commemoration. That is now forbidden. And since 2007, throughout Spain, many names of streets, squares, and buildings reflecting support for Franco's regime have been changed. In Logroño, seventeen street names were erased. History is a weather vane. With its twists and turns, one is left to wonder if the dictator's remains, removed from the Valle de los Caídos in October 2019, will be moved back at another date. At home, back from the Camino, I would watch a clip of the cortege on television: about two dozen glum sympathizers, one of them wearing dark glasses and energetically chewing gum. Bad enough for the Generalissimo to pop out of his coffin.

Bypassing Logroño today, I wonder about its forbidden street names, about its history. In Spain, I never ask about Franco unless a Spaniard broaches the subject. There is a rather rude saying: 'If you disturb shit, a foul smell emanates'. In Camino encounters, better leave the ground intact. Whose country has a flawless past?

The River Ebro

I wonder if Chloë's and my name and the date we walked by are still on the wall of the underpass along with all the messages left by other pilgrims. One is never too old for a bit of graffiti. Was this our effort to be part of history for a while?

Will I see the vineyards and the tall cypresses from the bus? Alas, for too much of the drive, my ear is bent by a pilgrim who has been hiking alone. "I love the solitude," he says. My eyes are heavy, my throat itchy. I am coughing nonstop. He doesn't seem to get the hint that I would like to sit quietly all the way to Burgos. He rambles on about his equipment not living up to the advertisement. I soon close my eyes and feign sleep. I am back on the Camino, walking.

In my first *credencial*, a favourite stamp is from the tourist office at the entrance to Logroño by the bridge over the Ebro. A purple oval with a pot-bellied *cántaro* (a water jug, the name of numerous pubs, restaurants and hostels), a fig leaf, a couple of figs, a shell, a Knight Templar's sword, and four words: *Felisa* (the name of a legendary local woman who helped many pilgrims) *Higo, Agua y Amor* (fig, water and love). The second longest river in Spain, the Ebro is like the Seine of Paris, the Rhine of Köln, the Danube of Vienna, of Budapest... History abounds along its banks. Wide and deep, it flows under the many bridges old and new, of Logroño, and is the fruit of the confluence of seven smaller rivers coming down from the mountains to the Rioja region where they merge. A lifeline for many, it rushes across north-east Spain to the Mediterranean, watering rice paddies at its delta. It flows through Tortosa, a small town south of Barcelona with a Moorish past, where live my friends Brid and José, an Irish-Catalan couple, one of the multitude of mixed European couples in Spain. They met in Ireland when José was studying medicine and Brid, science. More often, young people used to meet when Northern Europeans hoping to escape their dreary climate piled kids, granny and Fido in the Volvo and drove to the Costa del Sol. Many enduring love stories started with teenagers seduced by the weather, and by the suave, handsome Spaniards. It is no wonder so many Dutch nationals on the Camino speak fluent Spanish. I have met a few of those couples. Some of them own and run hostels. They seem a wonderful combination. The blond hair and blue eyes of the northerner blend beautifully with the olive skin and deep brown eyes of the Southern Spaniard.

I was visiting my friends in Tortosa during what I call the Second Battle of the Ebro. Fortunately this second, passionate battle is one of words, not of swords. It is a battle of petitions, demonstrations, debates, opinions and newspaper articles. Over a few decades, embittered citizens downriver fought and demonstrated in large numbers, all the way to Barcelona to stop what they perceive as mismanagement of water from up-river. Water is a scarce resource in Spain. Catalans worry the flow of the Ebro will continue to dwindle due to different factors, including the introduction of dams for thirsty customers and polluters upstream. As usual with these conflicts, the whole thing is shrouded in politics, the two sides each brandishing their different versions of the facts, but no one can deny the effects downstream of what happens upstream.

The 1938 Battle of the Ebro was of a totally different nature, with devastating loss of life, especially on Franco's opposition, the Republicans. On one of my visits to Tortosa, I had joined in commemorations of that Battle of the Ebro in which tens of thousands had died. When the present king's great-grandfather, Alfonso XIII went into exile in 1931, a new Republican government was formed. In a bid to overthrow that government, Nationalists under Franco's leadership, eventually aided by Italian fascists and German Nazis, entered into a bitter battle against the Republicans who received help from the International Brigades from countries like France, England, Ireland, Germany (anti-Hitler), and Russia. Many Jews also fought on the Republican side.

Hemingway, George Orwell and others who later gained fame, were on the battlefield at the Battle of the Ebro. After a fierce and courageous battle, the Republicans, with their inferior arms and a dire lack of air force, suffered a terrible defeat with at least 15,000 dead from the International Brigades. In the dog days of summer, they endured hunger, thirst and crushing heat which could wilt a garden in an hour. Fighting on rough terrain, they built bridges across the Ebro. Nationalist air strikes bombed them. They were courageous but naïve fighters who hoped to defeat Franco's forces with such inferior war machines. Had they anticipated the extent to which Hitler and Mussolini would come to the dictator's aid, they might have put down their arms sooner, prevented countless massacres. Alas, the Brave too often go into war blindly. The Ebro teems with barbarous history. Rivers all over the world have been scenes of bloody conflicts. They carry nutrients to the lands through which they travel, but along their beds, like large unmovable boulders, lie sleeping, centuries and millenniums of humankind's stories of cruelty, misery and strife.

As the bus nears Logroño and the Ebro today, it is a strange feeling to think of my friends downriver. I wish I could sail to them.

The One-armed Pilgrim and the One-legged Pilgrim

Andrea and I will never forget a bizarre incident which happened in Logroño. We had arrived at the hostel well before opening time and placed our backpacks in line. This would allow us to leave while reserving our spot. The day was stifling hot. Half-a-dozen pilgrims sat in the shade or soaked their blistered feet in the fountain at the centre of the large courtyard. We hung around for a while, then realizing we had at least an hour left before opening time, I offered to show Andrea around.

Before we left, we noticed a one-armed pilgrim, a man perhaps in his fifties. He did not seem interested in mingling with anyone. With his multitude of tattoos, he looked scruffy and rough. It made one wonder how he had lost his arm. From the corner of my eye, I noticed how dexterous he was: shedding his backpack, undoing the laces of his hiking boots, slipping off his socks and, after meticulously inspecting his feet while muttering to himself, pulling out ointment and tape from his backpack and taking care of his blisters before putting on clean socks and softer shoes. There was nothing he seemed unable to do. Later, we would witness his intransigence.

Logroño is a town full of interesting murals, sculptures, and buildings. Andrea and I walked to the square with the marble-inlaid designs and large, numbered dice that serve as seats. It was the famous Game of the Goose, a sort of Camino Snakes and Ladders. Pilgrims progress along squares with different illustrations. Some squares move them faster to destination, others set them back. A fitting metaphor for the perils of the long hike.

Near the game with its grim reaper, its maze, its white geese, and other representations incrusted in the stones of the large square, at the church of Santiago Real, we snapped photos of the patron saint brandishing his large sword, separating Moors' heads from their bodies. The legend has been the source of many impressive works of art. Inside the church, framed by gold-plated columns, another sculpture of Santiago Matamoros adorns the apse. It is the same depiction of our man in his wide-brimmed hat, astride his horse and with a Moor pleading for his life at his feet. Andrea was wide-eyed and full of questions most of which I was at pains to answer.

The fourteen stations of the cross were carved and elaborately framed. My favourite sculpture was of a life-size freestanding Jesus clad in blue from head to toe, burdened by his cross. Although I don't normally care for this kind of gruesome depiction, something about this sculpture was so reminiscent of the Pieta, it was difficult not to admire the art. It seemed as though the Jesus with that cross was the one who would soon be in his mother's arms in St. Peter's Basilica. I am amazed at how inured we, Catholics, have become to these savage scenes of torture. What is it like for someone who was not brought up in any faith, a religious virgin, so to speak, to view those images for the first time in adulthood? Is it like me staring at Ganesh and Shiva, or even at a lingam, in a Hindu temple? Or is it like watching a violent movie?

We had time to stroll under the arcades among pilgrims and tourists here for the *vendimia*, the wine festival, and to watch the procession of dancing *gigantes*, the giant puppets we find all over Spain, representing historical and fictitious characters.

Back at the hostel, minutes before check-in time, we found about twenty pilgrims eagerly standing in line beside their backpacks, *credencials* in hand. The door opened and, as a volunteer signalled for us to file in, a tall, distinguished-looking French gentleman in his sixties or seventies arrived with his wife. He was wearing short trousers. We all noticed his artificial leg.

Those of us at the front simultaneously said, "Please go first." But hearing us from his bench at the back, the one-armed man shouted angrily, "Why should *he* go first? He can wait in line like all of us." Twenty jaws dropped, twenty heads turned to the back and twenty pairs of eyes popped out of their sockets, staring at the angry man.

"You go ahead also," we said in unison. But he refused to get special treatment and was adamant the one-legged man should also wait at the end of the queue. Obviously not used to attracting attention to themselves, the French couple were visibly embarrassed by the whole hullabaloo. If the man wore short pants, it was probably only because of the searing heat or in case he had to adjust his prosthesis along the way.

There followed an outburst of shouts of approval at letting him go first. Bizarrely, two pilgrims, fortunately just two, sided with the rabble-rouser. One of them was a burly fellow with a three-day old chin shadow. The other, a wiry, nervous type, appeared to be his companion. The Frenchman's face showed no expression. His wife was floored. She shook her head. "Never in my life have I ever experienced anything like this," she uttered. After most of us insisted, the couple went ahead of us. It took me a while to shake the scene off and even now, as I recall it, I have a hard time believing it. Surely, all who were there have that scene imprinted on their minds.

Bricks and Stones

With its eight-hundred-year-old Church of San Bartolomé, its large avenues lined with brightly lit stores, its abundance of life-size metal sculptures, Logroño has one foot in ancient and the other in modern history. We had enjoyed posing beside some of its sculptures. One of them depicts two young and healthy modern pilgrims. Except for their walking sticks, they could be schoolchildren on an afternoon outing. One sculpture that intrigued us was of a man's torso with just one arm and the fingers of his hand spread out towards some bizarre chunk of sharp, twisted metal. Did it represent a broken man and the damages of war? I found it repulsive, and was frustrated at not knowing its significance. I assume it represented war because part of the wall behind it was built of large blocks of cut stone, yet one could see the rest of it was ancient, with stones roughly hewed and irregular. Often, with old buildings in Spain and in other coutries where bombs and bullets have left their scars, one can see this juxtaposition of old and new stone. Was it indicative of reconstruction after war damage? Was this sculpture representing those whose lives had been destroyed by war? Apparently, about two thousand people from here were murdered by Franquists. Logroño has more than its share of dark history: a tribunal of inquisition during the XVI Century; a century later, witches burnt at the stake. And more recently, Logroño was one of the cities in this area whose citizens suffered immensely during the Spanish Civil War.

Not far from the sculpture, standing back between buildings, a tall, imposing, tapered brown brick chimney towers above the town. I asked an elderly man about it. "It used to belong to a cigarette factory. My grandfather, my father, my brother, my uncles, my cousins, and I all worked there," he said proudly. "I met my wife there. She worked there until our children were born." The factory closed decades ago, and many found themselves unemployed for a while. The old man said they had kept the chimney for history's sake. In Seville, I had visited what was once the *Real Fábrica de Tabacos* (*real* means Royal) where they used to make cigars; it is now part of the University of Seville. The *Fábrica* served as Bizet's inspiration for his *Carmen*. Will the Logroño chimney remain as a monument to history?

Later, in the courtyard, while Andrea (whose parents are German) enjoyed speaking with a couple from Düsseldorf, I fell into a long conversation with Lenn, a retiring Australian. He seemed happy for the companionship. He showed interest in what I was saying, but did not contribute much unless I asked him questions about himself. Not at all gregarious like other Australians I had met before, I guessed him to be about sixty. He was a friendly giant with tanned skin and trim, muscular arms. I could imagine his strides twice the length of mine. Not fair, I wanted to say. His hands were huge and sun-baked. His back was slightly bent forward, maybe from bending to meet the faces of the people with whom he was talking. His hair could have done with a trim. He wore regular clothes, not hiking trousers nor sandals, like most do after a day of hiking. I asked him about his work. "I was a sheep farmer," he said humbly. Although I have never been to Australia, I knew sheep farmers ran stations on hundreds of thousands of acres with hundreds of thousands of sheep. He and his brother, both single, had inherited their father's station. Shortly after, his brother had died. Lenn had sold the station, and moved to a tiny apartment. He had been travelling around the world for three years, only returning home for a couple of months a year. I imagined he had always been single.

We talked about the churches along the Camino. I confessed I usually only make a cursory appearance inside some of them. When I do, I particularly like to compare their Stations of the Cross. They can be magnificent works of art. And in the hundreds of churches I have visited all over the world, I don't think I have ever seen two the same. Of course, they are all rather gory. But you need not subscribe to any religion to admire the breathtaking art religions have produced. "My parents were hippies before their time," said Lenn, "I had never been in a church until my mid-thirties at my grandparents' funeral. I am still trying to digest all that religious stuff. I never cease to be amazed and appalled at the same time." I was surprised by his sardonic tone. It didn't fit with his gentle personality.

I confessed I had drifted away from religion in my teens, but I added, "had it not been for Christianity, Islam, Judaism, Buddhism, Hinduism, and hundreds of other religions, I think our world might not only be poor in art, music and literature but it would be without millions of treasures of architecture. Notre-Dame de Paris, the Blue Mosque in Istanbul, the temples of the East, none of them would exist." He agreed. Although he was more interested in nature than in large cities, he had enjoyed visits to many of these historical monuments since his retirement.

Maybe it was the wine, maybe it was the relatively easy walk that day, or a combination of the two... we (mostly I) talked and talked, about religion, history, the Camino... "Temples are great for the safekeeping not only of art but of history," I said. "And of fiction," Lenn added. Did I detect a hint of sarcasm? I agreed with him, but thought there were two kinds of fiction inspired by the Church. One was the kind that floated Santiago's bones in a stone coffin across the Mediterranean to the west coast of Spain. The other was that of writers or painters. "Could you, while admiring Notre-Dame-de-Paris, forget about Esmeralda in the arms of Quasimodo? And who can't

'remember' Napoleon crowning himself emperor in Notre-Dame-de-Paris?"
I asked him.

Lenn topped up our glasses regularly. It was his wine we were drinking, so
I assumed he was not bored or wanting to escape from me. It must have been
the depiction of Santiago severing heads, in the church here in Logroño, that
took me back to a scene some years ago in Paris and amused Lenn when I
related it. Standing in front of a gruesome fresco at the Basilique Saint-Denis
where a man on bended knees seemed to be offering his severed head to
another man, I overheard a tour guide explaining that following the decapi-
tation of Saint Denis, he had carried his own head from Montparnasse to the
site of the Basilique where he was to be entombed. I could never summon
such a leap of faith, at least not since I was a child. To make sure the event
would not be forgotten, it is depicted for posterity in the sculpted fresco. (By
the way, my French friends, the Basilique Saint-Denis is also where the good
Roi Dagobert lies enshrouded, he who wore his trousers inside out until the
good Saint Eloi pointed it out, after which he good-naturedly turned them
the right way out before being chased by a rabbit.)

I am always interested in the history associated with churches and cathedrals, no matter how phantasmagorical it may be, but for beauty, I prefer
the softness of Islamic art. When I visited the Blue Mosque of Istanbul, I
thought if I lived there, I would gladly wear long sleeves, shed my shoes at the
entrance, cover my head, leave my ham sandwich at the door, and penetrate
that spiritual space when in need of quiet time. Unlike churches, mosques
are not cluttered with distracting art. Of course, their walls are plastered
with verses of the Koran, but for those of us who can't read Arabic, they are
nothing but elegant arabesques. Our churches and cathedrals can be osten-
tatiously opulent. They contain too much gold. I cannot look at all the gold
without thinking of the Aztecs and Mayas. Of the conquest. Without the
Church, though, what would Michelangelo have painted? Imagine a world
without the Pieta, without the Sistine Chapel. Nietzsche, Diego Rivera, and
company can claim that God is dead. The art Gods have inspired is alive
and well and living all over the world.

Andrea was getting up to leave her group. It was time to turn in for the
night. Half-an-hour later, as I was about to fall asleep, the patio filled up

with minstrels in their red and white attire, playing music and singing for us pilgrims while others poured a round of wine. This was the *Vendimia*, the Wine Harvest Festival of San Mateo. I would be tired in the morning. At least I would return home with some interesting photos including some taken in the afternoon of a group of handsome university-age men all wearing identical sneakers and white bobby socks, and not kilts but short, flair, colourful, woven skirts. Not a sight I would likely encounter in my country. I did not see Lenn again. His giant steps must have taken him far ahead of Andrea and me the next day and all the days after.

Puta

My bus zooms by the Pantano de la Grajera, the large reservoir with swans where hopeful fishermen cast their line and where Chloë and I enjoyed a break munching on fried calamari. Then in September, Andrea and I paused here too and met a Canadian boy hiking alone. He wore a top with the sleeves cut out; a baseball cap sat backwards on his head. His sneakers looked ready to abandon him. He was sweet as can be but confessed he used to have terrible conflicts with his father, a strict man. "I've smartened up," he said. "I have a lot of respect for my parents now." He had witnessed his father taking care of an ageing neighbour asking nothing in return. "Dad mowed her lawn; fixed things in her house, shovelled her snow in winter. I have learnt to respect other people's values even if they are different from mine," he said. "Now I know it is your actions that count." He walked with us for a while up the steep and sinuous path to Navarette.

Today, I will miss the wildflowers, the prickly thistles with their lovely purple blooms, and the large vines amazingly growing among stones the size of grapefruit. I never tire of vineyards, although when one really thinks about it, they are perhaps one of the worst examples of monoculture.

I must have been feeling really unwell when I slept in Navarette with Chloë on our first hike because the only thing I found later, jotted down in my diary was 'El Cántaro, nice *hospitalero*. *Lluviendo a cántaros* (raining pitchers)'. Idioms can be quite revealing of other cultures. In Vietnam, the

A place to pause

The game of the goose

mice don't play when the cat's away, but the hens grow shrimp tails when the rooster's away. To each their own fun.

Somewhere around Navarette, the base of a marble sculpture had been defaced with nasty graffiti. *Puta* (whore) seems a word of choice on the Camino which I suppose is as good a target as any for vandalism. Somehow, I find it less offensive than a certain four-letter word that can stab like a dagger. At least, the sound is soft. The age of evil, my mother called teenage years. I knew what she meant. Saint Augustine would have known what she meant. The pranks he and his buddies loved to play! My conscience is not totally innocent of those evils, but regret, like worry, is a waste of time. I have long ago forgiven myself. Hopefully, I have atoned for my own misdeeds.

The sculpture stands on top of a four foot high pedestal on which pilgrims have been building a cairn. A man, a bull at his side, holds three stems of wheat and a tall, rough walking stick without the hook of the shepherd's crook. A representation of the virtues of agriculture?

Arancha and Maite

After Navarette, a few pilgrims exit the bus in Nájera where I celebrated my birthday on my first hike with Chloë. Since Pamplona, we had not noticed one single pastry shop. Lo-and-behold, minutes before afternoon closing time, fifty steps from our hostel, three cakes beckoned to us from a window. Five minutes later, we came out of the bakery carrying one decorated with a shell, an arrow, and the number 70.

Shielded from the sun by the wide canopies of venerable trees along the Rio Najerilla, Chloë and I had rested while waiting for the hostel to open. Very occasionally, in some areas, we sense a less than cordial attitude towards us. In Nájera, the locals seemed friendly and accepting of our intrusion into their daily lives. We have become an inevitable part of their environment. Of course, there are those who benefit financially from our passing, but we are not exactly five-star tourists showering Spain with Euros.

I remember a couple of octogenarians on a bench. They looked sad. Their feet didn't touch the ground. We were struck by how small they were, shrunken with age. I acknowledged them with a discrete smile which the man returned. He was holding his wife's hand. She seemed in her own shrunken world. They were staring at the river. I wondered what tragedy had befallen them, or was it the sadness of things to come? In my head, I started singing Jacques Brel's song, *The old folks don't talk much*. People of all ages were strolling, walking their dogs, getting a breath of fresh air. Some were pushing wheelchairs. Was there a long-term care home nearby? Many, recognizing us as pilgrims, smiled at us and wished us *"Buen Camino."*

That first time in Nájera, I was sick; the third time, Vicki was sick, and today, it's again my turn. What is it that doesn't like us on this part of the Camino? I am particularly disappointed at not staying here tonight. I had hoped to learn more about the house that is now the hostel. It would likely have an interesting history. And I had been looking forward to seeing Arancha and Maite, our kind *hospitaleras*. They had been so good to me when I had arrived with my birthday cake. After I had placed a note near the check-in desk inviting the other pilgrims to help celebrate, they had set up a table for everyone and placed a vase of flowers on it. I still cherish a pretty Camino pin Maite had gifted me to remember the day.

We were a dozen around the table. One especially interesting man, a kind-looking eighty-year-old German photographer, had walked from Köln in Germany. He was going all the way to Santiago. He told us about his trek up to Base Camp in the Himalayas with his fifteen-year-old granddaughter. And this was his fourth time walking the Camino. Not a big man, he carried his backpack and heavy camera gear. He could have boasted about his exploits, but he was humble and only talked about them because we enquired. Later, as I walked past his dorm, he was sitting at the edge of his bed, removing his socks, head bent over to prevent banging it on the wooden frame above. With his permission, I took his photo. I enjoy going through my pictures and I always stop at his; it is a good representation of the routine of the Camino, and less of a cliche than many we capture along our path.

The next morning, until time for our bus to Santo Domingo, Arancha had let us wait in the living-room by the unused dining-room with its massive table and upholstered chairs. The house must have belonged to a comfortable family. Old paintings and fading family pictures still hung on its walls.

It had a museum quality to it. I wondered how long it had been welcoming pilgrims. There had to be a story there.

We would stay at the Puerta de Nájera also the next May with our four friends. Across the road, Randall, Janine and I went down to the riverbank while waiting for it to open. As usual, Vicki, Joanna and Chloë had arrived an hour before us. Chloë and Joanna were resting on the grass. Vicki, stretched out on a bench, was pale as a ghost. "You don't look good at all," I said. She gave me an evil look and closed her eyes without saying a word. Later, she had enough of a sense of humour to laugh about it "coming out both ends". Maite lent me a bowl to take up to her. Chloë wasn't feeling great either, but after a nap, she woke feeling better. Fortunately, although Janine and I had beds in the large dorm, our four companions had scored a four-bed dorm with its own small. cozy living-area with couch and balcony. For the first time in my life I saw black stuff coming out of a person's stomach. Vicki's sense of humour was unwavering. "Thank God I wasn't puking in front of thirty pilgrims," she said laughing weakly when, the colour drained from her face, she had spilled the entire contents of her guts into the bowl.

She asked about a doctor. Maite said there was a clinic, but she would be there for hours. The doctor would say, "Rest, drink lots of water and wait for it to pass." "We see this all the time," she said. In the morning, Vicki was determined to walk with us. We had to be firm in our refusal. "You're much too weak," we insisted. "Rest here tonight. You can take a bus tomorrow and catch up with us in Santo Domingo." She was adamant that she would walk every inch of the Camino, and absolutely refused to take a bus for any part of it. She finally buckled and took a day's rest in Nájera. Each of the following three days, she would walk far and fast in order to catch up with us in Burgos.

As for Janine, unforeseen circumstances called her back home. I was sad to lose her. Our friendship had developed on the Casa Ivar chat group. Before meeting in the flesh, we had talked online about art, politics, history, travel... We had become friends. In some ways, we were very different; in others, very similar. A good recipe for friendship. I had enjoyed hearing about her two beautiful daughters, one a successful visual artist, the other a yoga and meditation teacher now living in the south of Spain with her Andalusian partner. I had developed a lot of admiration for her. Her moral strength. Her stoicism. We all have our crosses to bear, but those crosses don't all have the same weight. In our two weeks together, I had learned how her mother in her early forties, and a few years later, her only sibling, a brother, had died in tragic circumstances. One of her best friends had been murdered point-blank in front of her. I had talked about my childhood in the nuns' boarding school; about my mother who had felt trapped all her life, burdened by six daughters, six pregnancies, mostly unwanted. We had discussed at length the differences between our generation and our parents', both realizing our good fortune. We had so much more to talk about.

That night, in Nájera, Janine had been on her phone for what seemed like hours trying to coordinate her return home. In the morning, before I left, she produced the diary which she had picked up in Estella while I wasn't looking. She had hoped to be with me to celebrate my 71st birthday. Back home, each on our side of the border, almost in a straight north-south line, a day's drive away, we would continue our friendship.

Kirikiki, Cocorico, Cock-a-doodle-doo

The next day, somewhere after Nájera, near a picnic table, a young man pulled an entire Café out of his tiny Cleo. It was amazing to watch him set up in the middle of nowhere, take out a folded table, baskets of fruit, small cakes, cookies, juices, a large thermos of coffee, an insulated box with cold drinks and a container for refuse. Folding chairs, even. It was far enough from the next watering hole for pilgrims to want a break. I marvel at the resourcefulness. I hope he can make a living from his little enterprise.

Our bus pulls in at Santo Domingo de la Calzada. The fellow beside me and a few locals and pilgrims get off. This would have been my fourth time here. The first time, Chloë and I stayed in the large, modern Casa de la Cofradía del Santo with its chickens in the backyard, reminding us this is a town with yet another insane legend. The scenario has a myriad versions, all with the same ending. Rich girl in love with boy. Boy rejects girl. Girl places silver object in boy's pocket. Boy falsely accused of theft. Boy hanged. Boy's parents pass by, see boy dangling from rope, alive. Boy's parents run to mayor. Mayor having dinner. Says he: "Boy as dead as chicken on my plate." Chicken on plate starts clucking. Mayor runs to boy and severs rope. And they all lived happily ever after. And attracted a lot of tourists and pilgrims with the live chickens and their artistic representations in Santo Domingo.

The Casa de la Cofradía had a great kitchen. A group of pilgrims were hogging it while cooking an elaborate meal. Yes, sadly, it happens often. One Korean woman was washing dishes under fast running hot water; another pilgrim came over and turned off the tap, scolding her for using too much water. Like us, I think he was frustrated at having to wait too long for a chance to prepare his meal.

There were signs everywhere: *Not wear boots and sticks to the room; You can't wash clothes in the toilet. Do in the garden; Not to put backpacks on the bed; No smoking; Please no cures into the rooms - go to the area of the cures* (by 'cures' they mean when people are taking care of blisters). *Scrub the dishes after use; Do not hang clothes on windows and bunks; Wifi and lights turned off at 10; everyone up by 7; everyone out by 8.* They are the same rules everywhere. Having them posted made it feel like Boot Camp. Some people need reminding often.

I wondered if this would be a place where, before internet, all pilgrims would assemble in the evening and sing international songs like *The Rooster's Dead* in all languages, or *Alouette* (a song I can't stand!) in French. Nowadays, as I would later learn, for a timid person, the Camino can be a lonely place.

At ten o'clock on the dot, a volunteer turned off the lights in the dorms; at seven o'clock on the dot, he woke all late risers. "This would be a good place to train regiments," said the pilgrim next to me as he dragged himself out of bed. But what I remember most was the stench in our dorm. I had not noticed it until it nearly knocked me out on my return from a midnight visit to the loo. Thank God my dinner was far down in my stomach. Never before or since have I experienced such reek.

The following September, Andrea and I were fortunate to find a bed in Abadía Cistercenses, a decrepit nuns' convent at the entrance to the small town. And again, the next May, while Vicki recovered at Puerta de Nájera, Chloë, Randal, Joanna, and I found beds with the nuns.

At the Abadía, the beds are old and creaky; the mattresses are thin and sagging; the floor coverings have seen better days; the thick wool blankets make you wonder if you should use them; our bathroom reminded me of the one in my grandmother's house. If you don't make sure its door is closed, the sewer smell invades your room. The rooms are cold. But the atmosphere is warm and welcoming. By coincidence, when I stayed there with Chloë, Randal and Joanna, I had the bed Andrea had the September before.

The room Andrea and I shared had only three beds. After we settled in, a charming old man arrived to occupy the third one. Was it his accent or his deep voice? He reminded us of Richard Burton. He introduced himself: "My name is Malcolm. I am Welsh. But I don't snore." Do the Welsh have a reputation for snoring? He snored like a rusty trumpet all night.

Andrea and I explored the parador with its sculptures of angels and saints, its cast iron chandeliers, its thick rugs on marble floors. Surrounded by the arched stone walls, arrogantly, we sat on the comfy couches, basking in the sort of elegance we would rarely encounter in our New World country.

We visited the cathedral with Santo Domingo's tomb. Its carvings, its sculptures, its golden retable rivalled many I had already seen on the Camino. In the light filtering through the high windows, five or six pilgrims were walking around, admiring the artwork. Only one knelt, seemingly absorbed with the divine.

I could find no one to explain the meaning of the sculpture of two men clinging to Santo Domingo de la Calzada's robes on his tomb. Bizarrely, true to what I had read in Brierley's guide, in a small grassy enclosure behind a fancy metal grate, high within the walls of the cathedral, a couple of fluffy white fowl pecked and clucked the days away. Oh, my! Spaniards love their miracles. They make sure they don't vanish into oblivion.

Andrea walked back to the convent. Perched on a low wall by the cathedral, to catch a bit of the late afternoon sun while jotting in my notebook, I soon became absorbed in the monologue of another pilgrim. I had him in the corner of my eye. He had an unusual accent which I could not pinpoint. Scandinavian, perhaps, or was it that he reminded me of the old men around the table in *Babette's Feast*? His straggly grey beard hung down on his chest. He wore unusually shabby clothes, weather-beaten hiking boots, and an immense large-brimmed, beige hat of another era. A soiled backpack lay on the ground beside him. A typically well-off pilgrim sat near him. They were obviously not companions.

"I'm sick of those tourists. This is supposed to be a pilgrimage, not a parade," the bearded one was saying, peppering his tirade with an occasional colourful expletive. There was no argument from the other pilgrim, so he droned on. "The Camino is full of atheists. The next thing you know, they'll have a gay parade." Upon hearing him, another pilgrim approaching the square skirted the area. In all my kilometres along the Camino, he is the only pilgrim I ever heard complaining that way. The fellow beside him stretched his arm out of his long sleeve a little too conspicuously, and glanced at his Fitbit. He stood up almost abruptly. *"Buen Camino,"* he said. And before the bearded one could utter another word, he was out of the square like a bat out of hell. My head was bent, my eyes hidden by the rim of my Tilley hat. I could only see the lower part of the complainer's body. Still sitting, he spun in my direction. I refrained from saying *Amen,* and went back to writing in my diary. He didn't seem interested in me. I was ready if he had started a conversation: *"Lo siento, no hablo Inglés,"* I would say. Then the most unexpected thing happened. He grabbed his backpack, got up, walked past me. Curious to see his face, I raised my eyes. He gave me a beautiful smile, wished me *"Buen Camino,"* and went on his merry way with the gait of someone who hasn't a care in the world. I nearly fell off my rocker.

Santo Domingo of the Roadway

I had many questions before my adventures on the Camino. I found answers to some. My impression had always been that saints were poor and humble people. When I heard of saints building hospitals, churches, bridges, and roads on the way to Santiago, I was confused.

The story of Santo Domingo was puzzling. A thousand years ago, Domingo García built the sumptuous parador and hospital for pilgrims in what is now Santo Domingo de la Calzada. García also improved roads and bridges along the Camino. Hence his posthumous name De La Calzada (Of the Roadway). He started off as a poor, illiterate man. Turned away from the monastery

Through the vineyards   *Shadows*

at San Millan near Santo Domingo because of his lack of sophistication, he became a hermit. Eventually, the Holy Spirit or perhaps his own cogitations (or are they synonymous?) made him realize he was not serving God with his unproductive life. He could use his talents to help better humanity's destiny by making man's toil less arduous. He became an engineer. Realizing his immense potential, Alfonso VI, then King of León, along with other rich nobles, granted him land and funds to build roads, hospitals, and hospices for pilgrims. Then they had him canonized. Now I understood.

Radio Camino de Santiago

After the legend, the chickens and the saint, don't blink or you might miss Grañon. Unless it is morning, your stomach is grumbling, and after being lured into the tiny but beautiful bakery by its wafting aroma, you notice a few steps further a bright blue sandwich board with the words *Desayuno donativo* outside the Casa de las Sonrisas (The house of Smiles). That is what happened last May to Chloë, Randall, Joanna and me. Inside, in front of a bookshelf lining the wall, was a long table all set for breakfast with everything any of us would hanker for, a long bench on one side and enough chairs for more than a dozen pilgrims. We couldn't believe our luck. I went back out to check the words on the board. The *hospitalero* assured me we were welcome to breakfast. On the table was a tin with a slot for donations. Before leaving, we thanked him profusely. When I asked his name, he produced a card with Radio Camino de Santiago details on it. Ernesto is one of the directors. I have become a fervent listener.

Now we had enough fuel to make it to Villamayor del Río past Redecilla. We were sorry Janine and Vicki had not got to experience the lovely gesture of hospitality.

Hotel Redecilla del Camino

Less than two hundred souls live in Redecilla, an hour's walk uphill from Grañon. Past the municipal hostel and the small church, the one star Hotel

Grañón

Redecilla

Vilamayor

Belorado

Villafranca

Agés

Burgos

N

Redecilla with its three large flags fluttering above a large coat of arms is where Chloë and I had stayed on our first hike.

Across the path, at a cluster of red tables, six women were having an early lunch when the two of us arrived. Their walking sticks propped against a wall by their backpacks, they were having a lively conversation while tortilla de patatas, ham sandwiches, chocolate pastries vanished from their plates. Since the owner and her helper were minding the bar without a second of respite, tending to an unending queue of thirsty, hungry pilgrims, stamping *credencials*, refilling water bottles, collecting dirty dishes from the counter, Chloë dropped her backpack in a corner and we, too, enjoyed brunch. We would wait to check-in until the hustle and bustle stopped.

Our platters cleaned, we mingled with other pilgrims, but soon realizing that the Redecilla was like Madrid Airport's Arrival Hall and there would be no hiatus in the traffic, we informed the woman that we had a reservation. Lourdes' smile was contagious. Only head and shoulders above the counter, her presence was radiant. Her sparkling eyes lit a permanent smile. Tied in a thick bun, her light hair was just starting to show silvery streaks in harmony with the discrete pearls on her ears. She managed the hotel with elegance and competence. She was obviously doing a job she liked.

The Redecilla is an impeccably clean little hotel. I hear it was quite the opposite until Lourdes took over. For no reason, she upgraded us to a room with private bathroom. Chloë took one look at the room. "This is one-star?" she asked, obviously pleased.

Rich amber-colour drapes gathered near the bottom were in harmony with the wall behind our bed. Instead of headboards, someone had painted on the wall two six-feet-tall pointed arches, like stained glass windows, gothic-style, with multicoloured pastel squares. Above, in the centre, a painting of a shell. Lourdes had placed fluffy towels at the foot of each bed. With a modern bathroom all to ourselves, this was many notches above the conservative, no-name decor of the very few expensive hotels I have stayed at including a five-star in Delhi. (A friend working for an NGO had invited me to share her room for a few nights.)

It didn't take us long to explore Redecilla. It was not as deserted as some of the other villages, but there was *nada* to do. Settled into the cozy armchairs of the small lounge while Chloë read and I did a little research, we were joined by Jacob, a Dutchman, (or Cloggie, as he laughingly called himself), newly retired, and his dog, a small, well-behaved terrier who travelled in a basket on his bicycle. Jacob was happy to have found this hotel. Few places have facilities for pilgrims of the canine variety.

Dinner with Friends

Later, in the small dining-room, Jacob was at the next table. We were exchanging comments with him and with Roland and Gwen, a British couple from Devon at another table. A retired French couple sat at a fourth table. We were craning our necks in this and that direction until I suggested we place our tables end to end to form one long table. "We are not walking the Camino," said the French woman, hesitant to intrude on pilgrim's conversation. They were driving back to the north of France from a holiday in Morocco. "Aren't we all life's pilgrims?" replied Jacob.

When Lourdes arrived with our soups and salads, she approved of our rearranging the tables. For me and for many others, multinational exchanges are very much what the Camino is about. Sadly, with cell phones and internet, they are quickly vanishing the way of the dodo.

Roland and Gwen were in the antique business, on the Camino for only two weeks. With inexpensive flights from England, they can do that once a year. Back in England, their loaded van was waiting at the airport for them to get right back to work. It was fascinating to hear how this antique business works. I had always thought of it as a hobby rather than actual 'work'. Around the table that night, I developed a lot of respect for their trade. It sounded like a lot of work, and definitely not boring.

Some people are born entertainers. Roland was handsome in a wholesome way; he had a definite twinkle in his eye. So did Gwen. They were passionate about their work and made it sound like fun although it is obviously not a big money-maker. "You have to know other vendors' buyers as well as your own," said Roland. Their trade was as much with vendors as with Sunday strollers. "Once in a while, you land a treasure. But those are our little secrets." He looked at Gwen, and she giggled. "At times you feel like a thief," she said, "because, when people die, sometimes the heirs are in such a hurry to get rid of everything and get to the money, they give away treasures. We'll never get rich, but every time we go on the road, we know it could be a bonanza day. They don't happen often, but they do."

The food was delicious. The wine flowed; I refilled my glass a few times because Chloe and I had already decided to stay another night. Everyone was having a good time. I asked Gwen the vegetarian when she had stopped eating meat. "Ever since I was a kid, the butcher shop smelled like death to me." I was glad I had waited until dessert to ask.

The next day, all morning and afternoon, pilgrims arrived alone or in small groups. Thirty years ago, they were less than five thousand a year on the Camino. This year, there would be over three hundred thousand. The Camino is bursting at the seams. It needs more accommodation. The well-heeled and older pilgrims often shun dorms. This is good news for a country whose economy relies heavily on tourism, and although the Camino itself might not be a huge source of income, it does create employment, and many of the pilgrims spend time in other parts of Spain after Santiago, or come back later and spend more lavishly.

Sunday afternoon, a van stopped for several minutes on the road in front of the church, the driver reciting some undecipherable sentences through his loudspeaker and playing a melody. We were about fifteen at the tables outside. We all turned and stared in the van's direction. Was it some sort of religious preaching? Suddenly, the van started up the street quickly past us. We realized alas too late it was an ice-cream van. I hadn't seen one of these on our streets at home for decades. I ran after him, but he didn't see me. It would have been a rare treat around here. He must have been disappointed. He obviously did not realize his music meant nothing to us. Did he think we were a bunch of cheapskates?

The AK-47 Pilgrim

That evening, Maryse and Herman, a Canadian couple, joined Chloë and me at our table. At the next table was a couple in their mid-forties. The man recognized our accents. "Are you, Canadians, aware of Mr. Trump's shenanigans?" he asked. I told him we followed American politics closely. "We are so ashamed," he said. I didn't feel like talking politics, but Maryse jumped in and said, "What I don't understand is the need for guns in your country. Why does everybody want a gun? Why would anyone own an AK-47?"

His wife was silent. Because I could tell they were kind, gentle people, his candid answer startled me. "Actually," he confessed, visibly embarrassed, "I own an AK-47. But I keep it in a locked unit. Our teenage son doesn't know where the key is." "What if his friends' parents have an AK-47 and their rules aren't the same as yours?" Herman asked. "Why would you need an AK-47?" His reply did not surprise me. It was something I had also thought about. "I am afraid there'll be an insurrection. We'll need to defend ourselves."

They were a friendly couple, but it was as though the AK-47 had opened an unbridgeable chasm between their table and ours. We made polite conversation until our food arrived. After dinner, the husband leaned over and asked Maryse, "At what time are you leaving tomorrow?" She shrugged. "I don't know." "How far will you be walking?" his wife asked me. "I have no idea." Maryse had told us they would not be leaving too early. We had planned to walk with them part of the way.

The next morning, from our bedroom window, I watched the AK-47 couple leave with their heavy backpacks. They had all the expensive gear. She was a small woman. They were the ones who, on their second day, had shed $500. worth of equipment on a bench along the way. They were good people. Had it not been for the guns, we would have had a lovely hike with them.

We said goodbye to Lourdes and Christian, her helper. It was heart-warming to see them at work, gliding past each other. Christian, perhaps in his late twenties, had been working for Lourdes for seven years. I could not imagine either of them ever raising their voice at anyone. Hospitality was written all over their faces. Smiling came naturally. Chloë and I were sad to leave our one-star hotel. We are fortunate to be XXI century pilgrims; the Camino would not be the same without people like Lourdes and Christian, without these oases of beauty, comfort and kindness.

Mr. Brierley's Slow Guide to the Camino?

It is less than four hours' walk from Redecilla to Belorado. It was mid-morning by the time the four of us left the charming hotel. We had chatted too long over our huge breakfasts, refilling our cups too many times. Belorado, only twelve kilometres away would be our next stop. Within a few days, we could forge ahead, making up the kilometres. The sun shone brightly, but a bitter wind slapped our faces. Plodding under a cruel sun on the rough shadeless path would have been as much fun as strutting into hell. It is easy to wrap up, but no matter what the old song says, you can't take off your skin and dance around in your bones.

Maryse and Herman were sailors. That year, they were giving their sea legs a rest. We enjoyed listening to their fascinating tales of adventures at sea, all the while picking our way carefully around the large snails. I have never been fond of slimy creatures, but like the fat silky black ones peppering the Camino before, I found the ones on our path that day beautiful. Their bodies were a pale amber covered with white dots, their thick feelers almost translucent. Their yellow and brown variegated shells will turn into pretty houses. I wondered what the farmers thought of them.

Although we were enjoying the couple's company, since we would not be walking as far as they would, we said good-bye to them at the tiny hamlet of Viloria de la Rioja, where a rickety old bench welcomed us against the sunny side of a house. The elements had been pitiless to it. Its green paint had peeled and its wooden slats looked quite rotten. Hesitant to plop our bottoms on it, we tested it with our thumbs, and sat gingerly, one at each end, spreading our weight in case it decided to give up the ghost that day. The house's shutters were closed. Although not totally dilapidated, it looked untended. Waist-high weeds and pretty yellow wildflowers had taken root in the soil that had migrated to the base of the wall. The arched front door looked as though I could poke a hole through it with my finger; it could use some plastic wood. What was left of its green paint matched our bench. Thick weeds grew within inches of it.

The many abandoned houses we passed made me sad, like vanishing songs, customs, words, expressions. The older we get, the more we would like things to remain the same, the more we find ourselves starting sentences of disapproval with "when I was young..." We are happy to accept the improvements, but we forget that they have a cost. We forget that evolution means shedding something and adding something. Disappearance and replacement are the natural order of things.

There are apparently a couple of tiny hostels here. Wouldn't it be something if the Camino could bring people back to this village? With the pilgrimage growing in popularity, I hope these houses will be restored to accommodate pilgrims before they have entirely fallen prey to the elements.

I remember hearing years ago about a small Spanish village where most people were related, and could find no one to marry. The mayor, worried about the exodus of young men needed to work the land, had invited dozens of young women from a nearby village for a weekend of fiesta. They had been billeted in the locals' homes. Eventually, weddings were celebrated, babies were born. I suppose that mayor would be called a visionary philosopher. It is sometimes good to think outside of the box.

I wondered if our slowly disintegrating bench had originally been placed there for pilgrims, or was it where the family sat on a hot summer day when the sun had gone around the side of the house. Benches abound along the path. They are always a welcome sight. I assume it is not rude to sit on them while watching fellow pilgrims go by.

A few hundred steps took us past the last house in the village. The large, old building in dire need of re-pointing had a line of well-tended flower pots along its wall and a single flower pot on a low windowsill. All its windows were shuttered. Beside it, a large sign caught my eye: *Santo Domingo merece más que unas ruinas* (Santo Domingo deserves more than just ruins). Santo Domingo was born here in 1019, exactly a thousand years ago.

We saw more flower pots on windowsills and, high on the side of a wall, clothes drying in the sun. Despite the decrepitude of some of the buildings, there were at least a few people living here. Later, I found out that there were seventy-three inhabitants here in 2004 and forty-six in 2010. Who knows how many there are today. Maybe it is time for Mr. Brierley to come out with a 'slow' Pilgrim's guide with fifty stages instead of thirty-three to

Amaryllis

lure the more apprehensive would-be pilgrims and to help revitalize those 'in-between' hamlets too often ignored by the one-stage-a-day pilgrim.

The Town of Three Lies

From Viloria, snow-capped mountains in the distance reminded us we were still at the foot of the Pyrenees. After a while, we walked along a highway with large trucks zooming by. It was not exactly idyllic. Fortunately, a wide expanse of tall grass separated us from the road proper. Having read about pilgrims hit while walking along roads, we appreciated the path.

We passed a building that still looked sturdy despite its weather-beaten exterior and a profusion of foot-high weeds growing out of its tiled clay roof. We had reached Villamayor del Río, known as the Town of the Three Lies: Not a town. Not major. No river. I was happy to spot more children's clothing flapping in the wind. We continued without stopping. In September, Andrea and I would stay in this tiny Village of Three Lies at the San Luis de Francia. Entering the village, we could see a large building about a kilometre off the main path. Was it the San Luis? It had been an unbearably hot day, and we weren't too keen on adding more steps to our hike. Andrea accosted a woman coming from that direction. Her name was Cathy. She was staying at the San Luis. Yes, it was the building in the distance.

We recognized a Canadian accent. "Where are you from?" asked Andrea. "A small town in Ontario: Kingston." We had to come all the way to Spain to bump into someone from our own town! A retired massage therapist, Cathy had set out on the Camino with a companion who covered many more kilometres daily than Cathy was comfortable with. Because she suffers from a mild heart condition, Cathy was happier walking four or five hours a day in a relaxed manner. By the time we met her, she was walking solo.

The next morning, and most mornings after, Andrea, Cathy and I started out together. As each of us fell into our own pace, distance grew between us. We would meet at our hostel at the end of the day. We each had our own style of walking. Andrea usually led the way. Sometimes, I would see her ahead in the distance, walking in an army-like step, raising her knees high and moving her arms vigorously, as if pumping air into her lungs. She

Cathy from Kingston

Andrea

would march like this for a minute or two, then resume a normal step. I walked fast when it was cold and slowed my pace as it got warmer. A tall woman, our new friend walked long, deliberate strides, with hiking sticks. If the topography was such that her doctor would not recommend walking, she would hop on a bus and meet us in the evening. Andrea usually got to destination first and tried her best to save us two good beds.

María Carmen, the owner of the San Luis, keeps the place spic and span. Helped by her teenage son, a bright young man who spoke English quite well, she served us a generous and delicious dinner. The next May, after Janine had to go back to Philadelphia, while Vicki, having recovered from her stomach flu, and determined to walk every kilometre, was still rushing like a madwoman to meet us in Burgos, Joanna, Randall, Chloë and I slept at the San Luis. I had the same bed in the same room as with Andrea and Cathy. María Carmen had taken their son to the dentist. Her husband Roberto was left alone to prepare the meal. He rose to the occasion with flying colours.

It was a bitter, cold day at the end of May, too cold to take advantage of the garden. Joanna had gone under the blankets immediately upon arrival. This was no country for Hawaiians. I could almost hear her bones rattling despite two heavy wool blankets. I taught her to sleep with her clothes folded under her blanket so they would be warm from her body heat in the morning, and to place her pillow between the blanket and herself for added warmth. Fortunately, in the other building, a fireplace with a roaring fire awaited us. She managed to stop shivering in time for dinner.

I wonder how María Carmen and Roberto can earn a living, let alone make ends meet with €5 beds, €3 breakfasts, and €8 dinners. I have heard the odd pilgrim grumble that the locals are "raking in the money from us, pilgrims." All I can say is these pilgrims don't know how to count. The business woman in me can't help but count: there are 26 beds. If every bed is filled, if every pilgrim takes dinner and breakfast, that brings in €406. Subtract the cost of food, hot water, electricity, cleaning, stolen toilet paper rolls, property tax, insurance, repairs, half-filled nights, five months empty... There is no doubt in my mind, *hospitaleros* work hard; they deserve every Euro they earn.

Too bad I am not walking today. I am sorry to miss the San Luis. On this warm sunny day, I would be enjoying the garden.

A Hidden Gem

After Villamayor, Belorado welcomes pilgrims in all its splendor. If not staying there, it is easy to bypass the town and miss the Plaza Mayor, one of the nicest between Pamplona and Burgos. Chloë and I had arrived much too early to settle into our dorm. We had lots of time to discover the large murals, some of which run the length of a block. They make Belorado very different from other places we had passed. In the square across from the large arcaded building with an avian painting covering its entire façade, amid the plane trees with their mottled bark and their strong, rugged limbs, the market vendors were getting ready to go home. We sat on a bench while I described to Chloë how in the evening and on Saturday and Sunday the locals would congregate in the square. In Spain, a family home is very private. People don't invite friends over on the same scale as we do in our Canadian homes. They fill pubs and restaurants. In clement weather, they come out for the *paseo*: dressed in their best finery, the entire family, including little children, have their social life in the square. By ten o'clock, they start thinking about going home for dinner. Maybe it is better to meet like that, on neutral grounds. The Belorado square, with its profusion of benches and shade trees is perfect for such a custom.

Later, we bumped into Gwen and Roland, the antique dealers. Gwen's knee was bandaged, but she made light of it. While Chloë and I had stayed an extra night in Redecilla, they had stayed here. They would stay here tonight again. We ate dinner together. We would end up hiking on and off with them up to Burgos. The sun sets late in Spain. After dinner, we were greeted by a rainbow before reaching our shelter for the night. The Camino knows how to end a day. I love Belorado. It has spunk. Today, I will miss its open-air art gallery.

Of Fakirs, Ascetics, Saints and Men who Live at the top of a Post

At 6:30 the next morning, Chloë and I were back on the path through orchards with snow-capped mountain in the distance. Villambista greeted us with the pink wall of a large house. Casa de los Deseos. Hmm. The house of desires... what sort of desires? Apparently brothels are not shunned as much here as in Canada. I even heard of one that has adapted a room for the handicapped. The Casa de los Deseos isn't listed in Brierley's accommodation section. Later however, I did meet two women who had stayed there and loved it. A young couple runs it. The women could not say enough good things about them. And apparently the food was filling and delicious. I had been planning on staying there this time. It will have to wait.

Further, at a restaurant in Espinosa, Chloë and I bumped into Roland and Gwen, and realized we had all reserved beds at the same place. It was a blistering hot day. The long hill to Villafranca seemed a lot steeper than it would on my next visit, when the weather would be a bit cooler.

Although it doesn't have that designation, the recently restored XIV Century Hotel San Antón Abad in Villafranca Montes de Oca is like a parador. Art and antiques adorn every nook and cranny. Perched high on a hill, it is part elegant hotel, part hostel. Reception for both areas is in a long lobby lined with comfortable armchairs. Marble floors and pillars, and wide, arched doorways confirmed we were in an ancient pilgrim's *hospital*. After his pilgrimage, the owner had wanted to give something back. We are the beneficiaries.

Down the hill, across the narrow, terrifying N-120 on which large buses and heavy truck after heavy truck barrel down without pause, is a small grocery store for pilgrims reckless enough to brave the crossing. Either there is no change of speed required, or if there is, it is totally ignored. (Spaniards can be quite anarchic. I remember one man on a train who, when tapped on the shoulder by another passenger who pointed to the no smoking sign, responded with "Sí, Señora. Sí, Señora," and went on smoking.) Apparently there are plans to re-route the N-120, the main street of Villafranca, a narrow village less than a kilometer long. I hope the trucks aren't carrying flammables. I have not forgotten a telephone call from my mother following a catastrophic accident on a winding road near Taragona on the coast. It was during the summer of 1978. She wanted us to know she was safe. She and her friend were about twenty minutes away from Alcanar when a truck containing liquefied propylene exploded near a camping ground. Apparently, in order to avoid toll fees, the driver had taken a narrow road; the truck carried much more than the allowed volume of the highly flammable material. More than five hundred people from a camping ground and near it were killed immediately or died from their wounds in the weeks following the explosion.

While our clothes dried in the sun at the back of the building, Chloë and I sipped Sangría with Gwen, Roland, a retired South African psychologist, and his wife at a table under a large umbrella. The couple had retired in Britain and for years they had been coming to Spain's Mediterranean beaches. We were commenting on the declining populations along the Camino, compared to the hugely overdeveloped Costa del Sol, often home to retired Germans, Brits, Dutch, Russians and people from all corners of the world. The couple were thoroughly enjoying the Camino but could not imagine coming to live in the area in retirement.

I had done my research. I pulled out my notebook: "The villages we passed since Belorado, it is no wonder we nearly missed them," I said. "Tosanto, Villambista, Espinosa del Camino, Villafranca, not one of these has more than sixty winter residents." I didn't know when the census was done. It probably wouldn't make much difference.

The psychologist was more interested in the name San Anton Abad and the names of other villages than in populations. I knew nothing about San Anton Abad. He assumed the name of our hostel was given in honour of an Egyptian saint, a man who lived in the desert and in cemeteries. "If you read about the lives of the saints," he said, "you will soon come to the conclusion that many of them were what we would call marginals now." "I have often wondered about all those fakirs, ascetics and saints," I told him. "Legend has it," he explained, "San Anton lived to the ripe old age of 105." Well, maybe… About those who lived a long time ago, if they ever lived at all, it is hard to separate fact from fiction. Didn't Sarah give birth to Isaac at ninety-one? I hope I will be forgiven for questioning that 'fact'. If San Anton's story is true, I would tend to agree with the psychologist. I wonder if the saint's behaviour would, today, be classified as sainthood or schizophrenia. I mean, a man from a wealthy family leaves everything behind. He goes off into the desert where he will befriend animals away from people; he lives amongst tombs, has visions of God... I assume itchy creatures have nested in his long matted hair, his dusty beard reaches his navel, his clothes reek and are full of holes, his body is filthy, riddled with open wounds... I guess I was not the only skeptic. Besides, I had read plenty about ancient Syrian stylites, those ascetics who fasted, prayed and preached, perched atop a post. All stories to be taken with at least a modest dose of skepticism, I think. Who makes up all that stuff?

Our conversation skipped from one subject to another as though we had been old friends. Over a couple of drinks, we had touched on philosophy, religion, architecture, and the history of the Camino.

In the evening, in the large dining-room, surrounded by art, and under the light of elegant chandeliers, we continued our palaver. The couple were planning on walking to Finistere and then down to Lisbon. I enjoyed listening to his perspective on history. His wife was self-effacing, and I am ashamed to say only when I came to write in my diary that night did I realize we had hardly given her a chance to speak. I promised myself I would ask her about herself when we met again. Sadly, we never did.

Next morning, before darkness had completely lifted, I was rewarded with one of my favourite Camino photos. The San Antón Abad is on a hill. Its dorms occupy the upper floor. Looking out from our dorm, through a large window with its two vertical panes open wide against a rich avocado green wall, I had the perfect frame for the scene of tall, slim cedars and, down from our hill, a large stone building, a rolling hill in the background, and the thin sliver of a rising sun, all part of the Camino offerings. It was only a matter of reaching out to capture the scene.

Devorah

From the bus today, I am following in the wake of history. Not only did Napoleon's troops come through, and Frenchmen settle here, but Romans, Visigoths and Moors all left their marks in this area. It seems only Hannibal didn't. With his elephants, he stuck to the coast on his way to the Alps. Tragically, in more recent history, the blood of people whose children and grandchildren are still alive was spilled near here.

The view: San Antón Abad

There is one site near San Antón Abad I will never forget. It was my first time on the Camino. Faced with many steep hills, I had sent my bag to San Juan de Ortega only half a stage away. The first hill was a killer. Chloë and I climbed on a narrow path through dense forest for what seemed like an eternity. When faster pilgrims showed up at my back, I had to stop and make myself skinny at the side. I was no match for the six-foot giants in the prime of life whose long, bouncy strides made their backpacks look like bags of feathers. After large purple bushes, we passed a ghostly area with the charred remains of tall trees, lugubrious skeletons of devastation, followed by a symmetrical, reforested pine grove.

When we climbed a hill, it was impossible to know where it would end. I was thankful for my visor shielding me from the crest which would always seem too far. At last, we would reach the top and down we would go for a while. Then, another steep uphill and downhill, and another and another... I let my spirit soar over the hills on the ascents, and caught it on the descents.

This is where the next September, Andrea and I would come upon, lying on their backs, hundreds of dead beetles. Chemical poisoning? Whatever the cause, it was not a good sign. A French woman had pointed out that around here, the cultivated fields have no weeds. "The Spaniards are very good at generating electricity with wind power. Now they need to tackle their use of pesticides," she said. When it comes to the environment, who, from a rich country, should be the one to cast the first stone?

Three times have I walked that part. The third time, downhill would be quite a challenge for Randall, our Hawaiian friend. I cherish the memory of a woman Chloë and I met at a monument on top of a hill. We were catching our breath in front of a large billboard at a burial site with its photo of a gathering of people, relatives of Civil War victims. In the picture, men are scratching at the soil to expose more of the skeletal remains. We were at the Monumento a los Caídos (Monument to the Fallen). I translated the inscription for Chloë: "In this common grave, on August 30, 2011 was discovered a mass burial ground. Thirty bodies were exhumed, plus another thirty that disappeared due to work on the Camino. They were assassinated between July and December 1936. This work was made possible thanks to the engagement and perseverance of their united families..." The murders had happened at the beginning of the Civil War. There are apparently more than a thousand such burial sites.

Many pilgrims give the Monumento a los Caídos a cursory glance and move on. It deserves more than that. It is important to know the horrors of history in order not to repeat them. I wanted to spend a minute in meditation. Beside us, a woman about my age, petite, with dark, wavy hair was trying to decipher the inscription. "Can you read Spanish?" I asked. "Would you like me to translate?" "Yes, please," she said. When I had done so, she nodded and closed her eyes. Then she started singing a heart-wrenching song in a language I did not recognize. Two Oriental pilgrims were approaching. Upon hearing her sing, they stood, listening intently. Her song went on for a while, rising in the still air like a prayer. When she stopped singing, there was hardly a dry eye around the monument. There was no need of a translation. We gathered around her.

"What was that beautiful song?" I asked. "It was the Yiddish song for the Dead," she said. We stood there for a few more minutes. The Koreans said, "Thank you, *Buen Camino*," before walking away quietly.

Chloë and I walked with her for a while. Her name was Devorah. She told us about the Jewish death ritual. "In Jewish custom, we have a special committee for when a person dies." Members of the committee wash the body and prepare it for burial. "We gather around and sing songs and talk about the deceased; we cry; we laugh; we sing; we even tell jokes." I assumed the ritual would be much more sober when people had died in the same circumstances as the victims in the mass burial.

Garlic Soup and Bread

Soon after the monument, it had started spitting. The day was getting warmer. The tiny drops were not enough to bother with rain gear. As Chloë and I entered the village of San Juan de Ortega with its two dozen inhabitants, the rain started coming down more seriously. We were now in a village composed of a church, quite pretty, with three bells, the Augustinian monastery with arched facade, a bar with tables outside sharing a wall with the monastery, and across, a tiny cluster of houses.

The monastery, where I had sent my bag and where we hoped there would be beds for us, would not open for another hour. The clouds burst, pelting with huge raindrops all the pilgrims who could not take refuge fast enough inside the restaurant, or under the arched entrance to the monastery or in the church. Chloë and I made it almost dry inside the church where we found Gwen and Roland, and which over the next fifteen minutes filled up with less fortunate, soaked pilgrims.

The rain came down *a cántaros* for a long while. I could think of worse places to take shelter. Churches are often as good as museums. I could appreciate the art, but not the macabre crosses with the bleeding Jesus. Some of the marble artwork was quite extraordinary: chopped heads, naked cherubs, women in long dresses kneeling in prayer... even the devil had a place of choice. But lions and camels? And the lion with the human face carrying a load on its back? The monks with hoops of cord? And whose ghost comes out of that marble tomb in the church at night? I would need more than a hike on the Camino to decipher all this fascinating if often grim artwork.

Our new friends had also hoped to stay at the monastery for the night. I pulled out my Brierley: we would be going to mass and eating garlic soup with bread for supper. Gwen is vegetarian but... It was early afternoon. The rain abated enough to make it possible to walk without getting soaked. The luggage van arrived. I retrieved my bag. We pulled our rain capes over our heads, and while Chloë and Roland, disregarding my protests, each grabbed a strap of my bag and started swinging it between them ahead of Gwen and me, we skedaddled to Agés, an hour away. "There should be more action there anyway," said Gwen. "The book says sixty inhabitants."

Marcial Palacios Colina's Charming Little Museum in Agés

Ruben and Raquel, a young couple, welcomed us into El Pajar de Agés (*Pajar* means straw loft). They were a cheerful sight, and the accommodation looked clean and comfortable. We could tell they loved their work. Ruben's tidy, full black beard and long ponytail spelled 'don't sweat the small stuff'.

If we had asked, they might have let us pay for only three beds since Gwen and Roland always slept head to toe in the bottom bunk. Apparently Roland snores. When he does, Gwen pokes him lightly in the chest with her toes, and it is enough to stop him.

In the morning, at a four-person booth like in an old diner, our hosts produced bacon and eggs with generous glasses of fresh orange juice, coffee and Cola Cao. All that for a few meagre Euros. I didn't know it then, but I would be back at the Pajar de Agés the next September with Andrea. Cathy would meet us in Burgos, having wisely gone by bus and skipping the steep climb between Belorado and San Juan.

One thing I didn't know about Agés, and which I would discover thanks to Andrea, was Marcial Palacios Colina's retirement hobby. Inside a large room (an old barn or workshop perhaps), the man has set up a charming display of his wooden miniatures: two-inch long farm implements, toys, kitchen tools, the old village school complete with furniture... All of these he delighted in explaining to us. "Can you guess what this was used for?" he asked of this or that object. We were five or six visitors. I translated as well as I could, but didn't always have the vocabulary. He also had wise sayings here and there on the wall: "*No llega antes el que va más rapido; si no el que sabe donde va.*" (Don't walk behind the fastest one but behind the one who knows the way.)

The old man also has a tempting hard-cover book for sale. His buyers must come by car or be the descendants of those who lived here. I like the humble title: *Paseando por mi pasado, la pequeña historia de mi pueblo* (Revisiting my past, the little history of my village). On the wall is a hand-drawn map depicting the houses of Agés' residents in the decade 1940-50. Below it, a list of each household with father, mother and children. Some of the names are a delight: Eusebio and Paula with their children: Epifanio, Segundo, Bienvenido, Marguerita. The first one must have been born on the feast of Epiphany; the second was, well, second... the third was welcome... the last one, born on St. Marguerita's day. In the third house lived two fecund couples, each with eight children... What surprised me most was the majority of families only had two or three children. In Canada, it would take another three decades for Catholics to start using birth control. Or was it that many women here had died in childbirth? Or children in early age?

Near the exit was a small bowl where one could deposit a coin or two. Some pilgrims pretended not to see it. The old man enjoyed sharing his work and the story of his village. It seemed right to show our appreciation.

Chloë, Roland, Gwen and I had missed the museum the previous May. The next day, we had walked together from Áges along a quiet road. After Atapuerca, it was quite rough going, with a stone-strewn brown earth path. Everywhere we looked, especially at the top of church steeples, were humongous nests with giant, prehistoric-looking white and black storks flying in and out. They looked like they had been here forever. What stories did they tell their young about the villagers, about the passing pilgrims? Did the ancient inhabitants of Atapuerca hunt them? Sometimes, if we were lucky, we could spy two or three chicks sticking out their heads on long slim necks in anticipation of a fresh frog perhaps, or a grasshopper, a lizard from the mother. At other times, thick fog patches obliterated the view. After the narrow path along cultivated land, we came to a rocky area. No path here. Just the rock. It was not easy for Gwen with her injured knee, but as long as we watched our step, all was fine. When the fog finally lifted, the blue sky was again striped with dozens of jet trails all going east-west, following the Milky Way: the sky pilgrims. Despite the yellow gorse pushing its way among the stones, the hilly area reminded me more of Ireland now than of Scotland.

In Cardeñuela Riopico, while the others stuffed their faces with croissants and chocolate eclairs, I gobbled up a tall strawberry smoothy, not needed after my huge, high protein breakfast, but who could resist?

By the time we got to the outskirts of Burgos, the air was heavy; the sun was pounding down on us. We were walking around the perimeter of an airfield on a busy, curved, hair-raising highway with occasional trucks, cars and buses zooming by at what seemed like inches from us. There was no going back now. The nasty stretch seemed to go on forever; it is an area I will never hike on again.

Eventually, in the humid air, with our shirts stuck to our backs, we reached the outskirts of Burgos. While the others refilled their bottles at a fountain, I went to enquire about a city bus. We were only five hundred

With Andrea

steps to a bus shelter, and waited happily for half an hour in the shade for one that eventually took us close to our destination, the Casa del Cubo.

Today I am sorry I have missed all these tiny villages, but not the part around the airport. The 'greener' alternative into Burgos that Andrea and I would take the next September was not great either, but it was not dangerous. For those of us here because of our love of nature, the entrance to large cities is often best skipped.

The Escape Artist

At the last stop before Burgos today, a short, barrel-shaped woman with thinning grey hair waddles aboard and takes the seat across the aisle from mine. When the bus has come into the terminal, and we are standing in the aisle, she blurts out: "You know, I'm an escape artist. This is my third time on my own on the Camino." It turns out she is running away from an intolerable situation at home: her middle son has been suffering from breast cancer for two years. "Yes, men can get breast cancer," she assures me. (I was sadly aware of that; we lost a friend to it in his forties.) Her other son is a drug addict, bipolar, in and out of jail. Her daughter has become estranged from the family because she cannot stand the dynamics. I didn't ask about a husband.

My life has not been without obstacles. Whose life has? Once in a while though, the vicissitudes of my own life seem rather inconsequential. I can see why the woman finds the Camino soothing. As I walk, day after day, my spirit rises far above my inner turmoils. Even though I don't think I am running from anything, except perhaps the noise of lawn mowers, leaf blowers, garbage collectors and partying students, I know the blissful rest walking the Camino can offer.

La Casa del Cubo

Across from a vibrant outdoor Café in Burgos, near one of the most grandiose cathedrals of Spain, where El Cid lies entombed, sits the imposing Casa del Cubo where I will not be staying this time. Welcoming, immense, clean, comfortable, and ridiculously inexpensive at €5, it boasts several floors of accommodation, a spacious, well-appointed kitchen, a comfortable lounge, good laundry facilities. Pilgrims enter the grand XVI Century stone building through its high, arched doorway. It is not unusual to see a line-up of dozens of pilgrims waiting for the door to open. The men minding the desk when Chloë and I stayed there with Gwen and Roland were efficient and friendly, but the clinical modernization of the building's interior had destroyed some of its soul.

Inside, apart from its high ceilings, one is at a loss to find vestiges of its past. I love sleeping in an old two-room school with creaky wooden floors, where children's desks have been replaced by cots, where the *hospitalera* stamps *credencials* from behind a solid oak desk, and I can imagine the village children spanning nearly a decade in age, putting logs in the stove, writing on slate, dipping pens in inkwells, throwing paper airplanes at each other. Other pilgrims, of course, appreciate the modern facilities and don't waste time bemoaning the past.

Blankets are not provided at the Casa del Cubo. Chloë and I were not carrying sleeping bags, nor had we needed them until then. We would have to find something to keep us warm. Not easy in this historical part of town with its fancy, expensive tourist shops. After a while, meandering through the old quarter, I bumped into Gwen and Roland. They had visited the cathedral and were now strolling around like a couple of young lovers. They had seen some dog blankets at half-price. I hurried over to the shop. Luckily, there were two left: one with a Mickey Mouse design and the other with Tinker Bell. At €5 each, I did not ask if they had other designs in the back.

Chloë and I had several days left before our flight. Pilgrims are only allowed one night at the Casa del Cubo, we would have to find another place to stay and a way to fill our days. I could think of worse cities to explore and, on the Camino del Norte, a couple of hours from Burgos by bus, Bilbao beckoned. "How about a day trip to see the Guggenheim?" I asked Chloë. From her enthusiastic answer, I could tell she had inherited my vagabond gene. Not that I didn't already know.

Hostel Burgos

Roland and Gwen had another night in Burgos before their flight home. Above the bus station on the other side of the Arlanzón River, we got beds at Hostel Burgos for our second night. It was more expensive but still reasonable, and it included breakfast. If the Burgos boasts no ancient vibes, its pluses outweigh its minuses. Unfortunately, the multilingual receptionist was using a new computer system. It took her over twenty minutes to process each guest. Chloë and I waited in line for almost two hours along with sweaty pilgrims, some of whom had walked a fair distance and had been too late for a bed at the Casa del Cubo.

We knew by then that every dorm has its own challenges. We were issued access cards to our eight-bed dorm whose heavy fireproof door closed with a jarring clunk and locked automatically each time one of us left the room. Worried I might forget my card on my midnight excursions, I slept with it in a small pouch on a string around my neck. The hallway lights stayed on all night. Each time one of us got up, whoever was sleeping by the door was disturbed by a bright flash. Some got up twice in the night. The door handle did not turn from the outside so the door slammed disturbing everyone in the room. I would end up staying there many times. I learnt to keep the door ajar by slipping a sandal on the floor between it and the jamb. I also learnt that not all dorms are equal at Hostel Burgos. I know now which are the best; it might remain my little secret.

The Burgos has many redeeming features: no curfew, no limit on the number of nights we can stay, and we can wander in and out during the day. Breakfast is served until 10 a.m. We can linger in bed while the real pilgrims shove their noisy crinkly plastic toiletry bags inside their backpacks, zip and unzip compartments, and exit the dorm, leaving the heavy metal door to slam behind them. I don't think any of us got forty winks that night. After breakfast, we dragged ourselves to the Museum of Evolution with its displays from the valley of Atapuerca. Of huge archaeological interest, the Sierra de Atapuerca, now under the aegis of UNESCO, was used from time immemorial as passage from Europe to the Iberian Peninsula. 800,000-year-old human remains and artifacts have been found, making the Visigoths look like modern settlers.

Later, in the large breakfast room which is open all day, Chloë and I met Celia, a Canadian teaching ESL in England, and Marcia from Ohio. Marcia's husband had recently died after a long illness. This pilgrimage was her new beginning. The six of us wined and dined together near the plaza and celebrated Celia's 60th birthday. Before we realized it, Roland had picked up the tab.

Marcia pronounces her name Marsha. I have a Jewish friend who was called Marsha. I therefore assumed this woman was Jewish. I told her about my friend changing her name to Malka because Marsha means warrior, which did not suit her personality. I talked at length about all the ancient Jewish quarters and synagogues Malka and I had visited in Spain, in Toledo, in Córdoba, and in Italy. I talked about my visit to Terezín in the Czech Republic. I asked her if she had been to a concentration camp. She hadn't. I told her about Devorah at the mass grave. Only when we exchanged email addresses did I realize she was Marcia, not Marsha. She was not Jewish at all; she must have wondered why I was bringing all this Jewish stuff into the conversation. I hope Humble Pie is gluten-free.

Gwen and Roland would be leaving mid-afternoon the next day but not before we could find a restaurant that served something they had not yet tried: *Churros con Chocolate*, the famous inch thick, foot-long, ribbed pastries, freshly fried, and the cup of thick-as-pudding hot chocolate to dip them in. Chloë and I would miss our friends. They had been such great fun. Roland: gallant, generous, always a twinkle in his eye, and Gwen the giggler.

Many friendships develop along the way. We would cherish the moments shared with them. We would miss them, but life goes on. From my solo travel, it is a painful lesson I learnt a long time ago.

Spain's Giants

A promenade along the river was what Chloë and I needed to chase our blues away. We walked towards the historical centre to the museum of *gigantes* with its giant knights, kings and queens, and other historical characters, including a Black African and a Chinese with long droopy moustaches. Some represented contemporary people. I had seen the *gigantes* in Tortosa and in Barcelona. And Andrea and I would see them in Logroño during the wine festival in September. Popular in Spain, they give Chloë the creeps. We didn't stay long. We later witnessed a funeral cortege passing through a line-up of these *gigantes* outside the church. Is this an honour given to local heroes? It reminded me, albeit on an infinitely smaller scale, of the honour bestowed on French presidents and other highly respected citizens like Rousseau, Zola, Victor Hugo, and Marie Curie, when their remains entered the Pantheon in Paris.

Pan con Tomate

For the few days before our flight home, Chloë and I had treated ourselves to a private room at Hotel Alda Cardeña, away from the historical centre. Oh, how wonderful it was to have privacy after weeks in dorms. Each morning, the staff laid out a generous breakfast in the dining-room. I was in heaven because it included *pan con tomate*. It was my first time seeing it on the Camino. Either they don't serve it because it is not a custom around this part of Spain or because, unfamiliar with it, pilgrims don't try it. Since this hotel was away from the beaten path, it did not cater to many pilgrims. It was normal to find the *pan con tomate* as part of its breakfast menu. Slices of toast are smeared with tomato pulp, olive oil drizzled on top. Sometimes a thin slice of *jamón curado* or perhaps a slice of cheese are added. If no cheese or ham, a sprinkle of salt will do. The heck with my gluten intolerance. And to taste a Spanish tomato is to never want to sink your teeth into a genetically modified greenhouse tomato again.

When one has seen video clips of the Tomatina festival in Buñol near Valencia, one can understand why *pan con tomate* is a staple breakfast for Spaniards. Every year, at the end of August, thousands of people, mostly young men, gather in a designated area of Buñol. Some climb a grease pole to grab a ham positioned at the top. When the ham is down, tons of tomatoes are downloaded from trucks onto the street, crushed by thousands of participants and thrown at each other until everyone is smeared from head to toe with juice, pulp and seeds. The tomatoes are grown in a special field for that purpose. I suppose the same kind of young person found at the Tomatina runs with the bulls in Pamplona in July.

I prefer the festival of colours in the spring, in India, when people decorate their elephants and throw washable dye of all colours at each other. I was in Jaipur, Rajasthan at that time, one year. Like Spaniards, Hindus take their festivals seriously. Shops were closed, wide avenues deserted, a huge contrast to the ordinary cacophony of traffic. Young people and children on the back of scooters zoom along the wide, empty avenues, throwing dye at pedestrians; it's all in good fun and, as a tourist, the more you get doused, the more of a celebrity you become.

After a blissful night at the Cardeña under fluffy duvets, our sleep prolonged by the absence of someone's inconsiderate crack-of-dawn alarm, or other early-morning pilgrims' noises, we indulged in a leisurely breakfast. It felt strange because here, guests nodded and smiled at each other, and, if they were Spanish, wished other guests a *Buen provecho* (Bon appetit). Otherwise they kept to themselves.

Old Stones of Burgos

Determined to put in our kilometres within the town of Burgos, Chloë and I borrowed quiet, winding streets up to the Castillo, a ruin of an old castle. The storks' giant nests were everywhere. Hypnotized by their long necks and wide wing span, we never tired of watching them. A long, gentle hill leads to the castle on a rough path, and near the top, shallow steps make the approach easy. The path was lined with delicate fir trees and tenacious red poppies. And although forts are forbidding grey affairs, here and there, at the summit, clumps of delicate purple and yellow wildflowers added a cheerful note to the base of the stark stone walls.

We enjoyed the stork's-eye view of the imposing cathedral spires holding court over the faithful of Burgos under the sun-baked orange roofs of the old city. The only other visitors that morning were a group of schoolchildren busy getting rid of their excess energy. Shouting, they ran helter-skelter in the large expanse at the top while their teachers chatted calmly while throwing an occasional glance towards them; they seemed pleased to see the kids enjoying their field trip. Soon, they all disappeared into a building to take part in a workshop.

Chloë and I were the only other visitors. Burgos' chief attraction is deservedly the Gothic Catedral and its surrounding area. Pilgrims, even those who take a day off here, don't have time to explore much beyond it and the Museo de la Evolución Humana.

After many convoluted paths, many steps up and down, we found ourselves back along the Arlanzón at the Puente de Besson. Across the river, a pleasant surprise awaited us: the XII Century Monasterio de las Huelgas, with its mixture of Roman and Gothic styles where about twenty cloistered nuns spend their days in prayer and meditation, their only words hymns to the glory of God. We arrived at an opportune time; there was only one visit daily. Along with a dozen Spanish-speaking visitors, after presenting our passports, and putting our bags through a metal detector, a guide took us across a patio through a stone passageway with arched ceiling and carved white marble pillars, to gilded chapels with precious woods and paintings. Our visit ended with the pantheon where lie Alfonso VIII de Castilla and his wife, English princess Eleanor, along with other royal family members. Sadly, the commentary was only in Spanish. There was no time for me to translate. Chloë's mind was somewhere else. She was pining for the Camino. Tomorrow we would visit the Guggenheim in Bilbao. That, I knew, she would thoroughly enjoy.

Sculptures of Burgos

At the bus station today, I spend a moment with the 'escape artist' before heading to the Burgos. As luck would have it, I get a bed with four other women in a six-bed dorm. My throat is so raspy I could grate cheese on it. I must get cough syrup or our dorm might turn into an Agatha Christie murder mystery in the night with yours truly as the victim.

The life-size brass sculpture of the policeman with his whistle is there to welcome me near the *farmacía*. I gulp down a mouthful of syrup before leaving the pharmacy and stretching my legs up to the *castañera* (the Chestnut Lady) with her handkerchief tied tightly under her chin, her thick cape around her shoulders. The *castañera* sits there, expressionless, roasting chestnuts, waiting for the other poor to part with their coin. That was her lot in life. Passing pilgrims, tourists and locals have been rubbing parts of the sculpture. It is something people do in Europe. Patina does not accumulate on the rubbed parts which shine like fool's gold.

I have snapped many pictures of sculptures. This being my fourth time in Burgos, they are old friends now. There is the pilgrim tending to his blistered feet; the girl, one foot propped on the low parapet, leaning over the river, enjoying the view; the one of El Cid astride his horse by the bridge. There are the musicians, elegant in their capes and fedora hats. One of my favourites is of the *viejecitos*: the old man and the old woman, side by side on a bench, his hands propped high on the crook of his cane in front of him. Silently, he watches the passers-by. Silently, she crochets a scarf, a bowl of yarn at her side on the bench. I plan on one day doing a walking tour of Burgos just for its art, although near the cathedral, I don't like the sculpture of the bare pilgrim with his blistered skin, his gourd, his pilgrim's stick and the shell around his neck. He reminds me of a victim of Hiroshima. Life-size sculptures abound in Burgos and not only here. We see them in many of the small and large towns along the way. And there is no lack of pilgrim representations.

With its sculpture of El Cid and other imposing characters, I wonder how come the San Pablo Bridge is not as celebrated as Prague's Charles Bridge. I even find it more interesting and more attractive than the nearby Santa Maria Bridge which seems the most popular, although with the grand arched passageway leading to the cathedral at its north end, I am not surprised. Every tourist and pilgrim wants to pose under the archway.

Weeping Willows and Plane Trees

By the river, the weeping willows bring a flood of memories. In the play area, at my childhood convent, one ancient weeping willow with carbuncular bark spread its long, thin, droopy branches like a hen over its brood. I always felt protected under it. Proust had his Madeleine. I have my weeping willow. For a moment, today, they make me forget my aching throat.

I also have sad memories from the convent, but they are few. I loved being there. It was a much better childhood than I would have had at home. Not every woman welcomed an uninterrupted string of six girls, as close together as beads in a rosary, in the days before the pill.

There is nothing left from my childhood. We had nothing 'of value' so nothing was kept. Memories are like seeds. Only some of them grow, and without objects to remind us of our childhood, many of our memories wilt and die. The house I grew up in was a wreck of a house. Once sold, it burnt to the ground. Clad in unsightly Insulbrick on which huge Coca Cola and Seven-Up signs had been nailed, the rickety, three-story rooming house sat between the movie theatre and the church, a foot away from the sidewalk on the main street. Between sin and virtue, my parents joked, although women were not allowed upstairs with the roomers who were all men. Maybe, after it sold, someone found it more expedient to put a bit of kindling to it. It meant I could never drive past it with my children and point to it saying "This is the house I grew up in." I could never knock on its door and ask if I could step inside for just a few seconds to get a glimpse of my childhood.

The nuns' convent where I spent ten months of every year from the age of six to eleven is now an apartment building. I was already in my forties when I revisited it in the tiny village of Ste Ursule. Its chapel had become a clothing factory. The whirring sound of sewing machines now filled the lofty space where our holy hymns had risen in childhood. The pews and the altar had vanished. Sold at auction, I imagine. I forgot to look up at the back to see if the grand organ that accompanied our singing had disappeared. I suppose it had. Women, bent over identical pieces of fabric, oblivious per- haps to the sacred space they were occupying, repeated the same motions a thousand times a day for a small wage. Light filtered through stained glass windows. Weeping willows are rightly named; they always bring me bitter- sweet memories. It is no exception in Burgos today.

Past the bridge, along the *Paseo* del Espolón, the alley is lined with plane trees on both sides as far as the eye can see. Some people find them ugly. I find them wholesome. How many lovers' hopes have floated up to their canopies? How many breaking hearts have they witnessed on the same benches along their alley? How many old folks have sat silently on the benches in their shade, hands resting on the crook of their canes? How many *paseos* have they graced? The upper branches of the trees mingle with each other, forming an arch where the thick foliage of spring and summer still shades the way for locals, tourists and pilgrims.

After my walk around the historical area, I retreat to my dorm, gulp down another spoonful of cough syrup, and curl up under my blanket, hoping for a miracle.

To the Guggenheim with Chloë

The north of Galicia used to evoke black smoke spewing out of chimneys, terrorism, kidnapping... Things have changed since my first trips to Spain thirty years ago. On the Camino del Norte, the Guggenheim, an imposing titanium-clad museum with soft, gentle curves, has put Bilbao on a different kind of map. There, pilgrims rub shoulders with art and architecture lovers from all over the world.

From Burgos, Chloë and I had taken a bus to Bilbao. We were close enough to the dramatic Picos de Europa to get a foretaste of them. Under a steely grey sky, rough escarpments appeared and disappeared at the whim of thick fog patches. Tall, slim cypresses and brown fields alternated with rich green valleys. I wondered if the Galician sky had inspired Gehry in his choice of material. Close to the Atlantic, and with the ocean air passing over the mountain peaks, fog must be a frequent companion around there.

We were happy for our conscientious driver. With the road occasionally rising to touch the clouds, the drive could be a challenge. We had our noses to the window. Tiny hamlets sparsely located and set among inhospitable craggy mountains brushed shoulders with lush pastures, playing hide and seek with us. This must surely be a land of poets.

Galicia is a province rich in minerals. We passed a few industrial villages with tall, idle chimneys, and houses low in the valleys; I wonder where the smoke can escape. When those chimneys were built, the environment was perhaps not part of the planning. Black smoke spewing out of chimneys meant employment, prosperity.

The museum is a pleasant walk from the bus station. My sister and I had visited it in 2001. The scene was different now, with tourists and pilgrims snapping selfies. A man was selling miniature reproductions of Louise Bourgeois' Mama, the large spider sculpture adorning the grounds. It is familiar to us Canadians: a replica graces the grounds of our National Gallery in Ottawa. Bourgeois lived less than two years short of 100. When her Mama was born, she was almost as old as Sarah when she gave birth to Isaac.

I talked to the vendor. He earned a decent living from his sales. "You could not have picked a nicer work area," I told him. He agreed. The only tool of his trade: a white cloth spread along a low wall on which he displays his miniature Mamas in all colours and sizes. This is no place for arachnophobes. "May I take your photo?" I asked. He smiled and nodded yes. The contrast of his ebony-black skin against the soft curving steely grey shapes and the thick white mist rising from a pool of water between him and the museum netted me one of my best shots.

Unlike the *manteros*, (from the word *manta* meaning blanket – a word useful in hostels) the brave Africans and Asians who spread their large cloths on the ground all over European cities near stairways to metro stations, this vendor was fortunate to have a permit. In Barcelona, the *manteros* sell everything from handbags to handkerchiefs and costume jewellery. The *manta*, the large square cloth on which they display their wares, has eight strings, their ends knotted in the centre: one from each corner and one from the middle of each side. Once in a while, they receive a call from a friend up the way. Grabbing the knot in the middle, they pull the whole lot of their merchandise into a balluchon and, with it over their shoulder, disappear down the metro stairs. A minute later, to pacify store owners, a couple of police officers stroll up to the area the vendors have vacated. I have seen these itinerant vendors along the Ramblas and at the Güell Park. They are clever. They are resourceful. Resourcefulness is a quality that disappears with affluence. In Gaudi's Güell Park, I saw earrings displayed inside an umbrella. Easy to fold when the *policía* arrives. These clandestine vendors are honest young people; maybe the police tolerate them. What are they to do? Deprive human beings of a living? They are not peddling drugs; they are not pick-pocketing.

Further down from the museum, near the spider vendor, were four prostrate buskers covered from head to toes with large, loose satin cloaks, each in a different, bright colour. Imaginary animals akin to giraffes, they moved gracefully to the sound of music. When someone deposited a coin in their metal can, they bowed to the ground in a grand motion to show their appreciation. They reminded me of Muslims at prayer. It must be exhausting work. Hopefully, they are adequately recompensed by the bystanders. Hopefully, there was no one collecting a percentage of their take.

Inside the museum, we were more impressed by the glass and the curved shapes of the open spaces and by the way the light filters through than by the art. Andy Warhol's Marilyn Monroe occupied an entire wall, but even Warhol did not impress us as much as the building's architecture.

Later, we watched some kayakers on the Nervión and spotted a group of ten young men crowded on a large paddle-board. Was it some sort of university student caper, or is it a sport around here? One man was not wearing a life jacket. We watched to see how many of them would tumble. None did. Oh! To be young and foolish again!

We had not much time to explore Bilbao. Past joggers and street musicians, our empty stomachs were lured into a shopping mall where we stuffed ourselves with all the delicious foods of a buffet lunch. Everything our hearts desired: Chinese, Italian, sushi, seafood, ribs, salads, even white asparagus. And for dessert, cakes of all sorts, cream puffs, lychees, ice cream... You name it, Mr. Wok had it. We were thrilled to have stumbled upon this restaurant. I wished I had a better appetite.

Flower gardens and sculptures lined our way back to the centre. I had not expected palm trees, yet here they were even though it was the end of May, and most people were wrapped inside warm coats. It seemed a contradiction in terms. I have since heard that nostalgic South-American expatriates imported the trees from other areas of Spain.

Sadly, we did not have time to explore the historical area, but we enjoyed the high Art Deco façade of the tourist office with its four-storey banner with the words: 'Ongi Etorri, Bienvenidos, Welcome' reminding us we were in

Basque country. Near the top of the seven-story brownstone building with elegant curved sides, stood a balcony with tall pillars and above it, a curved fenced-in rooftop terrace. Its clock must have been a good two-feet in diameter. You can always tell a building is old when it has a clock. What child would know that watches are a relatively modern luxury, that these clocks were necessary not that long ago?

Jesus of the Street

How often, in Canada, have I seen men on park benches reading books? Or well-dressed middle-aged businessmen walking their white poodle? How often have I seen elegant octogenarian couples, shrivelled with age, moving slowly arm in arm through the park? Their steps are unsteady. They are there for each other, silent, reading each other's thoughts. They try not to think of the day their clock will stop. She worries: what will he eat if I go first? He worries: whose arm will she hold when I am gone?

At home, I see retired couples who are fit taking energizing walks along the lake, but they are different. In Canada, old people are young. Their backs have not curved under the burden of oppression. Nor are the very old visible. There is such tenderness in the old couples I see here. Is it the tenderness that comes from suffering? Those nearing their end are old enough to have lost a brother, an uncle, or a parent in the Civil War. They are old enough to remember the whistle of a bomb between an airplane and the ground, the ratatatat of gunshots. Do they, like the British, have black-out curtains neatly folded at the bottom of a drawer? They are from an era when post-traumatic stress was not part of the vocabulary because everyone suffered from it. In Canada, some have suffered the loss of a brother, a father, an uncle in Europe in the war, but, except for our refugees, we have never known brother fighting against brother. Perhaps that is the main difference I saw in Spain in the traces of suffering on the old people's faces. Internecine. Fratricide. Those are infinitely ugly words.

But all is not doom and gloom. Chloë and I had a hard time containing our laugh when a tall, elegant man (he reminded me of Charles de Gaulle) with his tiny white poodle walked past an expensive-looking hair salon.

jesusdelacalle.com said the sign. Only in Spain would I find a hair salon called Jesus of the Street.

In the bus station, everything was in Basque first and Spanish second. *Itxarongela, Sala Espera; Bulegoak, Oficinas...* I know if I see k's, x's and z's I am probably looking at Basque words. If a word has the letter c, v, q, w, or y, I won't look for it in a Basque-English dictionary; Basque words don't have them. As for the Galician or the Catalan alphabet, well... forget it. But did you know there is also Valencian? And a myriad of other languages? All in Spain. Oh, la la! At least, except for Basque, they are all related and easy to decipher if you know *Castilian,* which is what we call Spanish.

Thieves

At the Burgos today, I wake from a deep, restorative afternoon nap. I am not out of the woods yet, but I feel a lot better than yesterday in Torres. In the large room with its dozen tables where pilgrims congregate at all times of day, I bump into Carole, whom I met in Orisson a week ago. She is not well either. She shared a taxi to Burgos with other pilgrims last night. Her walking partner, who is hiking more than a whole Brierley stage each day, will meet her here. Between Villafranca and Burgos, it can be quite challenging if you have a health problem or if you don't feel in shape.

"A pilgrim was robbed at the bus station today," says Carole. "A young man distracted her while his accomplices took off with her backpack, which she had placed on the ground beside her." I know how easy it is to let your guard down. I have done it a few times. Fortunately without consequence. This is a reminder to be careful. I hope the thieves needed the money they will get from it more than she does. How much work and expense it must be to have to replace everything. At least, it happened in a town with a large Camino shop, but this will put a dent in her time and budget. I hope she is not strapped for money. I am sad it happened yet thankful I heard the story. Although I am used to travelling alone and am normally vigilant about my possessions, on the Camino, I have been lax. From now on, I will keep my bag in front of me and slip my foot through a shoulder strap if I place it on the ground.

Now, off to the grocery store for a roast chicken and some vegetables.

Luís from Argentina

At the Burgos, I can use a basic kitchenette. I bought enough food for an army. I hope the others aren't all vegetarians. A tall, handsome, lanky fellow the age of my sons, with a full head of wavy dark hair, is sitting at a nearby table. When I catch his attention, I push a plate with the extra chicken and salad in his direction. Happy to oblige, he moves across from me. Luís is Argentinian. I am not in a chatty mood. When he sees me squeezing lemon into a cup of hot water, I point to my sore throat. I had looked for ginger in the store, without luck.

After our meal, in a second grocery store a block away from the one where I had gone, we find a good chunk of ginger. Luís then studies jars of honey and chooses one for me. Organic and local. A beekeeper, he is here supervising workers at a property he inherited from an uncle. His parents, both from this part of Spain, had met in school in Argentina, where their families had emigrated.

My new friend is a generous person but also a chatterbox. Back at the Burgos, I really don't feel like engaging in conversation. My throat is getting worse by the minute, yet I don't want to retreat to my room. I am coughing non-stop. As luck would have it, at another table, a large woman about my age, wearing a colourful, flowing Fabindia dress, an enormous diamond and emerald ring, a heavy gold bracelet, gold necklace and earrings, is holding court. Everything about her makes her look out of place: her dyed puffy blond hair, heavy make-up, nail polish, her Louis Vuitton handbag on the table in front of her, her loud, angry yak-yak. Apparently, a Spaniard told her he didn't like her. "For no reason," she says. I'm sure she is not a bad person, but pilgrims behind her are rolling their eyes. Everyone is trying to get away from her.

Although his English is patchy and the woman has less than ten words of Spanish, Luís seems the only one generous enough to voluntarily engage her in conversation. While I scribble in my diary, it's hard to ignore her. Sometimes, rather than enunciating a word more clearly, she repeats it louder. That is something I have often noticed from unilingual people, as though the louder the word, the easier it would be for its meaning to penetrate. I know I could help. But not today! When the woman despairs at not being able to use some function on her phone, Luís teaches her. He is patience and kindness incarnate, St. Luís of Old Women in Need.

Somehow, I cannot imagine that woman travelling solo. She is not a pilgrim; she is visiting art galleries and museums, and seems to know what she is talking about. I wonder why she is sleeping in a dorm. The next day, I overhear her telling Nuala, an Irish woman with whom I will make friends, and eventually spend time in Santiago, that she finds it lonely to visit museums and galleries on her own. She craves company in the evening.

The next morning, for a while, I feel peppier. Luís joins me at breakfast. He talks about his country. The only Argentinians I have ever met were a couple of retirees on a Greek cruise I had joined as a last-minute junket in the fall of 2002. I still remember their name: Malvestidos (Badly dressed). They had decided to use up their savings and travel around the world rather than let their money be swallowed up in Argentina's financial crisis.

I don't know too much about Argentina. Luís fills me in on its recent history. At the end, he says, "I remember my parents talking in a low voice about friends they had lost. Two of my father's close friends disappeared. One night, they just vanished. Another friend of my parents emigrated to France, where he became a famous writer. He was running away from death." Arrived penniless, the man had to prostitute himself in Italy until he found work for a newspaper. "All my life, my parents were afraid to talk about politics," he said. "There are names they never mentioned." They had warned Luís never to discuss politics with friends or even with their cousins. They lived in fear much of their lives. When I listen to him, I think how fortunate we Canadians are despite our many but relatively insignificant political quarrels.

Luís tells me about an old man here in Spain, who as a small boy had witnessed an execution, and kept his secret buried all his life. Towards the end of his days, he had led the police to the site of the massacres. "It is the same in my country," he says, "That is how mass graves are uncovered."

"In a country like Canada, we can't really comprehend what it must be like to live under dictators or tyrants. Some people think of Canada as boring. I'll take boring over fear anytime," I tell Luís. I spend three nights at Hostel Burgos enjoying many long conversations with my new friend, mostly listening. I could fill a book just with his stories.

Nuala

Over the next two days, I am in no mood to sit in restaurants by myself. One minute I feel cured, the next, I am feverish, my throat is on fire and I am hacking and coughing. This bug will end up staying with me for two weeks. I am happy to have Luís and Nuala to share meals concocted from the grocery store. Nuala is from Westport, on the west coast of Ireland. Like me, she is putting in time, healing. Despite hobbling on one foot with the aid of her hiking poles, the wisp of a woman, well at the end of her seventh decade, always looks elegant. She hurt her foot on the Camino and has been limping for several days already. She is determined not to return home early to bleak Ireland. "I am taking a bus to Santiago and staying there until my flight," she says.

From our time in Burgos to when we meet again in Santiago, I will see not one iota of improvement in Nuala's foot. Eventually, back in Ireland, her doctor will diagnose an impacted fracture of the tibia which will not stop her from going on a two-week vacation to Greece with her son and grandchildren a week after returning home. She is also planning to come back to the Camino. Anyone who has heard of Dervla Murphy knows some Irish women are made of hearty stock. Alone, on a January day in the early 60s, Dervla bicycled from the West coast of Ireland, across the Alps, through hostile lands, all the way to India. I can easily imagine Nuala doing some crazy thing like that in her younger days.

In Burgos, we spend time together until her bus a few days later. Nuala does most of the talking because every time I open my mouth, I risk a coughing fit. It is good to converse in English and not to have to serve as translator for a while. Incredibly enough, although I don't own a cell phone, I can even teach her how to use certain functions on hers. In fact, it is almost the same as an iPod, except that with my iPod, I need internet.

On my second night, I miraculously have the entire dorm to myself. I can cough away and not disturb anyone. Although we hear it is often difficult to find a bed on the Camino, I will have had three nights alone in dorms, including in one tiny village after León in a fourteen-bed dorm. My last night, four of six beds are occupied: Carmel Shalev, a gentle, kind and inspiring Israeli writer tells me about her book *In Praise of Ageing*. We discuss the situation in Israel. Carmel describes quite a different scene from what we, in the West, imagine. She talks about Palestinians and Israelis working together, and invites me to come visit in Galilea. There is also Michèle, an English teacher from a French village near the Alps. A solid woman taller and heavier than me, she looks strong. With her puffy, healthy-looking pink cheeks; she looks no older than sixty. When I confess I don't carry my bag, she chastises me. "You are not a true pilgrim," she says. "It's true," I tell her. "I never meant to be a true pilgrim. Besides, I'm seventy-one. I have nothing to prove by carrying a heavy bag." It turns out she is one day older than me!

I am determined to make it to Santiago this time. It means even if I weren't sick, since I only have four weeks altogether, I would still have to skip one part. What a dilemma: apart from the outskirts of large towns, there is really not one stretch I don't like; even the long, flat (and not so flat) walks between Burgos and León have their charm. Time is a great adviser. I will let it decide. There is a silver lining to my illness after all. I have walked twice from Burgos to León, but have never been past León. This morning, no need for me to deliberate. It's Burgos to León by bus. I am sorry to miss all the lovely places in between.

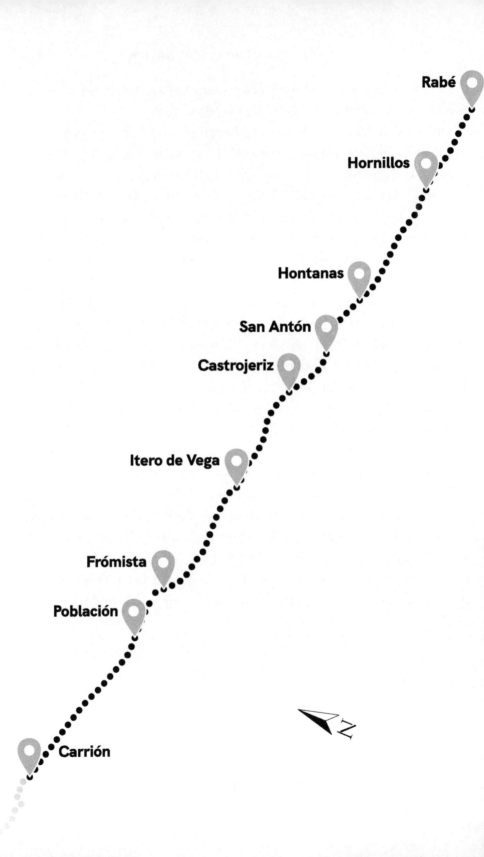

Rabé

Hornillos

Hontanas

San Antón

Castrojeriz

Itero de Vega

Frómista

Población

Carrión

N

Back on the bus – Burgos to León

The Most Handsome Grandpa in the World

A day's walk from Burgos, in Hornillos with its sixty inhabitants, lives 'the most handsome grandpa in the world'. Last May at hostel El Afar, hours after his grandchild was born, he tried without success to hide his pride. The staff teased him and called him *'el abuelo el más guapo del mundo'*. We joined in the banter, and for a few minutes, became part of his family. Time often seems to stand still on the Camino, but once in a while, a birth, a wedding, a funeral remind us that it marches on through rejoicing, loving, grieving, aging. The grandpa was my daughter's age. I had suddenly reached the venerable stage of great-grandmotherhood. Yikes!

Hornillos (the village name) means pottery kilns. My busiest Camino stamp is from El Afar: an earthen jug, moon crescent, shell, pilgrim, rooster, the Milky Way, and a wavy stretch of the Camino to a hilltop village. No kitchen sink. It uses two well-deserved spaces in my *credencial*.

While our clothes dried on the low stone wall, Vicki, Chloë, Randall, Joanna, and I stretched out on comfy lounge chairs in the sunny garden at the back. Alas, at dinner at the long wooden tables, with a dozen other pilgrims, while most were enjoying generous portions of artichoke paella, poor Vicki, was not impressed. She reminded me of a baby with its first spoonful of broccoli puree. At least, she has a great sense of humour. She left the table with an almost empty stomach, but we had a good laugh. It was a good thing we still had provisions in the larder part of my suitcase. That night, after we had all snuggled under our blankets, a thundering fart resounded in the dorm. We all burst out laughing, including the culprit, whoever he or she was. It was all sound and fury. Fortunately no aroma. No one claimed it.

El Fuego de San Anton

Near Castrojeriz, twice have I passed under the tall arches of the ruins of the once impressive Monasterio de San Anton. Now forlorn, abandoned, a tall myth has been erected in its place: monks with supposedly miraculous powers cured pilgrims suffering from a most excruciating disease: *Fuego de San Anton* or *Fuego de infierno* (Hell's Fire). People from as far away as

Northern Europe made the pilgrimage hoping for a cure to their burning, aching, gangrenous extremities. No smoke without fire; no myth without some truth. No one knew then that Hell's Fire, now called ergotism, was caused by consuming grains infected with a dangerous fungus. Pilgrims returned home cured. Often, after a few years, they came back for a second, even a third cure. The rye grains that made up a significant part of a normal diet in their countries were not popular in France and Spain. Absence from home acted as a detoxification cure. As their pilgrimage progressed, symptoms gradually lessened, often totally vanishing by the time they reached Saint James' tomb. Back to their fjords, harsh winters, and diet of rye bread, eventually, the illness would reappear. Superstitions abounded. Assuming God was punishing them for their sins, back to the Camino it would be, begging for forgiveness again, and making sure they stopped at the Monasterio de San Anton to receive the curing ritual of the monks. Perhaps, to please God, the repentant pilgrims left a generous donation for the upkeep of the Monastery.

Coincidentally last May an hour after the ruins, we were met at the door of quaint Albergue Rosalia in Castrojeriz with the aroma of freshly baked bread. I could not turn it down. At long wooden tables, we devoured garlicky home-made humus and a generous meal followed by chocolate mousse made with real eggs, real whipped cream and real chocolate. How could I ever forget that?

Randal, for whom going down steep hills was a challenge, was worried about his knees. Rummaging through the discards, Chloë fished out a pair of expensive neoprene knee braces. She had just completed an advanced sport injury management course following her third year of kinesiology. With the help of the braces and KT tape, in no time, she had Randal all organized. Once more the Camino lived up to its reputation.

It was there we met Priscilla. True to my habit of adding an epithet to each new name to make it easier to remember, when she introduced herself, I blurted out "Priscilla Queen of the Desert." "Please don't call me that!" she said, firmly. I didn't ask why. It wasn't the first time I put my foot in my mouth. Priscilla, not Queen of the Desert, was about my age. I don't know how much travelling she had done in her life. She had flown from

Figs, wonderful figs

Fargo, North Dakota to Paris, spent two days visiting the Eiffel Tower and the Louvre. Then, from Paris to London, then Madrid for a few days. From Madrid to Rome for an overnight. From Rome to Vienna... It seemed rather helter-skelter to me. "Why did you do it that way?" I asked. As though she had not a care in the world, she replied, "I should probably have looked at a map before booking my flights."

Figs, Wonderful Figs

Between Castrojeriz and Itero de la Vega, last September, near the excruciatingly steep hill, Andrea and I had been admiring a garden with a large trellis from which hung an abundance of green grapes when a man and a woman came out of the house. We complimented them on their garden. "We live in Burgos, this is our weekend home," said the man. "Do you like figs?" asked his wife. "We sure do." "*Momento*," she replied, and went into the house. She came back out with a large plastic bag which she filled with huge, juicy, ripe green figs for us. I have a cute video of her with her arm around Andrea's waist singing a beautiful song for us.

Hospital de San Nicolás

By the thousand-year-old bridge to Itero de la Vega, Andrea and I stuck our nose inside an ancient building. Until we passed through its arched entrance, Hospital de San Nicolás was an unimpressive, flat-roofed, rectangular stone building. But once inside, at first, we were sorry we had reserved a bit further. "This is the real thing," said Andrea. And she was right. The hostel consisted of only one large room at the end of which, below a crucifix, under a long, narrow window, stood a modest altar with a painted triptych with gold-leaf. At the other end, a table and a small area for cooking could not be called a kitchen, but apparently a communal meal would be prepared for the pilgrims. On the main floor were beds for men with the thinnest of mattresses. A rustic staircase led upstairs to the women's quarter. We were standing in a XII Century hermitage, in the kind of atmosphere a true pilgrim should experience at least once. But it was cold. Cold and damp. It was mid-afternoon and we were shivering uncontrollably. What would it be like later?

If we had stayed there, we could have been forgiven for waking in the night and thinking there were Templars standing guard outside. The place was dark except for a pale light reflected in the white stone floor, walls, tall pillars, altar and ceiling. Despite the cold, it would have been wonderful to experience one night here. We asked where was the bathroom. It was in a small building outside. No, thank you. We would be quite happy where we had reserved.

After a good night's sleep at our prosaic, comfortable hostel, the next morning, Andrea and I walked for a few hours until, by an old church at Boadilla del Camino, we paused for breakfast at the inviting restaurant of Albergue En El Camino. Past a courtyard with a modern metal sculpture of pilgrims, we found the large dining-room with pink walls hung with original paintings of pastoral scenes, and long wooden tables on which perched a fluffy white cat. Cat and art fit well with the beamed ceiling. We gobbled up filling breakfasts in pottery dishes prepared by a laid-back young man with short trimmed beard and wool cap. After breakfast, we couldn't leave without taking photos. We wanted to commit every inch of this garden to memory: a tall bush of delicate pink roses, a stone trough where more pink flowers grew cheerfully near grinding wheels, large smooth terracotta pots; metal frogs and lizards climbing walls... There was even a tiny pool. And lots of small trees under which a pilgrim could rest on a hot day. Just another garden of Eden. Unfortunately that morning, even though there were tables out in the courtyard, it was too cold to sit out there although, as usual, before late morning, we would wilt in the heat. After breakfast, we walked along the canal for what seemed like a long time through monotonous scenery, our only entertainment: workers dredging the canal.

Our bus bypasses Frómista on the other side of the canal where last May, the five of us landed at welcoming Albergue La Luz. A painted portrait of Anita, the Dutch co-owner, signed by her Spanish husband, adorned the wall near the reception. Upstairs was a piano room. You can't keep an old crooner away from a piano. We refilled Randall's glass with Rioja while he brought the ebony and ivory to life, and sang, and whistled some good old songs. What a delightful way to end a long, hot day.

Our dorms felt a bit overcrowded. We would not have noticed it had there not been a quartet of pilgrims who rubbed copious amounts of camphor on their legs which got me into fits of coughing every time I had to go by their beds on my way out the room. I wanted to ask them to please not do that, but this was the Camino; I must be tolerant. I'm not sure how tolerant they were of my coughing. It was too late to explain they were causing it.

Antonio

Last September, Cathy, Andrea and I had stayed a bit further in a two-room school in Población. Antonio, our kind *hospitalero*, looked about my age. I don't think he was born with the proverbial silver spoon in his mouth. I wondered if this was his permanent home. Alas, when I tried to make conversation with him, I could only decipher the odd word. He sat at a long table, stringing bracelets and necklaces with dyed wooden beads like I had seen at ten for a rupee in India, and he displayed them for *donativo*. Since our bed was only €5, I bought a few of his bracelets to encourage him. He had not an ounce of fat on his body. His muscular arms proved he was no stranger to hard work. Had the villagers taken him under their wing by offering him a roof in exchange for taking care of us, pilgrims? Later, in the pub-cum-grocery store, I found him at the counter enjoying a beer, perhaps with the Euros he had collected from his sales.

Bugs

Poor Andrea and Cathy were scratching all over. Cathy had been the first to notice the itch. Looking for a culprit, Andrea accused her of having passed it on. No matter how much I tried to get her to stop, she just had to find a culprit. "It could happen to anyone," I kept repeating. Miraculously, although she and I shared a bag, the nasty creatures never bothered me.

The next night, we slept in a huge dorm with beds rather than bunks, in a grand old nuns' convent in Carrión de los Condes. It had the best kitchen of the whole Camino. We were about eighteen in our dorm. It was like being back in my nuns' boarding school, except there, if my memory serves me well, we were five rows of sixteen beds. Here, the frames were not metal like at the convent. I could not entertain myself like I did as a child, by passing my nylon comb through my hair and hitting it against the metal frame in the dark, in awe at the sparkles created by the static.

Four or five pilgrims, all young women, were terribly sick with fever and vomiting. Exceptionally, it was their second night at the convent. Early morning, when I went to wash my face, one girl was retching and moaning, bent over a sink, her face white as a ghost. I asked what I could do to help. Just then another pilgrim walked in. Feebly, lifting her head slightly, the sick girl replied, "She's helping me. Thank you." We never found out what happened to them. It seemed they had all been at the same place the night before and probably had food poisoning. Or perhaps they had all drunk from the same contaminated fountain. Andrea was not feeling well, either. Fortunately, she was not as sick as the other women. Because of the aggravation from their skin rashes, she and Cathy were in no mood for hiking. We took our time in the morning, gave the kitchen a spring cleaning, and explored the town before catching a bus to Ledigos.

The Three Russians

With Chloë, Randall, Joanna and Vicki, instead of the nuns' convent, we stayed at the Santa Clara with its small rooms, large courtyard and quirky museum of hundreds of nativity scenes. Vicki, our snap-happy shutterbug, was quite miffed when informed cameras were not allowed in the museum. The scenes were constructed of all media including clay, paper, wood, metal, and everything in between. "It's like a Clint Eastwood movie," said another visitor. "The Good, the Bad and the Ugly."

Later, while we put together a tuna salad, two men and one woman, Russians, all twice or three times my size and a head or two taller than me, were talking loudly while picking avidly at the bones of large chops, and stuffing potatoes in their mouths. Their voices could be heard in the hallway outside the kitchen. They were still shoving in the food when they started

Ledigos

Terradillos

Calzada

El Burgo Ranero

Reliegos

León

N

interrogating us. How far had we walked? They had walked much further. How much did our bags weigh? Did we carry our own bags? They carried theirs and they weighed tons. How much had we spent on our equipment? They had spent much more. Where had we started? They had started in Saint-Jean many days after us. "How far are you going tomorrow?" the woman asked. I glanced at my companions. "I think we'll just mozie on to Calzadilla tomorrow," I said. I was lying. We all dreaded being invited to walk with them or to share a dorm. Terradillos de los Templaros, where we were in fact heading, was almost twenty-seven kilometres. It would be our longest day ever on the Camino, and where Chloë and I would catch a bus to León, then a train back to Pamplona for our flight home.

Late the next afternoon, approaching the entrance to Terradillos under an unforgiving, hot sky, we passed the Russians. The tallest of the three, the one with the biggest mouth, was sitting on a bench, a large tube of ointment beside him. His shoes and socks were on the ground. The woman was busy bandaging his feet. All three of them had huge sweat stains from armpits to waist. "Are you staying in Terradillos tonight?" asked Big Mouth. "No, we're hiking all the way to San Nicolás," I lied. San Nicolás would be another hour or two away. His eyes nearly popped out of his head. "*Buen Camino*," we said and walked another ten minutes to our hostel, the Jacques de Molay, with its definite templar feeling, its museum-like display of old farm implements and antique paraphernalia. When they arrived at the reception desk ten minutes later, there was no room at the inn. Comfortably ensconced in our seats at a table with our cool refreshments, we wished them again *Buen Camino*.

Wild Boars and Wily Old Men

Last September, somewhere between Carrión de los Condes and León, (you will soon understand why I don't say where), Andrea and I decided to explore the tiny village where we were staying that night. I often take pictures of textured surfaces. Curious about its building material, I was scrutinizing the wall of a house when three gentlemen came by. "Straw mixed with plaster," one explained. Another old man, who had been sitting on a stool outside his house, offered to show us inside. We gladly accepted. Once inside the house, the old man grabbed Andrea's head in an arm-lock and tried to kiss her. She was fast enough to move her face sideways and strong enough to get out of the arm-lock, but not before getting a peck on the cheek. We glared at each other. Should we make our escape now? The old geezer looked a bit too fragile to be frightening, and we had already seen enough of the house to know we wanted the tour. We stayed at arm's length from him, but kept glancing at each other and at him, secretly planning our escape if needed. I figured since the other three fellows had seen us enter the house, he wouldn't dare assault us. Andrea, once a bodybuilder, and I, assumed that between the two of us, we could easily overtake him.

His wife was away, he said, babysitting the grandchildren. He was obviously into that phase of life when inhibitions can fade away. No reason to take grandpa to court. He took us around the main floor, pausing in front of paintings with pastoral scenes inspired by Millet's Gleaners. Set in beautiful, soft-cornered frames carved by their son, they were his wife's work. He posed below a photo of himself with some of his cronies beside their hunting rifles and a very dead wild boar. The animal's hooves, now four gruesome coat hooks of polished black claws and fur, hung near the door. He led us to another room, stood under a huge stuffed boar's head and offered again to pose for us. We obliged, always keeping our distances.

In the interior court was an ancient well, its old rubber bucket still dangling above. Andrea and I looked at each other. Were we both thinking the same? Was the skeleton, backpack and hiking sticks of some young solo female pilgrim decomposing at its bottom? Probably not. Our tour guide's lasciviousness was likely an early symptom of dementia.

Pockmarked fruit dangled from the branches of an apple tree, and a dozen scrawny, miserable, filthy-looking chickens clucked away, crowded inside a long cage. Not a joyful sight, especially for Andrea the vegetarian. In another corner, a couple of fat, lazy cats sat undisturbed, oblivious to the chickens' lamentations.

"*No me molestan los peregrinos*" (pilgrims don't bother me) said the old man. I chuckled because the word for 'bothering' in Spanish is '*molestar*'. No wonder pilgrims don't 'molest' him. While his wife is babysitting, the old lecher perches on a stool outside his house, or in his living-room, behind the window that gives directly onto the path. There, he can enjoy the parade of young things in tight pants and padded bras, from early spring to the end of fall. For some, heaven is on this side of the pearly gate.

We thanked him profusely. Before we made it outside the house, he grabbed Andrea again. She narrowly missed a big wet kiss. The old man had to content himself once more with her cheek. I reached for the door and pulled it open. Recoiling, poor Andrea, hightailed it out of there.

I can't believe I did this, but I did: while Andrea was vigorously scrubbing her cheeks at the sink in the albergue, I grabbed one of my minuscule Canadian flag pins and went back to the old man. I found him again sitting on his stool outside the house, and pinned the flag to his sweater. He looked at it and said. "I will never take it off."

Michael and Kathleen

Between Carillon de los Condes and Reliegos, in El Burgo Ranero, Michael and Kathleen, a volunteer Irish couple, ran the *donativo*. At registration, I asked Michael where we should put our donations. "Wait until you see how you like it," he said, smiling, as he pointed to a slot in the wall near the door.

The next morning, while Cathy patiently waited and Andrea rifled through the box of discards from previous pilgrims, I was frantically searching for my sandals. Under my bed, in the bathroom, everywhere, without luck. I stomped down the stairs, fuming. "Someone stole my sandals. Thieves everywhere on this darn Camino!" I declared loudly. At the bottom of the stairs, Michael was standing, smiling, his eyes moving from me to my sandals and back. "Would these be yours?" he asked cheekily. I had placed them with the hiking shoes at the entrance after dinner out the night before. Humble pie for breakfast now?

Andrea was still busy pulling out treasures from the box of discards. Cathy was waiting patiently. It was a few minutes to eight. "Alright, pilgrims, time to go," said Michael. "I am staying right until eight o'clock," I said, "I want my money's worth." That's when the penny dropped... Not used to *donativos*, or to pay upon leaving, we had forgotten to put money in the donation slot! I hope other pilgrims are not like us.

We had a leisurely walk to Reliegos where Laudelino, our *hospitalero*, enrolled us as volunteers for arriving pilgrims while he went for his mid-afternoon meal. It was Andrea's and my last night. Cathy was continuing on to Santiago, but Andrea and I were already planning on coming back to walk the rest of the way.

León

This time, I am looking forward to walking from León starting tomorrow morning. From here on, it is all fresh territory for me.

I made a friend on our ride from Burgos. Susan, a Floridian in her forties, is hiking alone. She doesn't have enough time to walk the whole Camino, so she skipped Burgos to León. From the bus station, we cross the Rio Bernesga and walk together to Av. Republica Argentina and the León Hostel where she has a reservation, near the cathedral. I will be at the San Francisco de Asís, about a kilometre away. We make plans to eat together. "Call me when you're ready", she says. When I confess I don't have a cell phone, she can hardly believe it. Unlike one of my friends, Susan doesn't say, "Come on, get with it." She vows to put her own phone away one day a week back home. "I'll be at your hostel at 4 o'clock, if that works for you," I say. "Wow, just like that!"

On my way to the San Francisco, my bag doesn't seem heavy at all. Wondering if I shouldn't carry it after all, I soon smarten up. My walk today is less than an hour, not six or seven. In my experience, the weight of a backpack is directly proportional to the distance travelled.

At five minutes to four, I climb the three flights of stairs to the León Hostal in a narrow house sandwiched in a row of old buildings smack in the centre of the city. The León welcomes pilgrims in a bright sitting-room with comfy-looking couches. The furniture is IKEA style, unpretentious. It fits in just fine in the bright room with high walls decorated with old maps. Purple orchids adorn a small table. A vine climbs along a bookcase on the mantlepiece. The top part of the walls is covered with the original embossed tin, and a large marble fireplace keeps the room cozy in winter. French windows give onto small balconies where guests can sit and enjoy the procession

Murias Astorga Órbigo Valverde

of tourists and pilgrims below. The dorms are spacious, clean, and well-lit. This is a place the owners are proud of.

The *hospitalero* is out. I check the dorms until I come to Susan, asleep. While I stand there, debating whether I should wake her, her alarm sounds. I am happy not to have to make that decision.

A Feast for the Eyes

The old quarter is bustling with tourists. The restaurant has an artistic display of bright orange crab, huge pink prawns lined up like sausages with a thick slice of lemon for decoration, large scallops on their shells, some other creature from the sea, olives and slim yellow peppers, pale little fillets, anchovies perhaps, soaking in olive oil with flecks of red pepper. Among the *pinxos* (*tapas* in other parts of Spain), quite a few are mysteries for me.

Perched on high stools at a small table outside, we both order Russian salad. Minutes later, an uninspiring dish appears. In three less than bites, we have emptied our plates. "That was a bit of a disappointment," I tell Susan. "It was the worst and most expensive Russian salad I have ever eaten," she says, but the waiter was so pleasant that we still leave a generous *propina*.

Back in my dorm, the fever is back. I am coughing non-stop now. I worry about a roommate who is having a nap. This annoys me no end because at home, on the extremely rare occasion I feel something coming on, I tuck myself into bed with a hot lemon, ginger and honey and wake up the next day my normal self. On the Camino, the bug clings to me like a leech. I have no patience. It is often that way with those of us blessed with good health. I should just grin and bear it.

Susan and I had planned to walk to Villadangos del Paramo or even to San Martín del Camino about an hour further. We are to meet at the bridge near Plaza San Marcos at 6:30 before sunrise, but I need to shed the bug once and for all. I need my energy back. Internet is good, so I message her to let her know I won't be walking far tomorrow. No point leaving early. If I did, nothing would be open at my destination. I would have enjoyed her company. Such is the way of the Camino.

Suburbs

La Casa del Camino in Valverde is less than three leisurely hours away. After the historical centre of León, on the other side of the bridge, past the imposing parador with its dozens of medallions of who knows who, I pause under the red-tipped foliage of a chestnut tree, its branches laden with large, bumpy, pale green nuts. Further, before the industrial area, absorbed in my own thoughts, I am startled by a pilgrim sculpture in black cape and wide sombrero at the side of a restaurant. Complete with walking stick, modern hiking boots, rosary dangling from her neck, a gourd, she holds the breakfast menu below a sign: 'Buen Camino, 340 km'. I see pilgrims inside, but I will wait until I develop an appetite.

Further, imposing, shiny steel cylindrical storage tanks line the way. Full of Riojo, I wonder? Then, a small, whitewashed, dilapidated house catches my attention. It looks abandoned; its walls are cracked; large chunks of plaster have fallen off; ugly electrical wires run helter-skelter across the façade out of a door and into a window. But above a rotting door and a filthy, empty display case where perhaps daily articles used to be posted, a large sign in calligraphy: 'Diario de León.' Did the daily newspaper which boasts more than a hundred years of existence have its humble beginning here? The house is a sad sight. A window and balcony on the second floor seem permanently shuttered. The front door is rotting. But then I see, jutting out of the roof, on the third floor, a large modern window, and near the side of the house at street level, a modern steel and glass door. I bet someone lives up there in a modern apartment. Sandwiched between another old house fronted by dozens of mailboxes, and a modern, tall, brown brick apartment building where not a peseta has entered the budget for aesthetics, (the kind of building a beautiful country like Spain should be ashamed of), the Diario de León house must be slated for demolition. Unless its history has made it a monument. The area is a sore contrast with the historical centre.

Apart from the oaks with their long, erratic foliage laden with half-green, half-beige acorns, and apart from the interesting façade of a large, modern church with its giant sculptures of the twelve apostles, there is nothing for my camera. Much of it is boring and to be honest, downright ugly. I am in the suburbs now. The houses are modern, the road surface cracked, the surroundings uninteresting. But at the village of Valverde, La Casa del Camino is all the opposite.

Refuse, Reuse, Recycle

Marta welcomes me, and every pilgrim who comes for the night, with a generous glass of freshly squeezed orange juice. Realizing I am not feeling great, she invites me to join her and the cook for a lunch of thick, tasty, perfectly seasoned lentil soup with generous chunks of sausage. I see no reason to refuse. When Juan Carlos, the owner, arrives, Martha enquires about Alexandra, his wife who has been shuffling on one bandaged foot for a week from a frightening infection. She is usually the one in charge. I will get to meet her later when Juan Carlos drives up with her for a brief visit. "I just can't stay away," she will admit.

Everywhere I look, I can see Juan Carlos and Alexandra are recyclers. A white Art Deco lamp hangs above a white Naugahyde retro couch which reminds me of the one in my grandparents' house. The back could be lowered to form a bed with the seat if you didn't mind sleeping in the hollow where seat and back met. The display cabinet for dishes, the table and straight-backed chairs are also from the 60s. Every once in a while, when I point to an object, Juan Carlos says: "I got it for free." He despises waste, is proud of his finds. "You're a man after my own heart," I tell him. On my private tour of the garden, he points to the sliding gate lock. Most of his locks came from old trunks or rotten doors from his recycling business. In the vast yard, all the furniture and artifacts are recycled or re-used objects. An 18-inch long reclining Buddha and an ancient, white metal bird cage decorate a deep window ledge. Someone has placed a peasant's straw hat with a profusion of holes on top of the cage. A disused water pump reminds me of my childhood days at my grandparents' cottage. Transat chairs, like the ones I imagine went down with the Titanic, are there for us to stretch our weary bodies on. One of them is propped up with old bricks. Flowers of all colours, sizes and shapes bloom everywhere from old tree trunks or from abandoned objects repurposed by Carlos. And throughout the garden stand several large parasols. The piece he is most proud of is his solid desk-top, a five-inch thick, highly polished slab of wood. *"Nopal negro,"* he says, beaming. *"Muy, muy caro."* (Black walnut. Very very expensive). He found it amid the flotsam and jetsam of a demolished house.

Love on the Camino

As the temperature climbs; the garden is a good place to while away an hour or two and regain some energy. Near an apple tree, some pilgrims have taken refuge from the sun under a covered patio. At the edge of the property, a round gazebo gives shade to nine or ten hammocks, only two of which are occupied by a young couple. Romeo and Juliet are holding hands, gazing amorously at each other. She is one of those gorgeous young women who remind me life is unfair. He is equally handsome. With love blooming so near me, I hesitate to occupy a hammock. When I turn to go, Adonis says, "Please, please. There is room for everyone."

I am happy I have my notebook with me so I won't feel I'm intruding, but they are in a chatty mood and ask me about my Camino. It's hard to concentrate. They look so hot to trot! I can't imagine how they manage to sleep in separate beds. I'm dying to know how long they have been together. After a while, emboldened, I ask, "I am curious, did you two meet on the Camino?" "Yes," he says. "Near Castrojeriz." That explains it! By my calcu-lations, it is less than one week back. Beaming, she looks at him and asks, "Can I tell her?"

I must not look threatening or judgemental because she blurts out that it was love at first sight. There is one tiny inconvenience: he is married. "Yesterday," he jumps in, "I called my wife. I didn't want to be living a lie. I hate lying. I told her I had met my soul-mate and fallen in love." "She must have been thrilled to hear that!" I try not to sound too sarcastic. "What did she say?" "She said, 'go for it,'" he replies, seemingly unperturbed and obvi-ously relieved. "We had planned to meet two weeks from now in Santiago. She said she will still come." She wants to meet his new love. I am not too sure what to say. But it's not as though they don't know I will be jotting everything down in my notebook. I don't ask his name. I tell them I am collecting anecdotes for a book. "May I put your story in my book?" I ask. He hesitates a second. "Sure," he says. Shortly after, they continue on their way. Of course, I should have guessed they weren't staying here tonight. Nor will I meet them again. I suppose they found private rooms where they could live out their Camino romance to the fullest.

After they have left, I join a woman with a friendly smile under a large parasol at a table. Elena is taking an afternoon break. She is not sleeping here tonight, but I will bump into her again, and we will hike long stretches together before Santiago. A stuffed white rat, her pet companion, sits on her shoulder. After a few attempts at conversation, I realize her English is very limited, her French non-existent. A landscape artist from Ekaterinburg, smack in the middle of Russia, she speaks a smattering of German, and has taught herself the basics of Spanish before coming to the Camino via Barcelona where she had two weeks of tango lessons. Since my Russian is limited to 'bistro' 'nyet' and 'spasibo', we opt for Spanish as our common language. I learn many things from her today that will turn out to be erroneous. She is not fibbing, but her Spanish skills need a bit more honing than mine.

At supper, pilgrims are served generous portions of chicken. I swallow three bites and feel sick again. Grrr! I apologize and retire without dinner. My cough syrup acts as sleeping potion. In the morning, I wake up rested. It is not the lot of everyone in the dorm. As though he has been ruminating his words all night, a pilgrim spits out in anger to the man in the bed above his: "Do you realize how much you snore? People like you should sleep in private rooms." To which the snorer calmly replies: "Really? I didn't know snoring was forbidden. Do feel free to sleep in private rooms if you wish."

Marta has reserved a bed for me at the Verde in Hospital de Órbigo. The path today is flat as a tortilla. I am ready to hike a good six hours. I will take my time and rest often.

Sausage Fingers

I had few unpleasant experiences along the Camino, but there is one incident I probably won't forget. Maybe too many pilgrims make the same mistake, or maybe the woman's cat had died that morning. It did not happen any-

where near here. If I relate it now, it's because I wouldn't want her identi-
fied. It was lunchtime. Our rain capes had been put to good use. It looked
as though the rain would continue *a cántaros* for a while. If I knew what
dumb *faux pas* I was about to commit, I would not have stopped at the large
restaurant already packed to the gills with dripping pilgrims. The ambiance
was cacophonous. Groups of young, enthusiastic hikers with their guides
occupied most of the tables while quieter, solo pilgrims joined others at
tables with free seats.

An expressionless old woman, round like a Babushka nesting doll, only
head and shoulders above the counter, was busy serving and taking money
from customers. Elena and I waited patiently before attracting her attention until she shut the drawer of her cash register for the umpteenth time.
Elena ordered a croissant and coffee, and I, a drink and some tasty-looking
sausages displayed inside a glass cabinet. With her short stumpy fingers
which I imagined filthy since they had just been handling Euros without as
much as a wipe between the cash register and us, the woman grabbed two
sausage links, placed them on a plate and, without asking me, proceeded,
with a sharp knife, to cut them into chunks, sliding her paw all over them
ahead of the blade. With a look of revulsion on her face, Elena's eyes went
from the woman's hands to me and back to the woman's hand. I was thinking the same, but I was hungry. I said nothing. I tried to be philosophical,
to forget I had needed two consecutive courses of strong antibiotics to get
rid of giardia following a trip to India. Anyway, do we ever know what happens in a restaurant kitchen? Once in a while you have to live dangerously.
I already had the correct change in my hand, including a tip. I just handed
it over and thanked the woman.

Two pilgrims let us share their table. I pulled out some of my corn cakes.
Elena was carrying a tomato in her bag. She insisted I take it. I saw no reason
to refuse. When I finished my drink, I was still thirsty. I was carrying a can
of soda in my bag. Since we were near destination, I figured I may as well
drink it now.

Suddenly, the eagle-eyed owner pops up at our table and starts shouting at me. She is pointing at my corn cakes and at the orange soda. "Rude
pilgrim," she shouts in Spanish. "How dare you come into my restaurant

and eat your own food, bring your own drink?" She goes on and on in her loud voice. Necks are craned, all eyes are riveted on me. Now I realize what a terrible mistake I have made. Since the most common fare of restaurants has gluten, several times before, I have added something from my backpack to my meal. Normally I ask the owners. They never object. I always order some food and a drink. No one has ever reprimanded me or made me feel unwelcome because of it. "I am so sorry," I say, terribly embarrased. She cuts me off. "No being sorry," she shouts. "I apologize. I just wasn't thinking." But she keeps repeating, "No being sorry. Rude pilgrim..." Finally, I just shrug and let her be. It's a good thing I have a sense of humour and I don't beat myself to pulp for my stupid mistakes.

Dirty-Sausage-Fingers-With-Angry-Loud-Mouth exhausts her anger and plods back to her spot behind the counter to take more orders and fill her coffers. I take the time I need to finish my food, and Elena and I slip out quietly towards the door. But Old-Eagle-Eye is not yet finished with me. While I grab my rain poncho before making my exit, she starts shouting angrily again, pointing at me, telling customers who can understand Spanish to look at me, "the rude pilgrim"... I try to apologize again. She will stubbornly not hear of it. "No apologies, no apologies. Rude woman..." Finally, exasperated, pushing the door open, I lose my temper and shout back at her. I do it in French, a French-Canadian insult. Of course, she will not understand. One quick look in the room and I spot two compatriots, the only ones who get it, laughing behind their beards. Very childish of me. Sometimes the devil is quicker than you. He makes you do things. I refrain from giving her the finger; too much a part of the universal language. Considering I have walked over a thousand kilometres along the Camino, being shouted at once is no big deal. Losing my cool once is no big deal either. Outside, despite the unrelenting rain, Elena and I are bent in two laughing as she tries to tell me a joke about the woman. I think she is saying she wanted to poke her finger in the old lady's belly button and watch her fly to the ceiling like a deflated balloon. With Elena's Russo-Spanish and her gesticulations, I'm never sure, but she is good at making me laugh.

Yu Jin

At 6:30, I am ready to leave La Virgen del Camino. It's still dark. I wait at the exit gate until another pilgrim arrives. Yu Jin, a young Korean woman, had the bunk above mine last night. We had connected with only a nod and a smile because I was tucked in early. She is not keen on walking alone in the dark either. Together, with our headlamps, we brave the early morning darkness. I am happy for her name because I have a friend called Eugene. Her name sounds almost the same. I don't ask her to spell it; in my notebook, she becomes *Yu Jin*.

Soon, we leave the road and walk through dense bushes. It has been almost two weeks since the full moon; the sky is pitch black. We are happy for each other's company. This morning's stretch is definitely not the most interesting. The only thing breaking the monotony is a murder of at least a hundred rambunctious crows flapping their wings near us and creating a racket at the entrance to a village. What have they murdered? Or is that a funeral? I have read that crows gather to mourn a dead one of their members. I have seen it happen behind my house: dozens, maybe hundreds of crows darkening the branches of a tree above a dead one of theirs on the ground. They crowed for a long time before flying off again. Was one of them giving a eulogy this morning? It is fascinating to think many animals mourn their loved ones.

Later, across from a field redolent with the smell of India (and I don't mean the smell of spice markets) is a tall building advertising "*6 pisos llenos de sofas...*" (six floors full of couches). That's a lot of couches out in the middle of nowhere. Apparently some drug traffickers often use stuffed furniture for smuggling. A place this size would have enough to get all of Spain high at the same time. Then, as day dawns, come the cornfields for a short stretch of interesting nature. Without Yu Jin for company, it would feel like a long, rather boring walk. When I spontaneously reach for her and prevent her from falling as she trips on a large stone on the path, her immediate reaction is an expression of who she is. "You are my guardian angel," she says. It's easy to tell she was brought up in a caring environment.

Near Villadangos, another life-size sculpture of a pilgrim: mustachioed and bearded, with long curly hair, clad in a flowing brown cape with embroidered Templar symbols, he lurks in the corner of a small hotel. He carries a staff and gourd. Under his cape, a white, buttoned up shirt, suit trousers and even a fancy maroon vest. On his feet, old sneakers. He stands on a platform with wheels. Lucky pilgrim, he too spends the night inside. A stamp waits on a small table beside him for passing pilgrims. I stop for breakfast, and Yu Jin continues on her way. I will run into her a few times before Santiago. She is always cheerful, and she always runs to me, shouting my name. As if I were her best friend. She gives me a big hug each time I see her. Her presence is uplifting. Coming from a country where anyone above forty is invisible, I really appreciate her friendship. On the Camino, the path unites us. Few pilgrims find barriers to age.

In San Martín del Camino, friendly locals have placed benches along the houses. At the entrance, a large sign *"Prohibido la Venta Ambulante"* informs door-to-door salespersons they are not welcome here. It must be fifty years since we had door-to-door peddlers in my part of the world. I tried selling Avon when I was about thirteen. I lasted about three houses. I had the same success with Fuller Brush. And with the Readers' Digest. But I did make a dollar or two selling gift items from a Christmas catalogue. And during the summer, I sold our weekly newspaper, *l'Écho*, door to door. The selling price was ten cents. I made four cents from each sale. I would manage about ten sales each Thursday. By the time I had sold my papers, I had spent all my profits on candies. At least, it kept me out of trouble one morning a week.

I am taking my time today, walking leisurely. I enjoyed Yu Jin's company, and now I am enjoying being on my own. At Albergue Santa Ana, I poke my nose inside. Beds, not bunks; at least, the ones I see. It has an open garden at the back and the atmosphere looks friendly. Its sign says €5, which seems unreal.

Around midday, past the church with not one, not two, but three huge stork nests, near the entrance to Hospital de Órbigo, I bump into a few pilgrims who, after hearing me comment on the less than scenic hike this morning, scold me for not having followed the other path. What other path?

I pull out my Brierley. Will I ever learn? A green path is well illustrated starting at the exit from La Virgen del Camino. Yu Jin and I missed it in the dark. Sorry, Mr. Brierley, I forgot about you again today.

Hospital de Órbigo

At the entrance to Hospital de Órbigo, the mercury in my mini-thermometer has inched its way near the top. Time for me to slow down. What a pleasant surprise this town is after my long, lacklustre hike. The XIII century Puente del Paso Honroso (Bridge of Honourable Passage) has quite a history. Many of its nineteen arches were destroyed and rebuilt at different periods. The British wrecked part of it to ward off the *little Corsican's* troops during the Peninsular War. Napoleon himself wasn't here, but they were his men. What is the harm with a bit of name dropping if it can add stardom to a place? But considering the age of the bridge, all that is relatively recent history. The saga of Puente del Paso Honroso is long and complex. It is my favourite bridge so far. I even prefer it to Puente de la Reina.

Since I am assured of a bed for tonight, and it is not easy to get a good selfie, I volunteer to take pictures of solo pilgrims before crossing the bridge. One pilgrim also kindly reciprocates. I would not want to return home without that cliché, although I know that Neil, who has been travelling vicariously with me, sleeping in a comfortable bed and eating familiar foods, will have already surveyed my path and the bridge online.

The Puente del Paso Honroso has survived much turmoil. A large sign explains its history. An illustration with all the arches numbered recounts their destruction and reconstruction, and tells about those who have crossed Rio Órbigo through the ages. Before it was built, shepherds forded its bed with their flocks in the summer to seek fodder at the foot of the Cordillera Cantábrica. In Roman times, engineers were commissioned to build the bridge to ferry gold and other metals from the peninsula's northwest. During the first millennium, it was integrated into the official Jacobean itinerary. The hundreds of thousands of pilgrims crossing the Puente del Paso Honroso each year may be wearing out its stones, but they are also helping to keep the area alive. The bridge was declared part of World Heritage in 1993.

On the dry riverbed, since 1997, the festival of *Las Justas Medievales* (Medieval Tournament) in June commemorates the famous battle of Don Suero. According to history, in the summer of 1434, Don Suero, blocking access to the bridge, in two weeks, (or a month, depending on who is telling the story) destroyed the lances of hundreds of opponents (depending...). But why should numbers matter? Something important happened here for it to be recorded into the annals of history, for it to be enthusiastically commemorated yearly.

At festival time, spectators and participants don ancient costumes, and bring out armour, bagpipes, drums and flutes. Women wearing headscarves, shawls and wide skirts dance to Medieval music. Little boys carry wooden swords. Young maidens and older women alike are crowned with flowers. Some men dress as monks in brown cassocks of rough wool and walk alongside donkeys. On the stage, men strut in their flowing capes with fancy shields, suits of armour, and long metal lances, or sit astride armoured horses. Their entrance, capes flying in the wind, is accompanied by a cacophony of ancient instruments. A jousting tournament takes place. I have even heard of camels being part of the decor. The festival attracts people from far afield. Doubtless, pilgrims will join in the colourful celebrations. I wonder what it must be like trying to find a bed here during the festival.

There is nothing like an ancient bridge to catapult you through centuries. With these thoughts dancing in my head, I almost feel that pilgrims ahead of me are committing an act of arrogance, of impertinence. "Don't just strut across this old bridge," I want to shout. "Step with reverence on the cobblestones." I feel so fortunate to be living this moment in the company of knights templars, valiant soldiers, kings and queens, characters real and fictitious from Don Quixote, El Cid, and thousands upon thousands of ancient and modern pilgrims. On the Camino, time takes on another dimension. History is my constant companion.

Much of Hospital de Órbigo is paved with small, smooth stones like the ones on its bridge and on so many old streets and floors along the way. The stones continue into the courtyard of Albergue Parroquial soon after the bridge. An outside wall displays a coat of arms. As witnessed in its hand-crafted metal sign and wall sculpture of three pilgrims, there are talented

Susan and I would walk long stretches together

blacksmiths around here as well. In the albergue's open courtyard, on top of what looks like an ancient capped well, stands a display of shells, biblical pictures and quotations. The Camino is primarily a Christian pilgrimage.

Resourceful people run this place. The large backyard even has solar panels. It is heartwarming to see the environmentalism of Camino dwellers. I think guiltily of my polluting flight. I hope the things I do to atone for it redeem me to some extent. I can't just stay cooped up in my house all my life so as not to pollute. The simple act of living is polluting. Everything in moderation. I hope the Verde will have as much character as the Parroquial. The downside to reserving a bed is I often pass a place where I wish I were staying. I never want to be the pilgrim who cancels at the last minute.

Susan from Denver

Across the quiet, narrow street, I rest on a wooden bench in the mottled shade of a plane tree. I never cease to be amazed at the curve of tempera-ture around here. This morning, I wore hat and gloves. Now, I am thankful for the foliage which provides a modicum of shade. At the other end of the bench, her heavy-looking backpack and hiking sticks beside her, a pilgrim is taking care of her blistered feet, squeezing ointment out of a tube. She lifts her head and smiles to acknowledge my presence.

Susan is from Denver. She is wearing shorts and a short sleeve top. Her arms and legs are several shades more tanned than mine. Her sparkling blue eyes and her thick, wavy blond hair tied in a short ponytail, and stick-ing out through the hole of her sun cap take ten years off her biological age. This pilgrimage is something she promised herself years ago. She has been working with children most of her life. A decade ago, with a six-month commitment, Susan took in a child who had been moved through too many homes. Totally unplanned, she ended up adopting the girl who, despite many expected and unexpected hardships, has brought her immense joy. Susan's face lights up when she talks about her daughter. She is proud of how well-adjusted the girl is now.

While the girl was being transformed into a loving teenager and young adult, Susan heard about the Camino and promised herself that when her daughter started working, she would do the pilgrimage. She started from Saint-Jean-Pied-de-Port. Today, she is going further than Órbigo. When I wish her "*Buen Camino*", since she is ahead of me, I imagine we will not meet again, yet before the end, we will walk long stretches together, even enter Santiago together. Susan has a bed at El Encanto in Villares. It wears its name well. When I bump into her later, from her photos, I will see a pleasant interior court and balcony with rocking chairs. The owner dreamt of creating a relaxing refuge. She seems to have succeeded.

Looking back at my pictures now, I once again marvel at the magic of the Camino. I took my last picture of the bridge at 12:19; at 1:33, I was in my dorm at the Verde. So much had happened in that hour and fourteen minutes. So much had been shared. Unbeknownst to Susan and me, a friendship was born. We might not manage to keep it going because back home, we both have our lives, our families, our friends, our occupations. The memory of the times we will have spent together is another pearl in the long necklace of my life.

A Very Zen Oasis

A hundred steps after the bench, a hand-carved, colourful, curved wooden sign with the words 'Albergue Verde' and some footprints directs me to my refuge. The Verde lives up to its name. Its façade covered with thick ivy, the house sits behind a large multicoloured rose garden. In the courtyard, a delightful surprise awaits.

A welcome breeze and some patches of shade have kept me from wilting completely, but I am ready for a shower, and will be happy to settle in. The Verde is an environmental oasis with a special flavour, quite distinct from most places where I have slept. Its immense backyard has colourful Tibetan flags under a huge round gazebo (or perhaps it will be a yurt) with roughly hewed pillars, still in construction. I assume its owner has been to Nepal or Tibet. On the lawn, half a dozen pilgrims are sitting in lotus position on colourful mats. Some of the women are wearing loose multicoloured Indian cotton trousers, the kind made from recycled saris. Meditating independently from each other, they are waiting for the yoga teacher. Some have their arms extended, thumbs and index fingers forming two circles. Maybe they are humming a mantra in their heads. "Ommmmm, Om shanti Om." Other pilgrims are reclining on large garden chairs. While one older man is smoking in a far corner of the garden, a tame cat and a dog roam about aimlessly. A sign advertises massages, meditation, yoga. Later, many if not most of the pilgrims will join in the activities.

Up an exterior flight of stairs, after checking-in with a cheerful, welcoming host, collecting my bag, finding my bed, I enjoy a refreshing shower before heading back out to relax in the wide swing. Twenty feet ahead of me now, a dozen pilgrims are sitting on mats in a circle. This time, under a teacher's instructions, they stretch and fold limbs in unison; they stand and stretch their arms to the sky, open their hands and close them as if grabbing some ethereal object. They bend at the knees and, bringing their arms down, throw away the imaginary object. I am not initiated to these rituals. Are they shedding bad stuff? Eyes closed, they form an 'O' again with index fingers and thumbs. Then, with arms bent at the elbow, and hands up in front of them, as though pushing against a wall, they stick their tongue out as far as it will go. It reminds me of the haka dance of Maori rugby players. It is good entertainment for me. Everyone is happy. They're having fun; I'm having fun. And I didn't even have to pay for it.

Later, what a pleasant surprise it is to find Yu Jin in the dorm. But she has lost her warm jacket. Rummaging through a box of discards we find an extra-large man's windbreaker. It will do. Our dorm accommodates less than two dozen pilgrims. Crisp cotton sheets (organic, I imagine) and warm wool blankets are supplied for us all. No disposable sheets here. Why not use cotton and pay someone to launder them rather than throw away a set of disposable sheets and plastic bag every day?

Dinner is served around two large tables with white tablecloths. I did not know veganism could look so beautiful or taste so yummy. Every dish comes in ceramic or wood. A large plate of hummus topped with an appetizing layer of organic olive oil and a sprinkling of ground nuts is dished out with wooden spoons. Juicy, ripe tomatoes, olives, a bowl of mixed greens to which we can add a choice of inventive dressings, huge loaves of crusty, freshly baked bread, tasty, deep-fried cauliflower croquettes... And there are more mouth-watering foods whose ingredients I don't know. Everything possible is from their own organic garden, prepared and served with love. Every meal is an event here, a ritual as sacred, maybe, as mass or vespers in the churches on our path. What better way to honour our Creator. And the people who prepared it are as revered as priests. Water is decanted from refillable glass bottles. I could stay in this no-waste environment a long time.

After dinner, a fellow with a long ponytail leads us into a Camino song of thanks, and continues to strum his guitar for a while in the sitting-cum-dining area below a charming interior balcony. There I meet Francesco from Italy. I will bump into him sporadically over the next weeks. A laid-back young man, just like Yu Jin, he is a graphic designer who wants to change career. He has longish hair, ordinary, no-name clothes, and he carries a guitar. In the days to come, every time I will fall into step with him, he will be accompanied by an attractive young woman; at first, they are different ones. Eventually, it will be the same blond Swedish girl. I can see why so many young women like to walk at his side.

Money Talks

In no time, the conversation strays from the welcoming and environmental Verde to the depressing resorts on the Mediterranean coasts. We are half a dozen pilgrims with a whole gamut of arguments for and against the developments. Mostly against. I have seen the horribly defaced coast of Spain with its thousands of all-inclusives, its tall hotels, its hordes of tourists, fish-and-chips and German sausage stalls, its lack of green. Not to mention its mafia. I have seen them all in passing, but have never been tempted to spend time there. However, if someone asked me, does Spain need them? I would be hard-pressed to say. While irreversibly destroying its environment, they have pulled Spain out of misery. Things are never black or white. Still, I decide not to put in my two cents' worth, mostly because my throat is aching again. It's a good exercise once in a while to just listen to the arguments of others. These are all gentle people. No one seems to think his or her opinion is the only valid one.

The most interesting argument is that of an old man from the south of Spain telling us about his memories of a lot of angry, divisive discussions amongst members of his family when he was a child in the sixties because the Mayor of his small fishing village had begged Franco to allow foreign tourists to wear the bikini. The Mayor had done everything in his power to encourage the development of tourism with the millions of Pounds and Francs, Guilders and Marks and other world currencies it would bring to the area where he had grown up surrounded by misery. In those days, women were chastised not for wearing burkinis, but for not covering enough of their flesh. When the bikini-clad, blond-haired, blue-eyed girls with long limbs and shapely figures, avid of sunshine, and from less conservative countries, started covering their bodies with coconut oil, and stretching on the beaches of the Costa del Sol, the Mayor refused to bow to the wishes of his conservative people to ban the indecent bathing suit.

When the Catholic Church threatened to excommunicate him, which meant he would not be allowed to act as Mayor anymore, he drove for a whole day (on his scooter) to far-away Madrid to speak to Franco who, against the wishes of the Catholic leaders, bowed to his argument. Otherwise, the pretty girls, bait for more tourists with deep pockets weighted down by strong currencies, would have disappeared to more welcoming beaches in other countries.

Soon, teenagers were singing along with Brian Hyland strumming his guitar. The shy girl with the itsy, bitsy, teeny weeny, yellow polka dot bikini... she was here to stay. Soon, handsome, swarthy, well-mannered macho Spaniards and tourists were romancing gorgeous Northern European girls and producing pale skin babies from mothers with broken accents. Money rules.

In Minorca, the island has few if any of the offending beachfront highrises of Mallorca or of the Costa del Sol, apparently because it resisted Franco who therefore did not allow development for tourism. When the all-inclusives eventually sprouted on Minorca, environmentalism was becoming part of the discussion. Its resorts are not directly on the beach, nor are they as high as the ones on Mallorca or mainland Spain.

I cannot help comparing the evolution of the coast of Spain with that of the Camino which has metamorphosed from a religious pilgrimage to a

nature hike, an adventure for agnostics and even atheists all equally welcomed. From my experience, the believer is a *rara avis* on the Camino. But
rare also is the pilgrim, religious or not, who returns home without a deeper
appreciation for life.

Alone in a Fourteen-Bed Dorm

To beat the mid-day heat, Yu Jin and I start out in darkness. Her newly
found wind-breaker hangs down to her knees. The sleeves are long enough
to serve as mittens. She would make a good scarecrow. That would have been
helpful yesterday although the crows were not near any crop. I am wearing
my hat, gloves and a cashmere turtleneck under my warm hooded jacket.
When I offer my scarf, at first she refuses. "No, no," she insists, "you must
not get cold." Only when I point to all my warm clothes does she accept. By
ten o'clock, we will have shed all of it.

Last night at Casa Verde, we were instructed to take a shortcut to the
path at the back of the garden in the morning. "Please make sure you close
the gate after you. We don't want our cat to escape." Of course, one pilgrim
forgot, and four of us spent precious minutes trying to round up the cat and
incite it back to the yard.

An hour later, at the entrance to tiny Villares de Órbigo, in the middle
of the street, we pass, mounted on a two-step pedestal, a tall monument.
The bright golden glow of a streetlight illuminates a plain slab of rock with
irregular, carved edges. The cut-out of a large cross into the stone is in total
darkness. But the monument casts an eerie shadow on the path. There, in
front of our feet, the picture is reversed, and the cross is lit in gold. Impressive. Was it planned by the artist?

At a small village with farm equipment, young calves are busy getting
their breakfasts. A crow pecks at some tasty morsel near a large wooden
cross growing out of a mound of hundreds of stones. The sky, punctuated by
wispy stratus clouds, has now turned turquoise, and lights a small forest of
eucalyptus. I try to remember to glance behind at the sunrise. Most mornings, daybreak is a spectacle at our back. In front, the stones in our path
are gilded with the sliver of sunlight. "Follow the yellow brick road," says

Yu Jin. How does she know about the yellow brick road? What do I know about Korean literature?

Ten o'clock; the heat is brutal. The corn fields are a pretty sight, but they provide no shade. In Astorga, I stop to visit Gaudi's Palacio Obispal by the old defensive wall. Yu Jin gives me a big hug and wishes me "*Buen Camino.*" She has a long way to go today.

My iPod has died. I won't be able to take pictures inside the Bishop's Palace. With its many towers, it looks more like a medieval or even a fairy-tale castle. Not only have I brought home, from previous trips to Spain, many photos from the Casa Batlló, Güell Park, the Sagrada Familia, and other Gaudi creations in Barcelona, but I had the priceless opportunity to visit Colonia Güell in Santa Coloma de Cervelló, half an hour west of Barcelona where Güell, the artist's wealthy patron, had a whole industrial village designed by his protégé. There, a hundred years ago, textile workers had their homes, workplace, and place of worship. Colonia Güell is yet another one of Gaudi's eye-popping designs. The interior of the chapel in Santa Coloma is so beautiful, it is almost profane. As always with Gaudi, not one ounce of conventionalism entered its design. Even the columns are not straight; the stained glass windows are inset in amorphous shapes, the seats are of cast iron and carved wood. I could not find one straight wall or one right angle. Every shape is organic. In Güell Park, I have also visited Gaudi's minimalist abode. Maybe the lack of physical clutter in his life created room in his brain for his unbridled imagination.

Astorga is a small town. The palace-cum-museum receives a small portion of the attention which Gaudi's Barcelona creations enjoy. I don't have to wait in line for hours or even minutes. Compared to his Casa Batlló, the palacio's interior almost seems conservative, yet it is well worth a visit. It is a missed opportunity for pilgrims who pass Astorga without stopping. At least they get to enjoy its architecture from the outside. There are many buildings worthy of a visit along the Camino for their history or art. It is sadly not possible to fit them all in. It partly explains why one feels compelled to return.

Inside, I spot an electrical outlet at the base of a wall. I can squat on the floor near it while my iPod recharges. This is not the Louvre; nobody seems to mind. In twenty minutes, only a handful of visitors enter the room and they are too busy looking at the art to bother with me. Only later in Murias will I realize that the adaptor my Irish friend Nuala had generously given me in Burgos is still in the socket at the museum. Oh no! At least I have captured several photos to take me back to Astorga from the comfort of my home. Before I get back on the Camino early afternoon, I jot in my notebook: "Stay in Astorga next time. Spend a day here."

After the imposing cathedral with its twin towers dominating the town, a memorial plaque to a British hero of the War of Independence is a surprising sight. 'Sir John Moore, Commander in Chief of the British Army acting in alliance with that of Spain during the Peninsular War lodged at this house in late December 1808 just a few days before being killed whilst leading his troops at the battle of Corunna. Spain and Astorga are grateful for the glory of his memory and of his valiant soldiers.' It then lists the names of valiant soldiers. They must have been among those who defended the bridge at Órbigo. They are not the heroes I had expected to see memorialized on the Camino. War. War. War. Will it ever end? Nietzsche's prediction that wars would get more and more violent sadly seems to have proven right. If only people would start walking in nature, there would be no time or energy for war. Nothing in nature incites killing. Nature invites contemplation, rarely conflict, rarely aggression. Except of course, if one is a hunter. But that is entirely another matter.

Astorga is the beginning of Brierley's stage 23. It is late afternoon. Most if not all pilgrims are way ahead of me. I soon find myself alone on a dirt trail along a road. I don't mind until I come to a large sign. Due to road repairs, I must use a detour through dense bush. Dogs are barking in the distance. I hurry my step, telling myself I am being silly; there is nothing to worry about. Incidents rarely happen on the Camino. Half an hour later, unmolested, unbitten by mean dogs, I scold myself for being a scaredy-cat.

At Murias de Rechivaldo, my bed is reserved at Casa Flor. In the large, dimly lit, empty restaurant, I wait a long time for someone to acknowledge my presence. Eventually an elderly man takes my name, stamps my passport and leads me to a large basement room next door. Casa Flor is the fruit of a pragmatic businessperson. At the back of the adjacent building, several steps lead down into the immense dorm with green walls and low ceiling supported by half-a-dozen rectangular posts. I can just hear the owner: "We can fit fourteen beds, two or three bathrooms..." Nothing wrong with that. If it can help pilgrims and pad the owners' retirement coffers, why not?

I am the first one here, yet it is late afternoon. "Choose your bed," says my host. The beds on wooden bases, have ample space between them. They come with sheets and pillowcase and blankets and identical blue and white flowered comforters, the kind found in Ma and Pa motels back home. "Do you have many reservations for tonight?" I ask. "So far, you're the only one. We were full the last three nights. Today, it's just you."

Along one wall, a couple of inches below the ceiling, two windows let a stingy light into the room. At the entrance, (at the back of the building), by a wall of windows, is a large couch. For the straggling homeless pilgrim? Not needed tonight! Three wonderfully modern bathrooms are at my sole disposition. I am given the code for internet but will soon find out it doesn't work. Was I really expecting it to work? With its hundred or so inhabitants, Murias is not exactly a megalopolis.

Across the street from where I will sleep, is the old one-room school, La Escuela, with about a dozen beds where I recognize one of the pilgrims. When I tell her I forgot my adaptor in Astorga, she lets me charge my iPod using hers. One of the other pilgrims has an extra one which she generously offers me. The Camino provides... and provides... and provides...

Behind La Escuela, immediately on the path, an old two-storey house, Casa Las Aguedas, is abuzz with pilgrims. Although it has a kitchen, I prefer where I am for the luxurious bathrooms. I might be paying a couple of Euros more, but it is well worth it. If there is a sore point on the Camino for me, it is the shower stalls; they rarely have any place to put soap and other toiletries; most have nowhere to hang discarded or clean clothes, no soap dish... If I am not careful, my shoes will get soaked on the other side of the stall... At Casa Flor tonight, a full, modern bathroom is mine and mine only. Three bathrooms all to myself! I can lay my clothes on the sink counter, be sure my shoes won't get sprayed, take all the time I want, and not feel guilty.

In the restaurant next door I am a lone customer. I manage a not inexpensive dinner of a measly bowl of noodle soup, two tasty but miserly pork chops: large bone and three small bites of meat each, and a small portion of fries definitely not home-made. The staff is kind, so I don't complain. I think they are all family members. At least, the lemon mousse is home-made and delicious.

Back in my dorm, I see no other backpack, no sign of another pilgrim; I will be the only one here tonight. The owner doesn't mind when I ask for the key. I don't know if he and his wife live near here. I will really be alone. I lock the door and pull the curtains over the wall of windows at the entrance. Since Internet is not working, I cannot communicate with family or friends. Fortunately, I have an audiobook to listen to before going to sleep which I soon do only to wake at midnight. After midnight, insomnia is my only companion until I can safely leave in darkness and wait by the trail for other pilgrims with whom I can hike in the dark. It will be a long day. I hope my bag gets picked up today. The owner promised me it would. Fingers crossed.

The Dumb Waiter

Rabanal is only three or four hours away. I had planned on going further, but I am still coughing and, with a sleepless night behind me, I need to take it easy. In the penumbra, I stand by the path near Casa Aguedas. Inside, pilgrims are noisily cleaning up after their breakfasts. In the distance, three pilgrims with headlamps are approaching. They have about my pace. When I ask if I can walk with them until daylight, the three Swedish women are very welcoming.

In Santa Catalina, we come to a restaurant with a prominent sign showing a breakfast of bacon, egg, fries. It's time to take leave of my companions. I will get a good stick-to-the-ribs meal here. There's nothing like a heap of french fries to start the day. At the counter, I say good morning and ask for fresh orange juice, Cola Cao, fries, bacon and eggs. Without uttering a word, the waiter, a man with a stern face, points to a different poster near him: it says, bacon, egg, salad. I ask if I could have fries. He points again to the poster. I get it! No fries. The sign outside was just to lure me in.

It must be hard to be a dumb waiter. It must be difficult to have to communicate everything with nods in different directions and with signs. It's no wonder he doesn't seem too friendly. I should learn to be more compassionate. The man disappears into the kitchen and returns to wait on other pilgrims while my order is being prepared. Invisible now, I wait by the counter while other pilgrims are treated to the same wordless welcome. When my meal arrives, I take the plate, say thank you, and start walking to a table. "*Ocho cinquenta*" (Eight fifty) shouts the waiter. Startled, I put my plate back down on the counter and reach for my money. I wonder if he has had unpleasant experiences with pilgrims. It would not surprise me, especially since I saw pilgrims filling litre-size bottles of wine at the generous *bodega* in Irache. He is definitely not one of those who LOVE pilgrims. Too bad he paints us all with the same brush. Or maybe his wife was in a foul mood this morning. I have bad days too. Best to let him have his.

From Santa Catalina, it is daylight. I am enjoying the solitude. Despite my night of insomnia, I feel so light, I might just fly off like the birds swooping in the distance. I am one lucky person. How fortunate I am to live this experience. And for the fourth time in less than two years. How fortunate that my health allows it, that I have a husband who understands my need for a bit of adventure, that my kids are not worry warts who would nag me into staying home. And how fortunate that I am happy living out of a backpack and sleeping in a dorm with the occasional snorer.

Trudy Boukas

Just before Ganso, I stop to rest on a stone bench, a memorial to Trudy Boukas, 1942-2011. Two years less than I am now. Once again, I count my blessings. What happened to Trudy Boukas? What's her story? Accident? Heart Attack? One pilgrim I met early on, upon seeing an ancient woman with heavy backpack laboriously climbing, said to me: "She should not be here; she could drop dead from a heart attack." So what? Did Trudy Boukas' life end here? Or had she always wanted to do the Camino? And did a loved one do the pilgrimage for her? Maybe her ashes were spread somewhere here?

Nearby is a cross with two roses recently placed on it, and on the cross, a photo of a woman with short grey hair petting a tiger. She has a gentle face. Who was Trudy Boukas? Everyone has a story. Every story eventually fades. Someone who loved her has wanted to prolong hers.

Later, I find a tribute to Trudy Boukas on YouTube. Trudy Boukas has lived, she has loved, and she was loved. On a background of Antonio Molina singing his famous *Paloma Blanca*, someone has assembled photos of a life lived to the fullest. We see a baby in her mother's arms; a pretty girl with long braids in school uniform; a proud young woman with mortarboard and gown in front of a statue of the Virgin Mary. Later, she poses with handsome, bright-looking friends in the flower of their youth; with a man on top of a high mountain. Nepal? Surrounded by family and friends on her wedding day. Then comes the Volkswagen van, which becomes her home as she travels the world. She is scuba diving in what must be Greece, amid broken amphorae. Later, she is leaving happy clouds of dust behind her van in a desert somewhere. She is always climbing, always exploring, always living life to the fullest. Neither heights nor abysses frightened her. One minute she is belly dancing, the other, she is handling a sniper's rifle or, wearing a helmet, peeking out of a tank in the desert. Who was Trudy Boukas? She poses with children wrapped in warm blankets. From Nepal, perhaps? Later, she is in a classroom with more children. Kolkata? Mumbai? From parrots to cats and dogs, to dolphins, to wallabies, from elephants to tigers, they all loved her and she loved them all. She kayaked, she travelled in the desert. With her backpack, she poses beside a marker on the Camino. The last picture of her, a symbol of life after death: a large blue Morpho butterfly sitting on her hand. Then comes a white marble resting place with the name Gertrude Etten Boukas. Mary Elizabeth Frye's poem resumes her philosophy of life:

> *Do not stand at my grave and weep*
> *I am not there, I do not sleep*
> *I am a thousand winds that blow*
> *I am the diamond glint on snow*
> *I am the sunlight on ripened grain*
> *I am the gentle autumn rain*

When you awaken in the morning's hush
I am the swift uplifting rush
of the quiet birds in circled flights
I am the soft star that shines at night

Do not stand at my grave and cry
I am not there. I did not die

On top of the marble grave: a cross of St. James and a vase with a bouquet of bright yellow sunflowers. May you live a long long time, Trudy. It was lovely to meet you.

Of Orange Thieves and Vicious Cities

The day is foggy and raw. I am walking through clouds in a thick forest on a path often parallel to the road. Cyclists pass me by. Fortunately, it is not a road well travelled by cars, so the cyclists don't seem to mind the fog too much. I hope they are safe.

At El Ganso, the houses are ancient, built of local stone. Uncut, oddly shaped, the stones vary in size from an inch or two to a foot or more and hold together by the grace of God. Yet, the houses seem lived-in. One stone has a white shell painted on it; I have not strayed from the Camino. I don't really need a rest but a pilgrim has been walking at the same pace as me several metres behind me, listening to loud music. When I reach a small courtyard with its high piles of beverage crates and red tables, I remind myself it is part of my duty as a pilgrim to support the small businesses. I will put some distance between the can't-live-without-music pilgrim and myself.

I love the product names around here. On a case of cider: Ladrón de Naranjas (Orange thief). Another crate claims Sidra natural from Villaviciosa (cider from Vicious Town).

Later along the north side of the path, a wire fence, perhaps a kilometre long, is heavy with twigs forming thousands of make-shift crosses of all sizes. The most ancient ones are covered in moss. I pick two twigs of different lengths and, weaving them through the already laden fence, I form a cross.

Seventy-five

When I walk away, I wonder why I felt the need to do it. Has the religious ritual become just another pagan gesture on the Camino? Am I a usurper?

Rabanal, a Photogenic Village

Shortly after the entrance to Rabanal, I am catapulted onto the Asi Ghat on the banks of the Ganges in Varanasi. Rabanal is quite a change from other hamlets I have passed so far. Indian music is piped out of a loudspeaker outside a one-room grocery store advertising smoothies and ice cream (a bit cold for that today). Hariprasad Chaurasia, bansuri, sitar and tabla, they all seem out of place at the small *tienda*, but I am thoroughly enjoying it. Across the road, the atmosphere is definitely hippyish with its large open garden and huge artificial flowers in their own cacophony of colours. The gate is open; a sign invites one and all to sit and relax. Under a straw roof, tables are occupied by pilgrims snacking on their provisions. At the end of the garden, about a dozen blue and green tents will shelter pilgrims tonight.

In the store, I check out the merchandise. Since I am staying in Rabanal tonight, I might come back once I am settled. A heavy-set woman in her late thirties is busy conversing loudly (so she can be heard above the music) on her cell phone. She does not look at me, nor acknowledge my presence. I have got into the habit of saying "*Buenos días*" when I enter a small shop in Spanish-speaking countries, and of being greeted. I look in her direction. She makes no connection. Have we, pilgrims from less civilized countries, been spreading our ill manners along the Camino? In Canada, it is not our custom to greet the person behind the counter or to be greeted by them, perhaps because we are not used to small shops anymore. We walk around large chain stores. We often pay no attention to staff, nor do they to us. Our purchases are processed, our money taken and, except for the questions recited *ad infinitum*, and often without eye contact by the cashiers in one telegraphic sentence, "Any bags? Air Miles card? Debit or Credit?" there is, more often than not, no acknowledgement of the customer. Even a 'thank you' often does not receive a reply. Now, I guess I am just another moneybag in this little shop, another annoying pilgrim perhaps. Eventually, I pick up a container of juice from a shelf and hand the woman a €5 note. She reaches for it without interrupting her conversation, and gives me my change without ever making eye contact with me.

Outside, a young woman comes running to me. It is Yu Jin. "Danielle!" She gives me a big hug. "Are you staying here in a tent tonight?" "No thanks. I need a bed." Guitar-strumming Francesco is also here. I assume he too will sleep in a tent.

My bag should be waiting at the Gaucelmo. I will probably not sleep there. The Gaucelmo is run by the Confraternity of Saint James based in London. I have been warned they will not accommodate pilgrims unless they carry their backpack. No problem. I will find something else, but maybe I will first have a look. If I like it, I might just ask. Who knows, they might take pity on an old lady.

With its delicate purple flowers growing out of stone walls, Rabanal, population less than sixty, is a photogenic mountain village located at 3,500 feet of altitude. On my way in, I snap pictures of climbing roses and crumbling stone walls. When I get to the Gaucelmo, past a life-size sculpture of a *peregrino*, I survey the place a bit before collecting my backpack. At the large eating area are several chatty Korean pilgrims. They never ship their bags!

The Gaucelmo is ancient, spacious, cold and damp. I will check out the alternatives before asking if I can stay here. A few steps away, I pass a small hotel with a balcony on the second floor: El Descanso de Gaia. The sign says: *Habitaciones economicas. Alojamiento de calidad* (inexpensive, quality lodgings). A delicate wrought iron vine with green stained glass climbing along the marble arched doorway of the hotel reminds me yet again that in this part of the world, artisans are valued.

On the top floor, I am shown a bed in a bright room with four other beds in a large attic with skylights. Elias, the young owner, says I will have the entire room to myself for €30. There is even a set of fluffy, clean towels on my bed, and the bathrooms are five-star. Guests can use a small kitchen downstairs. I will get a good night's sleep. I check out the regulations sheet on my pillow; it's the usual, including check-out time: 10:59 and 'Dogs allowed (educated)'.

Elias is the right person to manage the small hotel. After his studies, his parents helped him acquire it. "In the winter, I rent the whole place to groups

Camponaraya

Riego del Ambrós

Foncebadón

Rabanal

N

El Descanso de Gaia in Rabanal

of *Madrileñós* who get together as a family during holidays. Or sometimes, people use it as a base for hiking in the area." In winter, Elias helps in his father's restaurant only open on weekends in a nearby village.

Rabanal is a photographer's delight: moss-covered rocks; more colourful wildflowers reaching out to the sky on top of abandoned walls, or climbing on houses still lived in; collapsed, caved-in slate roofs; five-foot high worm-eaten doors made of old planks, and with pale remnants of ancient paint, in field-stone walls, their access blocked by sturdy wildflowers; door handles and latches with venerable patina; tin roofs held down by large stones; tangles of thick, stubborn thorny branches and roots strangling field stones; pink and yellow roses everywhere... and, as if all that wasn't enough, a poem by Antonio Machado painted in elegant calligraphy on a large grey rock beside yet another weather-beaten wooden door:

> *last night, as I lay sleeping,*
> *I dreamt – marvellous error!-*
> *that I had a beehive here inside my heart*
> *and the golden bees were making*
> *White combs and Sweet honey*
> *from my old failures*

Wouldn't it be wonderful if we could turn our old failures into sweet honey? The bees would be unemployed.

The Shopkeepers of Rabanal

After the sitar and tabla grocery store, I had passed La Tienda del Camino where a slate sign with a stick-man drawing of a peregrino had attracted my attention. I was curious to know how a community of less than a hundred inhabitants could support two grocery stores, and I had planned on returning to ask the owner of the second one a few questions. On the way there, ten metres away from my hotel I pass a pretty, open garden with several wooden tables made of thick insect-scarred planks sitting on sturdy log sections; the chairs are carved out of two-feet wide tree trunks. Pumpkins and colourful, warty autumn gourds of all sizes and shapes adorn each table. The area belongs to a third grocery store! Three grocery stores for less than a hundred inhabitants? I must go in.

Between customers, Susana, an attractive woman with rosy cheeks, says she has been running her store for seven years, since her husband's debilitating work accident. Her thick, light brown hair piled at the back of her head compliments her round face with its engaging smile, and contrasts nicely with her stark black fleece jacket zipped up to her chin. She needs it to stay warm in the unheated room where a puff of cold air accompanies each customer. In front of her, on the thick wooden counter, a small calculator from the 80s. No "Debit or Credit?" here. No "Air Miles card?" Just *"Buenas tardes"* and *"Gracias"* and *"Buen Camino."*

Susana and her husband live in the village. They have chickens, pigs, rabbits, and four dogs. Although her husband cannot work anymore, he is not bored. They also had cows and sheep. After the accident, they had to cut down on the menagerie. Their two sons work in the city; she uses the word *fuera* (away). It could mean León, or perhaps Madrid. It means somewhere too far to come home on the weekend. One works for a bank and the other for Renault. At the mention of the word *fuera*, I see a shadow of sadness in her eyes. '*Fuera*' is a powerful word in these areas. It doesn't just mean 'away'. It is loaded with a sense of loss; it could be better translated with the word 'exiled'. But it is also the word sometimes used in graffiti by xenophobes along the Camino. Then, it means 'go away,' or something even more rude.

In these parts of Spain where family bonds are tight, grown children rarely go away with a light heart. Lucky are they who can stay and find work. Farming has mostly been swallowed up by large corporations. There is not much else unless one can find a way of getting pilgrim dollars. Susana knows her sons will probably marry women from far away; she will not see her grandchildren grow up like her parents did. If she stays here, she will be lonely in old age, unlike her own parents who have her. The richer a country becomes, the poorer family life becomes. In the end, wealth is a thief. It is not the first time Spaniards have had to look elsewhere. Central and South America are peopled with descendants of exiled Spaniards who fled poverty from Galicia and other Spanish areas. They left their families behind in an age when, for the poor who would often be just a little less poor in their new country, the separation would be permanent. Many were those who would never see their families again.

"It's a catch-22 situation," a Spaniard once told me. "Educate your children and they will find work in large cities or in other countries. The only way to keep your children near you is to let them quit school early and become artisans or journeymen."

Susana's one-room shop is the only one open all year. As well as a huge variety of fresh produce, cheeses, canned foods, drinks of all sorts, foot care products and toiletries, she even carries gloves, socks, fleece jackets and thin, light-as-a-feather daypacks. I ask her how she manages with the competition from the other two grocery stores. "We are all good friends," she says. "We all get together at the end of the season and celebrate with a feast before winter."

At times like these, I think, if I were young and single, I would move here. These people have values hard to find in our capitalistic world. They look after each other. They are proud of each other's success. Greed and ambition have no foothold around here.

At La Tienda del Camino, the second grocery store I had passed, the door is wide open. A fat tabby runs out. Sara has had this store for six years. Her parents also live in Rabanal. She lived and worked in Madrid for nineteen years in a large grocery store until it closed. *"Nos echaron a la calle."* (They threw us out in the street), she says, with less resentment in her voice than in her words. With the settlement she received, seeing the Camino was becoming more and more popular, she purchased the small grocery store. She stresses that the store already existed. The previous owner was ready to retire. It was the perfect opportunity. "I am open from April to November," she says. "Then, I go back to Madrid where I have my apartment and where most of my friends live."

Back at the first store, Navidad, a wisp of an ancient woman, sits outside on one of the cast-iron chairs with padded cushions along the wall of the store. Her feet don't touch the ground. In her rusty voice, she tells me she is named Navidad (Nativity) because she was born on December 25. I could have guessed! The frail old woman is knitting a pot holder. She owns the store which her daughter runs. Her sons live in Madrid. The family has cows, sheep, geese. Her husband died last year.

The Indian music is still blaring. I ask Navidad if her daughter and her son-in-law have been to India. They have. "They brought some of it back," I tell her. She smiles but adds nothing. Meanwhile when three pilgrims I have met before walk by, we acknowledge each other with smiles and "*Buen Camino*." I get a warm feeling from being part of this ever-changing Camino family. Now a teenage girl with purple streaks in her long brown hair comes out of the store. She is wearing the same kind of clothes as my own granddaughters, has the same air of assurance, and could be from just about anywhere in the Western world. "This is my granddaughter," says Navidad proudly, in a Spanish I find hard to understand. The girl is fifteen. She attends school in Astorga, gets picked up every morning and brought back in the afternoon. And she is an excellent student. "*Valiente y estudiosa*".

While I pelt the old woman with questions, pilgrims go in and out of the store in a long procession. Doubtless, this is a good business. Now I understand why the daughter behind the counter could not put her phone down when I was in; she never has a minute to herself. Eventually, during an unusual lull, I go inside the shop hoping she might have a minute for me. "How did you like India?" I ask her. "I have never been to India," she replies. "Your husband went alone?" "He never went to India."

By the church, in front of the Gaucelmo, is a life-size bronze bust of Julian Campo, an intellectual-looking, bald man with a bushy beard and thick eyeglasses. 15 May 1956 – 21 August 2006. He had renounced most of his earthly possessions and dedicated a significant part of his life to help-ing the most destitute as a volunteer in Calcutta. The memorial was erected here after his death in a train accident in nearby Villada. I assume he was a citizen of Rabanal.

I think of my friend, Dr. Jack, who I met in Kolkata in 2004 and who would turn ninety in the summer of 2020. Having lost close family members in Hitler's camps, he understood the pain of war. From the day he graduated as a mature student in medicine in Dublin, Dr. Jack dedicated his life to the destitute, displaced victims of political conflict and famine in Bangla-desh. Kicked out of that country for exposing corruption from officials in cahoots with a European NGO, he moved to Calcutta, (now Kolkata) where he worked as a volunteer for Mother Teresa. There, he founded Calcutta Rescue to care for the sick, offering treatment and sometimes cure to men and women otherwise destined for palliative care in Mother Teresa's house for the dying. He lived in Kolkata from a tiny pension in a tumbling down, mouldy, insalubrious hovel slated for demolition and which has since been taken down. He and his organization have helped hundreds of thousands in Kolkata, never receiving a penny for their work. His health failing, pressured by those who love him, amongst tears from his family of volunteers and those he had pulled out of misery, he finally agreed to retire in his 89th year. I hope that when he makes it up there beside Mother Teresa, the British will erect a monument to his memory in his native Manchester. I also hope he and Mother Teresa will get along better up there than they did in India.

Vespers

The tiny village of Rabanal boasts two churches. Across from the Gaucelmo, humble, ancient Iglesia de la Asunción with its high alabaster windows is the popular one. Even though I have long ago abandoned religion, I still enjoy the more pagan aspects of the Catholic Church. Vespers are celebrated in Latin every evening. There will be Gregorian chanting. I want to be there, to be plunged back into my childhood years. I imagine there will be a handful of pilgrims. I have not met many religious ones. At one minute to seven, I enter the small church and find its dark, damp, and cavernous interior with its primitive beauty overflowing with about a hundred pilgrims and locals. It is standing room only. Everyone is asked to put away cell phones and to refrain from taking pictures or recording. Soon, the monks' chanting lifts everyone's soul. At the end of the service, a German, a Korean and a Spanish pilgrim read verses in their own languages. The whole thing lasts less than thirty minutes. Believers, agnostics, atheists, no one is untouched.

In bed later, I think of all the wonderful people I have met in Rabanal. With its tiny population, it is a world rich beyond what I had imagined. Tomorrow morning, I will leave with dust on my heart.

The Bells of Foncebadón

I am still not out of the woods with whatever has been ailing me since Torres del Río almost two weeks ago, but I wake refreshed and take my time leaving Rabanal. I plan on walking four or five hours today to Riego de Ambros. The first half of the way is depicted as mostly uphill on Brierley's map, and much of it, especially at the end, will be rather steeply downhill. For the first hour or two, I am walking alone, taking my time, counting my fifty steps uphill, stopping to catch my breath. The air is cold. My long, slim shadow leads the way intermittently at the sun's whim. Apollo is playing hide-and-seek today in a sky strewn with billowing pregnant white clouds. Life is beautiful. I feel free as the birds soaring in the folds of mountains around me.

Mid-morning, I pass another village shorter than its name, Foncebadón. I keep repeating Foncebadón in my head. It rolls off the tip of my tongue like a hard candy. This handkerchief-size hamlet even has sleeping and eating establishments with tables outside where despite the cold some pilgrims are having coffee.

Everything is old in Foncebadón. The hamlet itself is over a thousand years old. Even the large information billboard at the entrance is falling into ruin. Words are missing, but we can still read that until the end of the 1960s, agriculture, animal husbandry and mining provided work for its inhabitants.

Many years ago, only a feisty old woman named María and her son remained, the others having gone *fuera*. (Maybe she became feisty after seeing herself abandoned by all the other inhabitants.) Apparently she was a generous soul who often gave shelter to pilgrims. The church, like many of the other buildings, was crumbling. One day, a priest, some workers and men from the Guardia Civil came to the village to take down the church bells and exhibit them in a museum. Warned of their coming, the old lady armed herself with sticks and stones and welcomed them perched at the top of the church. "I don't have a telephone," she shouted, "these bells are the only way I can ask for help." "The bells are useless," shouted the priest. "They don't even have a clapper." To which she retorted: "It doesn't matter, I'll use yours." Meanwhile, the son, sitting on a nearby boulder, threatened to shoot them should they try to take the bells down. They should be there to ring at his mother's funeral. "After she is gone," he said, "you can do what you want with them." The men left empty-handed. I gleaned this story from a Spanish pilgrim when I stopped for my hot chocolate. I say gleaned because his Spanish was very different from the Spanish I studied, and am not sure the part about the clapper is what he meant but I thought it was a good story. Just don't take my word for it.

Foncebadón is being reinvigorated thanks to pilgrims. I hope old María and her son lived long enough to see their village come to life again. The bells have not been taken away. Sadly, though, in 2019, disregarding the protests by friends of the Camino far and wide, the old stone road through the village was paved, obliterating a thousand years of history.

Om Shanti Om

After Foncebadón, the impressive Cruz de Ferro, the Eiffel Tower of the Camino, has about thirty pilgrims craning their necks to catch sight of the crucifix at the top. At the end of what looks like three telephone posts end to end and joined with wide metal rings, the iron cross is an imposing sight. Some pilgrims are adding messages to the base where previous notes are decomposing. Others have lugged a stone from home to add to the gigantic mound already surrounding the cross. Some are posing or just sitting by the cross, meditating. Fifty feet away, one pilgrim sits, eyes closed, in lotus position, arms extended and fingers of both hands forming Om. I glance at the tall cross, snap a photo, and go on my merry way. I sometimes feel like a fraud. I can only laugh at the irony of having fallen in love with the Camino. I had a history of travelling off the beaten path, yet the Camino is one of the most beaten paths in the world. It is no wonder I have been called an oxymoron.

In this area, the path is an obstacle course. Apart from trying to stay warm, there is no need to rush. Surrounded by bushes and trees, enjoying my inner solitude, I tread gingerly. Just before Manjarín, a small display of fruit and drinks beckons. It's the usual "*donativo*" so I help myself to a banana and a slice of watermelon. Manjarín welcomes us with a rather unattractive mishmash of flags and a Templars' cross sticking out of what looks like a pile of rubbish near solar panels and a shack with the words Centro Interpretacion Templara Medieval. It seems abandoned. Maybe it is more for tourists. A sign says I still have 238.4 kilometres to go. This part of the Camino is less than smooth. Beware ankles! I am so busy making sure I don't get a sprain that I almost miss at the next arrow, a black slab of stone, a cross, a bird, an inscription:

Michael Cura
03/08/99 21/07/16
The boat is safer anchored at the shore
But that's not the aim of boats

On another stone near it, one word: 'Silence.'

Suzanne

I am just about to leave, with the sobering reality of this young man's life having been nipped in the bud right here, when a slim woman with a bright orange t-shirt, knee-length hiking pants, wide-brimmed sunhat and a heavy-looking backpack that doesn't seem to bother her in the least, joins me at the memorial. A bicycle accident, we both assume. Suzanne has three children in their early twenties. She can relate to the loss. As I will later learn, Michael was a seemingly healthy cyclist from Swansea who died of a heart attack. His family has since started a foundation to help detect the type of heart condition from which, unaware, he suffered.

A French-Canadian palliative care nurse from a small town in central Alberta, Suzanne is here with her psychologist husband Paul who is lagging behind due to a serious case of tendinitis. I will meet him later at Acebo. We walk the next couple of hours together, enjoying the chance to speak French, shooting the breeze happily but a little too exuberantly, oblivious to the other pilgrims around us until one German woman passes us, turns around and says aggressively, "Are you deaf?" I could kick myself for not being quick enough to reply, "Pardon me?" At times like these, I miss my husband who, doubtless, would have had that quick repartee. We just laugh

Suzanne

it off discretely, but do lower our voices. I should remember this incident when faced with annoyingly loud passengers on buses and trains. And on the Camino.

In Acebo, Paul, tall, handsome, and gentle, arrives with another pilgrim. We all eat lunch together. It is good to see a couple enjoying the Camino without one being the leader, or obliging the other to go at their pace. Back home, Suzanne says, after work, they go biking together in a ravine near their home. Here, they are quite happy to walk together or to split when the occasion presents itself. Escorted by low mountains, she and I will continue on to Riego de Ambros. Paul, resigned, will take a taxi so as not to aggravate the tendinitis. A kind villager, approached by one of the restaurant staff, draws near us with his car. He will drive Paul to Molinaseca.

In Riego de Ambros, as in the previous village, the houses are built of fieldstones. Their wooden balconies with weather-beaten posts jut out over the cobblestone street supported by tall, thick, roughly hewed pillars. I wonder what it must be like to have your front windows right onto the sidewalk, your balcony ten feet away from the one across the street. This doesn't seem to bother the villagers. They have even placed the odd bench along the front of houses.

I'm sorry to have to say goodbye to Suzanne. After a warm hug and a "*Buen Camino*" in front of the small church, today's walking companion heads off into the distance, but not before a visit to the Ermita de San Sebastián, nor before we exchange contact information.

No Country for Vegans

Olivier, a French volunteer, and handsome to boot, welcomes me with kindness to the quaint, old Municipal hostel where I am thrilled to spot Elena, the Russian woman. She is sitting inside with her small white rat mascot on her shoulder. It has been a while since we met in the backyard at La Virgen del Camino with the two lovebirds holding hands and swinging in the hammocks two weeks before they were to meet the wife.

As usual, I am offered a lower bunk. I am starting to suspect that when someone calls to reserve a bed on my behalf, by saying "*para una señora*" rather than *"para una peregrina"* it means for an old lady. The Spanish are a courteous people. Whether or not I am right, I am not complaining.

Outside, the heat is brutal. Within the stone walls, I shiver with cold. Elena and I go up the hill to the sunny terrace of a pub. Ensconced in our plastic Estrella Galicia and Hijos de Rivera chairs, amongst a mixture of pilgrims, locals and road-weary drivers on a quick break, while enjoying a beer, we shoot the breeze as much as our language barrier will allow us. Because of her difficulty with Spanish, it takes me a while to get Elena's story straight.

I thought she had one husband. Now, I learn she had three. The first one died in a car accident. And didn't she have two sons and a daughter? "What daughter?" she asks when I ask the girl's name. I am still not sure if I have the correct version. Elena and I will end up as companions on and off, until San Lázaro, three kilometres before kilometre zero. She wants to arrive in Santiago with the sun at her back and see the cathedral lit up by the rising sun. By sleeping near Santiago, she will arrive in the early morning. Has she forgotten that Galicia is a province of morning fog? Rarely is the sun at your back, it seems. But I don't wish to be a naysayer. I say nothing.

Back down the hill, Olivier has prepared a humble meal of Spanish rice and fat sausages. Fortunately, there are no vegans around the table. Our host has put a large earthenware jug of fresh water and an equally generous pitcher of red wine on the table. Since he had said we could use the kitchen, having enquired about dinner, the vegans have either prepared themselves an appropriate meal or explored the restaurant. But I am not even sure there is a grocery store here, even a small one.

As always, there is great camaraderie around the table. We are only seven pilgrims, plus Olivier. On my photo of that night around the table are a blond Danish girl of about twenty, a dark-haired young man about her age with nicely trimmed black beard, and Pat, Christine and Morag, three sisters from Australia.

Their accent is different from that of other Ozzies I have met either from the Perth side or from the eastern states. "There is a reason for that," says Pat. "In 1963, our family emigrated from Scotland. Australia needed more settlers. It sponsored immigrants from English-speaking countries. My parents went over by ship for a £10 fare. I was just a kid then, and my sisters were born in our adopted country. My parents never lost their Scottish accent. Inevitably, we caught some of it." They are a cheerful threesome. They live far from each other, and chose the Camino as the place to meet for a month before heading off to Scotland to explore the ancestral land.

At night, Elena asks me, "How far are you going tomorrow?" I am planning on Camponaraya. "Do you mind if we walk together?" she asks. "As long as you don't mind leaving early. It is supposed to get really hot tomorrow." "*No problema.*"

The Old Oak Tree

At 6:30 in the morning, we are out the door, chatting away under a moonless sky. We forget to look for arrows and soon find ourselves at a frighteningly narrow highway with foot-wide shoulders along a dangerously deep ditch. An occasional truck thunders by, inches from us. I am scared to death I will break a leg by jumping off into the ditch. Elena is convinced we are on the right path. It is the same highway I had walked along for a short while yesterday, but here, it is all sharp curves. With dense forest on both sides, we can't see around the bends. Neither can we be seen by oncoming vehicles until they are almost upon us. The light from my lamp is almost dying. Elena doesn't have any light at all. Even if I had a lamp a hundred times as bright, trucks don't just change course on a dime. I obstinately refuse to go any further. "I don't want to die run over by a truck. This can't be the right way." But Elena is convinced it is. "It can't be," I insist. "It is the only way," she argues. I dig in my heels, then start walking back, fast, to the exit of Riego de Ambros where we got onto this road.

"But it is the right way," repeats Elena, her words drowned by the noise of another truck rumbling by inches away from us. "No way I am walking along this road!" I tell her. We are two stubborn women. I need a better argument to convince her. "Let's wait for other pilgrims," I suggest.

All the time glancing behind me as though that would prevent vehicles from coming, I walk back quickly to where we exited the village. This is nerve-racking. If I have to jump into the deep ditch, I risk breaking an ankle or worse.

When we are finally off the road, Elena pulls out her Russian guidebook, borrows my headlamp and insists that yes, it is the path because we are standing under a large oak tree. "It says here the path starts at a large oak tree." We have been walking amongst oak trees for days now. "There are oak trees everywhere," I say. But Elena insists. I pull out my Brierley and point to his illustration of Rabanal to Molinaseca. "You see, the path never goes *on* the road in this area. It does cross it at some point, but it is never *along* the road."

All the time, I'm thinking "it's going to be a hot day; we have to get going." Finally, after long minutes of arguing and no other pilgrim surfacing, Elena agrees to walk back up the hill with me into the village, to the hostel if need be because from places with accommodation, there are always arrows pointing the way. Near the top of the hill, I spot three pilgrims heading down a trail in a densely forested area. "Oak tree," I point out to Elena. "Oak tree, oak tree," I say, pointing triumphantly to another and another. Finally, laughing like two hyenas, we head down a dark, narrow, rugged but safer path between the trees.

After about fifteen minutes through this bush, we come out at a curve on the road where we must cross to pick up the path on the other side. There is a cross, a monument to a dead pilgrim, I suppose. I feel wicked in pointing it out to Elena. "See. See." But she doesn't comment. She is a fearless woman. I am not fearless, but we are two strong-willed women. I wonder how long we will hike together. I listen carefully for incoming vehicles and make a mad dash to the other side and back into the forest. It is 7:45. We have lost an hour. We will pay for it later.

The path is treacherous today. My eyes never leave the ground. Elena's stride is shorter than mine. She doesn't have a light, so I slow down. We must be on an old Roman road for sure this morning. It would not do to take our eyes off the path. Not even for a second. The large slabs of stone are often strewn with pebbles. I am right to always carry my tensor bandage. I have had enough experiences with sprained ankles, always during my travels in other countries. Always in Spanish-speaking countries, come to think of it.

The three shapes ahead of us are the Aussie sisters from last night. Before we reach them, I quickly pull out my notebook where I wrote their names so

I can impress them. Pat, Christine and Morag are having the time of their lives talking away rather loudly. I refrain from commenting. There are few people with us in the forest this morning. The sisters are carrying their backpacks so are slower than us. We wish them *"Buen Camino,"* and continue at a steady pace until the cobblestones of Molinaseca's bridge.

Camino Doloroso

"Que linda!" exclaims Elena at the entrance to Molinaseca. She is right, it is lovely. After resting a few minutes on benches by the Roman bridge, we spend time exploring. It means we will have to suffer the midday heat. So be it! We are resigned now. Who knows if we will ever have the chance to visit here again.

Past the bridge with its many arches, the narrow streets remind me of the Wild West with the upper floor of houses jutting out over sidewalks, supported, like the balconies of the previous village, by unpainted, rough, weather-beaten pillars. The passages they form would serve as rain shields for the locals who probably carry umbrellas anyway. I saw them years ago in Galicia. It was quite a sight: two hundred enormous umbrellas emerging from a church on a rainy Sunday. That image is deeply etched in my brain where I store all my travel memories. We are near the Bay of Biscay. Rain is a serious affair in this part of Spain. No wonder red geraniums abound, a sharp contrast to the stone windowsills and balconies they adorn. I bet they never need watering.

In two skips and a hop, we have crossed the village. Brierley will have us walking along the road for several kilometres this afternoon; that likely means no shade at all. *"Vamonos."* We say it at the same time.

A couple of hours later, at the entrance to Ponferrada, at the head of Puente Mascarón, as though they have been waiting for us, a disgruntled French couple, realizing I speak their language, decide to unload their griefs on me. They don't speak Spanish or English so they are happy to meet me even though I have "a quaint accent." They both retired early four months ago, the husband tells me. "We had been looking forward to this pilgrimage since our kids left home." They had prepared and trained for years, and had started over two months ago at the foot of the Alps, where they live. "We walked from the other side of Le Puy-en-Velay," says the wife, not without a fair amount of pride. "From our home to Saint-Jean-Pied-de-Port it is three-quarters the distance of Saint-Jean to Santiago." But they are extremely disappointed about the Spanish part of the Camino. All Spaniards are thieves. The food is *"pas bon"*, the prices *"trop chers"*, the accommodation *"terrible"*, the people *"mal élevés"* and much of the scenery *"pas belle"*, not at all beautiful like north of the Pyrenees. "They don't even speak a word of French," adds the woman. "It is much better in France." It seems they have enjoyed not one minute since they have crossed into Spain. I wonder which Camino they have been walking on. "Oh, I tell them," grabbing my daypack, which I had set down while listening to their griefs, and finding it hard to keep a straight face, "you obviously were on the wrong trail. You must have taken the *Camino Doloroso*." Before they can utter another word, I add, *"Excusez-moi*, we must keep going. We have a long way to go. *Bon chemin*."

I hope they don't hear us guffaw as we leave them with their misery, and cross the bridge into Ponferrada. Elena did not understand, but she is smart enough to have gotten the gist of it. "What was that all about?" "Oh, just a couple of disgruntled old farts," I tell her. *"Viejos pedos?"* she doesn't know what that means. Neither do I know the derisory term to describe this kind of old people in Spain. But now, I have to explain what *"viejos pedos"* means which I can only do with gesticulations at my backside followed by a pinch of my nose. Now, we are bent in two, giggling like teenagers. I turn around to look back towards the other side of the bridge. The Frenchman is glaring at me. He gives me the finger. Oh, he does speak another language!

After finding a grocery store we rest on a bench in the park and share anchovy-stuffed olives, paper-thin slices of cured ham, fresh green peppers and tomatoes. Elena breaks a fresh baguette in two, and stuffs one half inside her backpack for later while I spread some peanut butter from the plastic jar I carry on my corn cakes. We find ourselves of the same mindset when we decide to resist a bottle of red wine. We can have a drink at destination. As tempting as it is to have one now, one thing I know for sure is it is not a good idea to indulge during the afternoon. I am bound to need a nap if

I do. Having to turn down wine along the Camino is as sad as being blind in Granada.

Already, the heat is unbearable. Reluctantly, we skip a visit to the imposing Templar's castle, something I will later regret, but we are still too late to escape the savage sun. At the exit to Ponferrada, I spot a wild fig tree. "Don't wait for me," I tell Elena. "I'll catch up." I half-fill the bag I carry, only to find out later that the figs leave a horrible feeling on my tongue. The only thing to do is to dump them in a field.

Pepe Cortez

I wonder if Spain has an inventory of all the wonderful bronze life-size sculptures honouring its citizens of all walks of life. In Ponferrada, we pass one of a man with a small satchel at his waist; beside him stands a waist-high cylindrical metal tank similar to the acetylene tank my husband used in his goldsmith workshop, and topped with four knobs. The man's hand reaches for one of the pistons; his fingers are strong and knotty. What does he represent? Is he a miner? The name of this town contains the word 'ferrada' which might have to do with iron. We are in an area rich in mineral. But why does he have a coin purse around his waist instead of a metal lunch-box like my father used when he was a miner?

My intuition is quite wrong. Later, I will learn that I was looking at the legendary Pepe Cortez, a famous, kind-hearted *barquillero* who delighted a couple of generations of children now grown-up or departed. A *barquilla* was a small, rolled up, crisp wafer made of flour and cinnamon, without sugar, fat or yeast of any sort. The square where Pepe's sculpture stands today is where he plied his trade and became the children's hero. Beside him is a representation of the gas tank used to heat a hotplate to cook the *barquillas* on the spot. The sculpture celebrates a humble man who made friends with moms, dads, and children. It is a throw-back to a time when men and women were resourceful, tradespeople were valued, a time when there were less social services to take care of the poor, the illiterate, the ill. People worked, or they starved. Long live Pepe!

Where have all the poets gone?

After Ponferrada, we walk along a quiet road. On either side, the fallow fields are yellow with wildflowers, neither fluttering nor dancing in the breeze. Where is Wordsworth when we need him? Then, at our fingertips, vineyards tempt us with their plump and juicy fruit. Shamefully, we cannot resist.

An occasional car breaks the monotony. We are only about ten kilometres after the start of stage 25. Pilgrims who do it by the book passed here early morning. The mercury has already climbed much too high. It's a rare tree that blesses us with its shade for a few short seconds. Not even a miserly puff of wind blows to provide relief. Under my parasol, I walk at a steady pace, but not fast. Elena never misses petting the cats within her reach. They bring each other joy.

The road is an endless grey ribbon. Each minute seems longer than on winding paths. At a fountain with a bench across from a house with rotting, bare wooden windows and plaster falling off the field stones it once covered, we replenish our bottles and take a few photos. The lower part of the house shows signs of water-damage. Was there a flood here? Posted on a rotting green door to a small metal balcony, a sign '*Se vende*'. No matter how derelict the house, my heart aches each time I see the 'for sale' signs. Is it too far gone to restore? It would be a perfect location for pilgrims' accommodation.

A pilgrim forgot her hiking sticks at the fountain. I shout, "*Peregrina! Peregrina!*" She is too far ahead for my words to reach her, or she doesn't want to bother with us. We don't have enough energy to run after her. A local cyclist stops for a drink. When I explain the predicament, he takes the sticks and delivers them to her.

Before Fuentes Nuevas, a life-size sculpture catches my eye. It is something one would expect to find in a Marxist country: a peasant woman, handkerchief tied around her hair, a heavy load on her head, a child at her side: a monument to hard-working people who have built this country. I never tire of seeing how Spain celebrates its ordinary people.

It is after three o'clock when when we find La Medina, our hostel near the exit of Camponaraya. The name Camponaraya had me expecting a scenic town. Not so. And I had thought I would find a Marakesh or Fez flavour in the decor of La Medina. I was wrong; there is nothing of Morocco here.

For a couple of Euros more, we have reserved beds instead of bunks. At the entrance, past the bar, a young woman is helping other pilgrims. After a while, she shows us all upstairs where two pilgrims are allocated bunks in an immense dorm. The Australian sisters are already here, resting. They overtook us when we were wasting time in the towns on the way. Past their dorm, Elena and I are shown to a room with three solid-looking single beds and one bunk. "Choose the ones you want," the woman instructs us. We are both thankful not to have to duck under upper bunks tonight.

Nearby, outside a bar frequented mostly by locals, we order *cañas*, (small glasses of beer). The server brings us each a *pinxo* (a small savoury pastry free with our beer which only costs €1.50). At a table next to ours, two old gaffers are drinking a golden liquid in tiny glasses in the shape of hourglasses. They must contain no more than three ounces of the beverage. Curious, I ask what it is they are drinking. "*Cortos*", says one of the men smiling mischievously as he explains that it is the least expensive glass of beer and it also comes with the free *pinxo*. They are widowers, he explains. They come here each day for their *cortos* which cost €1 each. After three *Cortos*, and three *pinxos*, the old men are satiated. "At our age," he adds, "we don't have a huge appetite." I imagine many locals also come each day mid-afternoon for the generous, affordable three-course meal I am told Franco obliged all restaurants to offer. When they leave, I notice €6 on the table. Not one cent more. Elena and I compare pension plans in our countries. Our Canadian pension is five-fold her Russian one. I feel bad for having chosen this place and suggested beds instead of the less expensive bunks. Elena also prefers to buy her own groceries to paying for the pilgrim's meal. I will have to be more careful if I continue walking with her.

On her phone, my new friend shows me a series of paintings she has done. Some are Gauguin or Picasso-inspired, one Monet... I am no art critic, but in my humble opinion, they honour the masters. She is modest about her art, but I am dazzled by her multiple talents. Elena knows flowers and trees; she knows mushrooms, birds... She loves music, dances the tango... She is an avid skier. Nothing seems outside of her reach.

At a nearby table is a man we have not seen before. I wonder if he's a pilgrim. He is wearing shorts and sandals and on top of his white hair, the cutest peaked peasant's straw hat. "Shall we invite him to join us?" asks Elena. We pull a chair for him at our table. Enrique is Filipino. He has been living in California most of his life. Tall and lanky, he has long, bony fingers. His face and hands are splashed with age stains.

"I also ship my bag," he tells us. His son will meet him somewhere between here and Santiago. We don't get a chance to chat more because back at the albergue, it is time for the communal dinner for which he has signed up. Elena and I will sup from the food leftover from our lunch. We will cross paths with Enrique several times. He walks a slow, deliberate step in his sandals, his face shaded by the conical hat. "I usually walk until early evening," he tells us. He reminds me of Aesop's tortoise. And he always looks serene.

In the night, each time someone uses the bathroom off the large dorm next door to us, a bright sensor-activated light comes on and flashes in the faces of those in the bunks facing the bathroom. I am glad we are not trying to sleep in the dorm.

Art Along the Camino

This morning, an hour into our walk, the three Australian sisters are having coffee at a table outside the St. James's Way in beautiful Cacabelos. "Great place for breakfast," says Morag. Don't they feel the cold and dampness? Elena and I are shivering. We opt for a table inside where I order my usual stick-to-the-ribs breakfast. The waiter is very "*simpático.*" I wish our French 'friends' would stop here. I wonder what they would find to complain about. I suppose they would want a croissant. After our meal, Enrique appears in the distance. His pace is steady. He looks content. He must be a ray of sunshine to his family. We will walk with him for a short stretch.

On the way out of Cacabelos, all three of us stop at a well-executed mural on a building. In the background: a factory with smoking chimneys; in the middle: a prostrate man and, perched on top of his back, a monstrous man-machine with cogs inside its stomach; a large fig-leaf conceals the shameful secrets of industry, and long clawed feet dig into the enslaved man's back; to the right: a man wearing a dhoti, sitting in lotus position, hands joined in the *namaste* sign. Behind him, dead trees attacked by long, carbuncular fingers of smoke from the chimneys. At the bottom: a man with a German Shepherd, a cane, gourd and satchel, looks pensively at a vineyard and its winery surrounded by a low stone fence. Across the painting in Spanish: "Humanity suffers the consequences of its uncontrolled progress. When will we find a way to harmonize science and nature?" Two Spaniards come up to the mural. They stand in front of it for a minute and then, as they walk away, I hear one saying: "How does the artist think his paints are produced?" Further, another mural depicts ten-foot high, half-human, half-imaginary creatures with a distinct Egyptian flavour walking in a procession: a motley crew of pilgrims. I have no idea if the painting has a specific meaning. I love this place; it is kind to artists.

When we come to a disused, lovingly preserved stone press, I imagine a dozen short, sturdy, merry peasants dancing on the grapes, women holding their skirts up at their knees, men with rolled-up trouser legs. A wooden roof on tall pillars protected the fruit from the rain and the workers from the sun. The juice would run into the large trough below. Then would come the wine festival. This would have been pre-union, pre-nine-to-five, pre-minimum wage, pre-regulatory yearly holiday, pre-sick leave, pre-Sunday shopping at the mall. Surrounded by the old stone houses, the cobblestone streets, and the frequent antiquities, I am hiking across centuries.

Before long, we hear a young man singing and playing guitar. "*Francesco! Hola. Francesco. Cómo estás?*" He still looks as though he hasn't a care in the world. With his yoga mat rolled up on top of his backpack, he strolls along, singing and enjoying the day. Soon, a few young people arrive; one is a pretty blond girl I have seen hanging around our minstrel; she stops to talk to him while her companions continue. Their faces light up at the sight of each other. Enrique is already back on the path. After the press, Elena and I continue with Francesco and the blond girl, but soon, with raised eyebrows, we slow our pace, and stop to admire a large field with purple wildflowers, their small petals huddling together under the threatening sky. We take photos until we have left a respectful distance between us and budding love. This cool weather and our easy, flat gravel path help us progress at a good pace today. Eventually, we pass the love birds. *"Buen Camino,"* we say and move on ahead, quickening our step and hoping the clouds will not burst and douse us before we can shelter somewhere.

We are walking in silence when, with no one near us front or back, I start singing a song from the Buena Vista Social Club: *"Silencio, duermen las flores, las rosas y las azucenas..."* Elena immediately falls in love with the song. I don't know all the words. I sing it in a loop. She wants to sing along. We stop and prop ourselves against the railing separating us from the road while I write down the words I know. For the next while, we sing together, only stopping when there are other pilgrims near us. As most days, since we are not doing the official stages, most other pilgrims are far ahead. We will sing the song many times along the way. It's a gentle melody, almost a lullaby.

After Pieros, in the middle of nowhere, a marble sign in bas-relief in the style of ancient Greek sculptures depicts a sculptor with a mallet and other tools of his trade and the words: *Estudio de Escultura A Nogueria.* At first, I am surprised to find Portuguese here. *A Nogueria* means The Walnut Tree. In Spanish, we would have *El Nogal,* or *El Nogueral.* We are close to the Portuguese border. I had already noticed many names of places in this area where the articles *"el"* and *"la"* are replaced by the Portuguese *"o"* or *"a"* as in O Cebreiro and A Coruña. The explanation, of course, resides in the complicated history of the Iberian Peninsula. Languages evolve, but they are storehouses of history.

Unfortunately, the sculptor is not here today. Behind a high wooden fence, in the distance, at the end of a wide path and untended grounds where weeds have taken squatters' rights, is a tiny one-room studio, half-open to the elements. Even with its new roof, it looks forlorn under today's low grey sky. On one side are some partly finished sculptures; on the other, a tall finished one. Set on a pedestal, the organic shape has pieces of ceramic incrusted in its multiple walls. Cathedral-style, several peaks are topped by round balls and shards of ceramic. Gaudí's spirit roams in this area. Elena and I are sorry not to meet the artist.

A Fortunate Mistake

Vineyards line our path again today, then a fig tree spreads its branches, loaded with plump, juicy-looking fruit. It is obviously a wild one since it grows at the edge of the path. A ditch separates us from the tree. It is about four-foot deep on our side and eight-foot to the embankment on the other side. Carefully, Elena climbs up to it. After she samples the fruit to make sure it is ripe, I hand over my bag at the end of a stick. In no time at all, it's bulging with figs.

If going up to the tree was risky, coming back down is even more dangerous. After tying the top of the bag and passing it over to me on the stick, Elena makes it back to the path without too much dirt on her clothes and we continue on our merry way. As we are walking along, we notice that the ground, starting where the fig tree was, comes down gradually to the level of the Camino. After about fifty metres, a narrow, private road crosses the path at our level. Lo-and-behold, this is a *bona fide* fruit orchard. Private! *Mea culpa, mea culpa, mea maxima culpa.* Honest! We didn't know! But are we glad we didn't! The figs are plump, sweet and juicy: the best we have had so far. The funny thing, of course is, had we known, we would not have picked them, but had we known and wanted to pick them, we could have just walked a hundred steps further and gone in from the road.

Villafranca del Bierzo

Cats wander in and out of a derelict house at the entrance to Villafranca del Bierzo, a town of 3,500 souls. A profusion of greenery grows out of the house's roof and front wall. Those decrepit buildings are nature's art. They remind me of the Easter Sunday straw hats of my childhood that kept me entertained during mass. Elena is in her element. She gets to pet her feline friends. On our right, a sunroof sticks out almost at road level. It belongs to a hostel built into a precipitous hill. From our vantage point, we only see its roof and fifteen inches of its wall. Suddenly, I hear "Danielle. Danielle." There is Yu Jin again. She runs over to us and gives me her usual big hug. When I introduce Elena, she gives her the same treatment. Yu Jin is one of

Yu Jin and Elena

the highlights of my Camino. And, wouldn't you know it: fifteen minutes later, who should appear but Francesco strumming his guitar and singing, the blond girl at his side.

After Villafranca, much of our walk is along the N-VI, a major highway curving around a mountain pass. The road is quiet, and a waist-high cement wall protects us from vehicles. It's one sharp curve after another. I would not like to hike on the shoulder without this separation. I would not be surprised to learn that a few pilgrims have had their appointment with destiny in this area. Whenever I find a structure like this wall or an overhead pedestrian crossing over a busy highway, I imagine there might have been some tragedy to lead to its design. It is often how planning works. Remedies rather than prevention. I hope I am wrong. I am thankful for the Spaniards who look after our welfare. Way up in the sky, above my left shoulder, like two thin ribbons, rises an incredible feat of engineering: the *autopista* from Madrid to A Coruña or *Autovia del Noroeste*. From our vantage point, it looks amazingly fragile. Once in a while, we are startled by the loud rumbling of some heavy transport zooming by along it. When the sound reaches us, it is as though the vehicles were right above our heads. Their noise amplified by the mountains, they sound more like trains than road transport. Each time, I am caught by surprise. Elena's nerves are more solid than mine.

The Tiniest of Villages

At the entrance to Pereje, we leave the N-VI. Although it is not busy, the occasional cars appearing out of nowhere all seem to be going at breakneck speed. Perhaps it is just an illusion since there is not much traffic, but running across this highway to get to the old road into Pereje is a little scary. After the cemetery, past ten or twenty houses, the old stone school is there for us with our fourteen-bed dorm on the lower floor. Upstairs are a kitchen, and a pile of mattresses. I suppose they take care of pilgrim overflow during Holy Years. No meal is offered here. A restaurant is only steps away. According to Olivia, the cheerful *hospitalera* who drives in from a nearby village, only eight people live in Pereje.

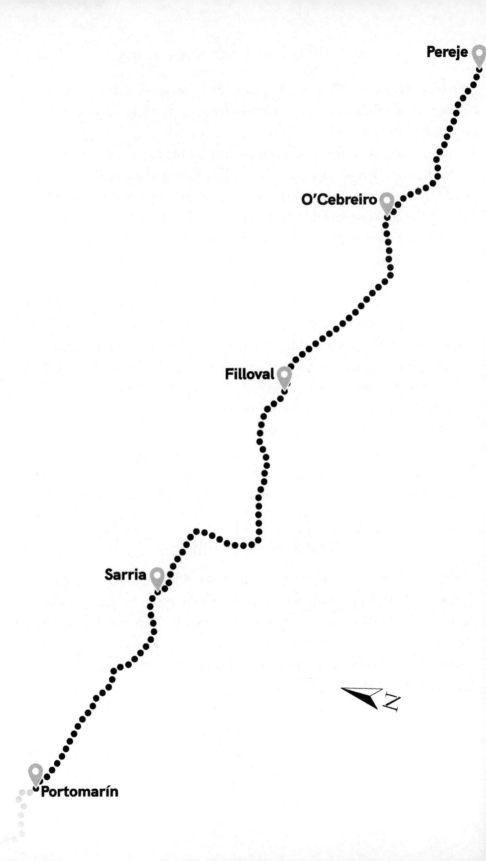

Pereje

O'Cebreiro

Filloval

Sarria

Portomarín

N

"How can the village afford to keep our dorm open and pay your wage?" I ask Olivia. The *ayuntamiento* (the town corporation) pays her salary. Less than half the beds are occupied tonight. At €5 each, they are not in the black with us, yet this is one of the best places to stay along the Camino. Our beds have clean linen and blankets. There are no laundry machines, but we can wash our clothes outside in a deep sink. Hanging laundry to dry outside on the lines is always a back-to-earth feeling.

We walk around the village, taking pictures. In five minutes we have seen it all. One house's balcony runs the length of its facade, full of healthy, potted red geraniums. Some houses might serve as holiday homes for their owners. Many of them are in an excellent state of repair. Others are past any hope of restoration. The stone walls of the schoolhouse and of the large restaurant look solid and well taken care of. This would have been a lively village before the new road which bypasses it.

Dinner With New Friends

Elena and I scribble in our diaries. Since there is no internet, we go for a beer at a table in the sun across from the restaurant, the only other building with any sign of life. It is late afternoon. Only an occasional straggler passes by without stopping. Three pilgrims sit at three tables; they all have beds in the schoolhouse. As always, we regroup around one table.

Richard, a tall, handsome, healthy-looking sexagenarian, is from Oregon. Hanne is a thirty-year-old German. Minko, middle-aged, is Ukrainian. She and the two men came alone to the Camino. Soon, another woman arrives. When she heads for a table by herself, we signal for her to join us. She hesitates, thinking we are hiking as a group. She doesn't want to intrude. "No, no, we only just met." That clinches it. She pulls a chair up to our table.

Richard's missionary and humanitarian work has taken him to many African countries. Now retired, he is enjoying the pilgrimage. He also has a smattering of Spanish. I love the gentle way he speaks to Elena. Their conversation sometimes requires my help, but again, I am quite amazed at how much one can get on with basic vocabulary and gestures galore.

Hanne quit his job in advertising before coming to the Camino. Another one who uses the pilgrimage as a transition between jobs. His work consisted in targeting people with the right advertising. "I was good at my work," he says, but it didn't fit in with his principles. He and his partner are minimalists and live in a tiny old home in which he rented a space from as far back as his student days. It has a large flower and vegetable garden. When the owner went into a retirement home, since she had no family, she sold him the house for a decent price. He and the old woman had become close, like grandmother and grandson. He visits her regularly in the home. His partner would have loved to accompany him on the Camino, but could not get away.

Minko is taking a year off from teaching, and going around the world. Marina is doing the Camino on her bicycle. Although gentle and quiet, you can tell she is strong mentally and physically. She apologizes. "I have to make an important call," she says, and retires to another table where soon, she is busy talking with someone in sign language on her phone.

A Cruel Disease

At the restaurant across the path, I find the place empty except for an old woman sitting by herself, idle, arms stretched in front of her on the table. In semi-darkness, she stares in the distance, a vacant look on her face. When I wish her "*Buenas tardes*," she doesn't respond. Without saying anything, the woman behind the counter throws a glance in my direction. I understand. She must be the daughter, or perhaps the daughter-in-law.

Dementia. A terrible disease. Sometimes I wonder if modern medicine hasn't done too much for our bodies. With our hip and knee replacements, our pacemakers, triple and quadruple bypasses, with our antibiotics, our blood pressure and high cholesterol pills, we live so long that our ghosts go to mush before our bodies are ready to give them up. Although I have the incredible good fortune of having no medical condition, except for my Camino bugs and gluten intolerance, if I stay physically healthy into my eighties or nineties, I run a good chance of suffering from dementia. A scary prospect! Many of my acquaintances are already living that nightmare. I can only hope a cure is found for my children's generation. I wonder what help this family gets, if any. I imagine the woman behind the counter never has a moment's respite. At least, not during pilgrims' season. There might come a day when she will have to choose. Mother or earning a living. The answer is clear but cruel. Life is like that.

There are no customers in the restaurant. I go back out with our beers and menu cards. The fare looks appetizing. No one is vegetarian around the table tonight. When I mention the old woman and when we have discussed what it must be like to live in a small village like this without help, we all agree to order the same thing so the cook will have less work. We all know someone with dementia. Who doesn't?

When our soup arrives, followed by yummy chicken brochettes, home fries and salad, we congratulate ourselves on our choice, and sit around the table eating and drinking wine past sunset, sharing vignettes of our lives until the stars shine brightly. Talking. Listening. Encouraging. Sympathizing. Atoms dancing. After a while, we each take our dishes into the restaurant before walking back to the schoolhouse together. Sadly, only then does it occur to us that we should have done that sooner. We were the only customers, the only other people in the village. The woman in the restaurant was likely waiting for us to leave so she could call it a day.

A million stars light the sky. Hanne spots a satellite doing its rounds. He points to it until we all find it. We stop for long minutes and stare, awed by the scintillating show. The moon is a thin sliver, a toenail moon. It is hard to leave this heavenly sight, but our beds are calling. Tomorrow we are tackling the hill with the worst reputation on the whole Camino Francés.

Today I have threaded many fine jewels on my necklace of friendships, but the only one of this group of four Elena and I will come across again is Hanne. He is a breath of fresh air. Ditto for Richard, Minko, and Marina. My life is rich with these moments spent in the company of pure strangers.

In the morning when I wake, the dorm is empty except for Elena and me. It is not seven o'clock. Quiet as mice, everyone else has already vamoosed. Oh, my! It's cold out there! I pile everything on: leggings under my pants, cashmere turtle neck, scarf, hat, gloves... the whole kit. We walk fast to stay warm. Whatever creature finds itself in our path is blindly squashed. It's not a morning for Buddhists or Jains. We are both inside our own heads, not in a chatty mood, as though talking will make us lose the heat our bodies have stored during the night.

Back onto the modern highway snaking around the mountain pass, protected by the waist-high wall, overtaken by many cyclists, we move at record speed. Some cyclists are courteous and either ring a bell or announce themselves. Alas, they are the exception. The sooner we can get off that path, the better. At least we don't have to watch our every step, but I like the more challenging surfaces where I feel transported, where in my imagination, I walk behind the man with the long beard, hair in a ponytail past his shoulders, weather-beaten hands and face. He wears a heavy, rough, full-length brown wool cassock, carries a gourd full of water. He trudges on, bent over a thick, uneven branch: his walking stick. A grimy balluchon containing stale bread, a pock-marked apple, and tied with a rough piece of twine, hangs over his shoulder. When I tell Elena what I am thinking, she laughs and says. "You wouldn't want to walk too close to him." That gets us giggling like two schoolgirls because just as she says it, we are passed by almost such a pilgrim. With his facial hair and straggly shoulder-length mane, his filthy, well-travelled boots that look like they might abandon him anytime, he is a link between the past and the present.

Later, we face quite a different challenge on what must be a Roman road. I know some would much prefer the paved area. But Elena and I must have a bit of the masochist in us; we pick our way carefully but enthusiastically among slabs of rocks, deep ruts, stones of all sizes. One second of carelessness and my tensor bandage will have to come out. I have no intention of using it so I walk gingerly, nose to the ground, lifting my head only occasionally to take in the huge chestnut trees laden with nuts, ivy hugging trees, apple trees heavy with fruit on bowed branches, well-tended gardens, a six-foot high pile of pumpkins against a barn door, more apple trees...

Apples in this part of the world can never compete with Canadian apples. With their rough, thick, greeny-brown skin, they all seem worm-eaten and inedible. But, when we go through a tiny hamlet, it doesn't stop a local gentleman from offering us some. Out of politeness, Elena and I accept one each. The man points to a tree behind a house along the road. He picked them from his absent neighbour's tree with his permission. "No point letting them rot on the ground," he says. I could imagine pigs being fed these pockmarked apples. I have eaten better. I wonder if he is going to turn his into apple sauce. With a lot of peeling, coring and trimming, it could be done. Or they could be pressed into cider. They would not be something to sink your teeth into blindly. When we are out of the man's sight, we look at each other and, laughing, catapult ours irreverently into a field. Further, a woman bent over a large straw basket is gathering wind-fallen nuts. Nature is generous in these parts if you are not too fussy.

In a small town, at a weekly market, Elena and I each buy a small enamelled pendant on a chain. At €5 each, they have to be from China, but they are pretty and well made. It's more to encourage the young woman behind the table than because we want them. Having spent many spring, summer and fall Sundays fund-raising for my friend, Doctor Jack, in Kolkata by selling trinkets at a Sunday market, I know the pleasure each sale brings. It will be for a granddaughter's stocking at Christmas.

By late morning, as usual, we have shed our warm clothes. The sun is getting nasty. In Madrid, the saying is *"Seis meses de invierno, seis meses de infierno"* (six months of winter, six months of hell). On the Camino, it's often six hours of winter, six hours of hell. Elena and I find a bench in the shade and pause to eat our fruit and vegetables from the market. Even in the shade, we feel like two of Dante's characters.

Road Apples

Sometimes ignorance is bliss. I wish we had not looked at my Brierley today. Laguna de Castilla lies two-thirds of the way to O'Cebreiro along the most punishing hill of the Camino Francés. White and brown horses clip-clop past us under a merciless sun. Lucky riders. With pinched noses, knowing that tomorrow our walk will be much easier, we detour around huge piles of steaming fresh road apples where armies of flies feast in a frenetic *danse macabre*. Aware this is a stretch skipped by many, we do our best to enjoy the challenge. We will still have the top third of the climb when we start tomorrow morning, fresh from sleep and in the cooler hours. I swear to Elena if I have the good fortune of coming back to the Camino, I will skip

Herrerías to O'Cebreiro. "No way I am climbing this again," But I know I will soon forget and, given the chance, I'll do it all over again. Thus is programmed the human brain; that is why women have more than one baby.

Hot and breathless, we soon find our dorm with its immense backyard in Laguna de Castilla. As usual, sit in the sun and roast or sit in the shade and freeze. There doesn't seem to be a happy medium.

The restaurant's fare looks appetizing. My supper starts with the customary thick lentil soup followed by yummy finger-licking pork ribs piled high on rice. Try and try, I can hardly get through half of it. Not used to wasting food, I feel terrible having to leave so much. Had I known, I would have asked Elena to join me. My meal would have been enough for the two of us. She could have saved her market produce for tomorrow.

Half-way through dinner, who walks into the restaurant but our Filipino friend from California. "Enrique, come and join me." I enjoy his gentle presence. We don't talk about anything too deep, but discuss the changing difficulties along the Camino. Enrique is the model pilgrim. He doesn't need to prove anything to anyone. He doesn't say why he is doing the Camino. He has loved walking in nature all his life. I don't ask if he is a believer. Why should it matter? I offer him my dessert, and he, thin and willowy, incredibly gobbles the whole thing up although he has licked his own platter clean.

Lizi

By the bunk next to mine, a puffy travel neck pillow perches atop a humongous backpack. The pilgrim, a woman in her thirties, has flown from China. She will be starting her Camino here. I can tell she is feeling intimidated. By now, most pilgrims have found a partner or two. "I haven't seen you on the Camino before," I say. Lizi has just arrived by taxi. She only has a week to walk to Santiago.

"Are you serious?" she asks, ecstatic, when I comment on the size of her backpack and explain about the transfer service. "Really? Ship it from one dorm to the next? I can do that?" She is almost crying with relief. After Santiago, she will meet a friend in the south of Spain, so she is carrying much more than Camino needs. She is not a big person, and was extremely worried, wondering how she would manage. There is no way she would have made it up the brutal hill today. Her Camino has started with a blessing in disguise. At the Madrid airport, as seems to happen often, Lizi's bag was nowhere to be found, so she lost a day. It meant no time to walk up the infamous hill. I can just imagine her with her huge backpack, picking her way around the flea-infested horse dung under the pounding sun. Impossible! Death on the Camino! Or at least, jettisoned backpack.

In the morning, it's pilgrim's progress in pea soup fog. We can barely see twenty feet ahead. Little by little, all around us, spectacular mountains pop into view. Elena and I are enjoying our young friend's company. A well-travelled woman from the south of India, Lizi works in Shanghai for a large advertising firm. She seems oblivious to the attention of several young men. She must be used to it, and would have all the reasons to be full of herself. Her hair, thick, shiny black, naturally wavy and half-way down to her waist, would have inspired an O. Henry. Her sparkling deep brown eyes attest to the fact that in the south of India live beautiful women. Elena and I are happy to have new company for the last uphill stretch between Laguna de Castilla and O'Cebreiro. Lizi is receiving baptism by fire this morning with an extremely laborious hike for a couple of hours. "I can't believe I was going to carry my bag!" she says, laughing at her naivety.

Breathless all three, it is still early when we reach O'Cebreiro. We had been looking forward to visiting a *palloza*. Unfortunately, it is closed. A vestige of roman times, the impressive, immense, round house with its low stone wall and imposing conical thatched roof would have been worth a visit. Apparently these *pallozas* were homes. The roof is about three times the height of the circular wall at the highest point. The livestock lived downstairs while the heat they generated rose to warm the family upstairs. Natural heating. A bit like the cow's breath on baby Jesus.

Can You Spare a Band-aid?

We expected the path from O'Cebreiro to Alto San Roque to be flatter. Nearer the top of the hill we have to stop and catch our breath often. Elena has been walking ahead of Lizi and me. After catching up to her, we walk silently as a threesome up to the colossal bronze pilgrim sculpture where we stop for pictures, hoping at least one will turn out. The fog has dissipated. The bright sun and strong shadows make it almost impossible to get a good picture. Leaning into the wind, peering into the distance towards Santiago, his hand a visor above his eyes, the giant rises from his high pedestal. Pilgrims with a sense of humour have put band-aids on his toes.

From here, in every direction we look, we are above treed mountains and valleys. The fog spreads its shroud over the lower areas, giving an illusion of lakes. It is a moment to take home in the treasure-box of memories.

José Antonio

By Alto do Poio, after Elena and Lizi have left me in the dust, I happen upon an old man sitting on the seat of his walker, a walking cane at his side. He is wearing a warm sweater, sneakers with velcro, sunglasses and a wide-brimmed hat, and is busy doing nothing more than contemplating the vista. I stop to say hello and comment on the beauty of this area. His name is José Antonio. A younger woman sits on a low wooden seat behind him. "Your daughter?" I ask. She is his *visitante*. José Antonio is the only inhabitant in his village. "Is it far from here?" "Two or three hundred metres that way," the woman says, pointing behind her. "Padornelo." I ask if I can take their picture. They don't mind. The old man has a beautiful smile and a twinkle in his eyes. He is 72 years old, which surprises me; I thought he was older, but his face is quite young. I had assumed he was older because of the walker and the cane.

I wonder what it must be like to be the last inhabitant of a village. I can't imagine him climbing to the roof of his church to throw stones at the priest below. They ask where I am from. Am I walking the Camino alone? Is this my first time? Am I enjoying it? "Have you ever walked to Santiago?" I ask. They both have. Now, he walks with his cane as much as he can, and then he uses his walker. After a few minutes of polite conversation, "It was lovely talking to you. I must move on," I say. "*Buen Camino,*" they reply in unison. I think often of the biologist and philosopher Albert Jacquard's phrase: "In life, we must multiply encounters; each encounter enriches us." I know I am richer for having talked to José Antonio and his caregiver today. There is a little spark in me that wasn't there before. A new bead on my necklace.

At a table outside a restaurant at the top of a very steep hill. Lizi is sipping on a soft drink while Elena pets a large, lazy German shepherd. It is enjoying the attention. "I am terrified of dogs," confesses Lizi, so I recount to her how I used to be afraid of certain dogs until my son adopted a Rottweiler. I was petrified. I thought I wouldn't even be able to go near it. Within minutes of meeting the dog, I was sitting in my son's armchair, the dog's head snuggling against my thigh; it was love at first sight. He was the gentlest creature I had ever met.

When we resume our walk, the three of us with no one behind, no one in front, Elena and I sing the Cuban song. We are in a corner of paradise now, in areas of purple crocuses, trees laden with scarlet berries. I think it's the kind they use for a liqueur around here. A woman in wellington boots calmly leads a cow somewhere. Earlier today, we passed a large barn full of healthy-looking cows in their smooth beige coats. There are more of them now enjoying their siesta in emerald-green pastures. Living a life of *far-niente*. They know nothing of their distant cousins, the cattle destined for fast-food restaurants in feed lots all over the carnivorous world, packed a thousand together under large roofs, prisoners of their master, born slaves, dying slaves, spending their life in the stench of mud and dung at their feet.

After the well-tended garden of Mesón Betularia, in Biduedo, we stop by a tiny one-room stone building. It is not open. Is it a church? Was it once a church? A structure above the entrance looks as though it might have once housed a bell. Is it in a museum now? Was there no one with sticks and stones and a son with a gun to protect it? Flat, naturally tapered stones, some as long as my arm, form the arched entryway. They hold together by gravity. A feat of engineering. I wonder who invented the arch. I stand there, admiring the building. We see this kind of construction everywhere in this part of the world. I like it because it uses the materials at hand. No mortar. The stones are as they find them. It is a matter of fitting the right one into the right space. The building, like the cows, fits perfectly into its surroundings. Whatever its use, I bet it will stand centuries from now, after the modern homes and apartments we live in now have been torn down, after millions of pilgrims have walked by it. The funny thing, though, is someone has planted large, colourful artificial flowers at its entrance.

On our way to Fillobal now, where we will stay tonight, are many low stone walls. We stop often to take in the vista: more emerald green fields and stone, like Ireland. There are mushrooms too, but Elena says "*No toques*" (Don't touch).

In Fillobal, we have a twin room. I hope she doesn't mind. I would be happy to pay the lion's share, but she will not let me. Her tight budget is developing into a bit of a problem because, frankly, I have had enough of dorms, but I don't want to impose. Roubles don't translate into too many Euros. Elena is obviously happy for the company. Lizi, who did not reserve last night, gets a bed in a dorm down the hall. Elena knows she could trade with Lizi, but she chooses the room. My conscience is clear.

Everything here is top-notch. Our host, a young man, is gentle and welcoming. Our bedroom is perfect. We even have a couch. On the wall, some-one has painted "*Solo aquellos que sueñan pueden volar.*" (Only those who dream can fly). Indeed.

After an excellent dinner next door, listening to the pelting rain, I think about José Antonio, calm, serene, a man at peace with his world. Maybe he has a choice of moving to a retirement home. He chooses to stay where he was born, where he married, raised his children, where his wife died. That is his home and where, one day, his caregiver might find him gone to eternal sleep. He will spend the rest of his days contemplating the beauty of the mountains, his mountains. Is that worse than ending in a disinfected room, among strangers, in a dying factory? It is not death, but the fear of death, that is tragic.

Of Mean Dogs and Men Hiding in Trees

Sarria is about six hours of steady walking from Fillobal. Although further than one stage, on my map, after the first hour or two, it is depicted as a relatively easy hike for those of us with good knees. At 7:30, under our rain ponchos, hoods drawn over our heads, we are ready to brave mist and rain. The visibility is about nil. I love mist. I love rain. So do Lizi and Elena.

Jean-Pierre, a true pilgrim

José Antonio and helper

Alone in a 14-bed dorm

Near the path, perhaps for pilgrims to enjoy, in a clearing in front of tall sunflowers, someone has arranged together three large, warty pumpkins, five or six green-tipped orange gourds and a green squash with white stripes like a sea cucumber. The still life pierces the fog with vivid colours, ready to be captured on canvas. Back home, this will be one of my favourite pictures.

Around the corner on a hill, a pilgrim is standing still, arms at her side; a German Shepherd barks menacingly near her. She is Riza, a Lithuanian whom we met briefly last night at dinner. She walks alone. Scared, she is keeping calm, waiting for braver pilgrims to calm the dog. Lizi is terrified. I am happy Elena is with us. The German Shepherd is a companion of choice in these areas. Not the friendliest-looking dog. Elena talks to it gently, and he soon retreats. I think dogs understand us more than we understand them. We walk with Riza for a while, wondering what it would have been like had Elena not been with us. The Camino used to have a reputation for dog attacks. Apparently there is now a law to prevent roaming dogs. Sadly, it also means that at a roadside home somewhere before Burgos, where an old lady sits at a small table offering to stamp pilgrim's *credencials*, hoping they might buy a small trinket from her, her young puppy has to spend the whole day at the end of a chain. There ought to be a Ministry of Exception.

Near Triacastela, on the right-hand side of the path, a tree reigns, mighty, imposing. The trunk is at least twelve feet in diameter. It must be the two-hundred-year-old chestnut tree I overheard a local woman describe to a pilgrim yesterday. She did not mention the man in the tree, yet he has surely been there for decades. The tree base is all knotty and bumpy. When I first saw it, I immediately saw the man. He stands, ten feet tall, naked, with his back to the pilgrim. I could clearly distinguish his legs, the cleft of his buttocks, his wide, muscular back. His left arm is at his side. His head is hidden about twelve feet up into the part where the trunk straightens. Most pilgrims pass by without paying it any attention. We are all different; we all have our own reasons for being here. On the Camino, my soul dwells mostly outside of me. For others, it is mostly inside; it is where they search along their Camino. The strange thing is that for me, at home, it is the reverse. When I walk, more often than not, my thoughts go to 'things to do today.' I don't notice my surroundings. What a luxury it is to walk the Camino without wondering if I need to get milk today, if I have defrosted the fish for dinner.

A True Pilgrim

The temperature has risen. Near a wide stream, I stop to talk to an old man, a pilgrim. Sitting by a low wall of stones, he is sweating profusely. He almost looks in distress. On the makeshift bench beside him, his old-fashioned backpack is bursting at the seams. He is prepared for all eventualities. He even has a rolled up mat. His staff is a tall branch. He seems happy for the opportunity to speak his language. "I have not spoken to anyone for three days," he says. Yet, I have met many French pilgrims. He must not be bold like me. I talk to anyone and everyone. And I like to listen to everyone's story. Jean-Pierre is from Bron, a small town near Lyon, north-west of Le-Puy-en-Velay. There he started his pilgrimage on his own. "Did you see the man in the tree?" I ask. He did. A true pilgrim in the religious sense of the word, he does not carry a camera. His wife could not accompany him, He connects with her each night. "Can I take your picture? I will send it to you." He seems happy at my suggestion. I note down his email address and we wish each other "*Buen Camino*".

Manton Lowe from Oxfordshire

After Jean-Pierre, I stop to photograph a pot of delicate purple flowers in the recess of a stone wall. Elena and Lizi are nearby, taking pictures. We are outside a one-room house: an artist's studio open to the public. Inside, sitting at an old wooden desk, an artist is busy placing a label on the back of one of his watercolour reproductions. Without interrupting his work, he welcomes us into his studio. A large poster of an exhibition featuring his work and with the theme 'Pilgrimage' hangs on one wall amongst his art-work. His paintings were exhibited at St George's Chapel in Windsor Castle three years ago. His art doesn't leave us indifferent.

Manton sleeps on a narrow cot in the corner of his studio. "Where is your kitchen?" I ask. He pulls a small multicoloured carpet away from the middle of the floor and, through a plexiglass trap door, shows us his living area below.

Arthur Manton Lowe is from Oxfordshire. Now in his sixth decade, he has been interested in art since he was a child. Like many artists, he started by copying pictures of birds and butterflies from Natural History books, and has developed a style very much his own. I find his watercolours, especially those of the Camino, quite striking. There is serenity and a sense of mystery and of the sacred in his work. His pilgrims are engaged in a mystical, abstract, tunnel-like passage in shades of blue, or gold, surrounded by beauty. I wouldn't mind hanging one of his paintings in my home.

How fortunate the artist who can live from his art. Near the door, I notice a small, discrete bowl where we can deposit a coin. I have always said art galleries should have a donations box for those of us who have already amassed too much art, and want to encourage artists. We deposit a few coins before leaving his studio. "*Gracias* and *Buen Camino*," he says.

Francesco Enamorado

Around a sharp bend, we are welcomed again by two large dogs. Fortunately, Elena is there to reassure us. She is trying to tell me something. I think she is saying, "Look, they are wagging their tails. They are friendly." She knows how to talk to them; she does it well.

We are in one of the lushest, most enchanting areas of the Camino. Every rock and twisted tree trunk is covered in emerald green moss. Looking at the small colourful stones on the path, mixed with the myriad colours of the decaying leaves, I see where our artist gets his inspiration. In one area the size of a handkerchief, I count over twenty colours among the stones: oranges, greens, greys, yellows, purples, beiges... a full palette; nature's gift to the artist. Nearby is a great place for a rest: a large semi-circular bench of stone slabs and picnic tables. Behind it, a huge green and white scallop. Pilgrims are welcome here, but we pass without stopping. We have already dilly-dallied enough this morning.

I laugh at the newer Camino markers. Until Elena pointed it out, I hadn't noticed that they mark the distance to Santiago not only in kilometres but also in metres. The one at Montán, after Triacastela, shows 124.926 kilometres to Santiago. We couldn't ask for more precision, could we?

After the Montán sign, past the cemetery and a tiny church with its two modest bells, Elena spots a large property, an open-air hippy haven with a large hand-painted *donativo* sign on a table covered with a white lace tablecloth and a cornucopia of everything anyone could wish for, including an assortment of fresh fruit and home-grown, organic apples. There are cakes, juice, and glass jars to drink from, olives, nuts, boiled eggs, home-made bread and jam... There is even a thermos of fresh coffee that gets replenished regularly. Even soy milk.

We are not surprised to find Francesco here, his guitar on the ground beside a couch where he and... the lovely blond young woman are snuggling. Cheek to cheek, the two of them are laughing, enjoying a break in this small patch of heaven. Oh, to be young again! "Don't you think those two are made for each other?" I ask Elena and Lizi, and they both agree. They are one of the little Camino miracles. I wish them happiness.

The couch is covered with blankets and a pillow. Someone must have slept here under the stars last night. This surprises me because if there are three things for which Galicia is known, they are rain, fog and mist. The large space is half under some sort of jutting roof. "They must move the couch under there at night," says Elena. Odds and ends of armchairs and other unmatched furniture are strewn around the place. There are books on shelves, long, straight branches-cum-walking sticks, an assortment of wide-brimmed hats hanging from hooks. I recognize a couple of Tilley hats, forgotten behind by pilgrims? They hang at the end of long sticks inserted in gaps in the stone wall; there is miscellaneous artwork, and bits of wisdom: "The Camino provides" "The Camino teaches you who you are"...

We breakfast, sing along with Francesco, take advantage of the quirky facilities (contemplating the scenery from a half-inside, half-outside loo) and stamp our *credencials* with blue footprints. But before we leave, we take a minute to photograph the large stone spiral amongst ferns and trees at the back of the building.

After the oasis, we follow a path with ten-foot high banks. From high above, large trees spread their thick canopy of leaves over us. It is like walking through a tunnel. Now we know where Manton Lowe got his inspiration for his painting of pilgrims going into a tunnel. A long tunnel is a good metaphor for the Camino. At the entrance, there is no knowing what awaits us. Some find love, some find new friendships, some find peace, some find God. Others, I suppose, find nothing.

There is a sign to La Casa del Alquimista, another art studio we have been told we should visit by the young owners at the hippy haven. Its arrow points to a location 350 metres off the Camino. With its inviting lotus sign, it probably would be worth the small detour. Maybe next time.

A Moo Moo Here, a Moo Moo There

At Furela, half-a-dozen healthy-looking black and white cows, Holstein perhaps, grace a large field. I used to have an area rug from Brazil made of the same black and white hide. These cows must have some distant South-American cousins. Here, they are happy cows, with clean, healthy-looking pink udders bursting with milk; they graze in fairyland pasture. Ahead, another tiny church, another restaurant, and it's back into our lush tunnel.

A little further on, the path is lined with mysterious, giant, cultivated plants with emerald green leaves the size of rhubarb leaves. They tower high above our heads. I capture them on my iPod, planning to ask a local about them. Of course, I will forget. Only back home, in Lyndon Penner's excellent book, *The Way of the Gardener*, will I learn that they are called Walking Stick Cabbages and that walking sticks are actually made from them.

Gabriela

At our six-bed dorm at Albergue Oasis, at the entrance to Sarria, we have dinner with a new friend. Mid-way through supper, Gabriela finds a bee in her pocket. It has been trapped there for a while. "I was wondering why my thigh was so itchy. It has been hurting since this afternoon." I had noticed her scratching on and off, exactly where the tip of her pocket would be. Fortunately, it is not what I had suspected, nor is she allergic to bees.

Gabriela is about my daughter's age. Like her, she radiates health and happiness. Slim and light on her feet, she is hiking alone but enjoys company. Before starting her Camino, she resigned from her job as reception-ist-secretary in a long-term care home. "I have been with them for almost twenty years," she says. "I need a change." They have asked her to recon-sider. "I told them I would give them an answer when I return." But she has already decided. As much as she knows they really would like her back, she understands the importance of following her own path in life. Gabriela is the tenth of sixteen siblings. Eight brothers and seven sisters complete a balanced picture. She has exactly fifty nephews and nieces. By the time she returns home, who knows how many she will have.

"Do you know all their names?" I ask her. "Absolutely. And their ages. The oldest is 36, and the youngest is..." she stops to think, counts on her fingers... "April, May, June... Seven months old," she says after a few sec-onds. "We celebrate each birthday." Her siblings all live near each other. Birthdays and anniversaries are not a quiet affair, ever. Not many families can boast of close ties with all members. I find it quite extraordinary. Her parents are alive. They must be happy together. The harmony between these siblings cannot have sprouted from an unhappy home.

Gabriela orders a pizza Margarita. It comes without tomato sauce. When she asks for some, the waiter produces a bottle of ketchup. Lizi and I order *arroz a la Cubana* (Cuban rice) which comes with tomato sauce and fried eggs. The best way to know what will be on your plate in another country is to find another guest eating something that looks good and to order the same.

Replete from our generous dinners, we are all in bed early; tomorrow might be a tough hike. Brierley shows a rather steep climb for the first part of the day, followed by an equally steep descent. Lizi is having problems with a knee; she is worried about the descent. Not one of us has hiking sticks we can lend her. We plan on leaving together early. By ten o'clock, when I am ready for sleep, I realize that since we are at the entrance to Sarria and we will leave in darkness, this is one place I won't get to explore. I wish I had thought about this before and done a bit of sight-seeing after supper.

San Juan Brierley del Camino

Galicia is fertile in many ways. For a town of less than 15,000 inhabitants, through the years, Sarria can boast having been the cradle of an impressive list of artists and other famous people. Four hundred years ago, it was the birthplace of Gregorio Fernández, the baroque sculptor who so deftly depicted Jesus' agony and the sufferings of Mary. Most of his sculptures now live in the Museo Nacional de Escultura de Valladolid north of Madrid. Others, including his own version of the Pieta grace religious establishments and museums all over Spain.

Not quite so long ago, Matías López López, another son of Sarria, brought joy to people all over the peninsula with his chocolate factory and his philanthropy. There is even a song about him. López López died in 1891, and his factory continued operating until 1964. It had been in operation for 113 years.

But if there is one man from Sarria to whom pilgrims are indebted, it is Elias Valiña Sanpedro, a visionary priest who lived from 1929 to 1989. (His remains are in the small church at O'Cebreiro.) With his large round eyeglasses, his slim figure, and Gandhi-like appearance, he is credited with giving new life to the Camino with his 1982 guide. Because of his work helping recover some long neglected paths, many villages were saved from oblivion, many jobs created in the hospitality sector. I don't know if he was the one who suggested the hundred-kilometre pilgrimage. It does sound like a plan that could have emanated from his mixture of pragmatism and spirituality. What more noble and holy cause than to help people earn a decent living? San Elias Valiña del Camino? One needs a miracle to be canonized. Elias Valiña del Camino's miracle is the revitalization of this ancient custom and the spiritual enrichment of hundreds of thousands of pilgrims walking its paths yearly. I wish to submit his name for canonization to the Holy Father. And how about San Juan Brierley del Camino? Or even San Bryson Guptill, for his concise version of a guide to the Camino Francés and excellent online map?

As for the pragmatic person who did think of the hundred-kilometre pilgrim, I say, "Good job!" Those pilgrims most often hire a guide and stay and eat in the more expensive hotels and restaurants. All good for the Spanish economy.

The Hundred-kilometre Pilgrims

With these thoughts still dancing in my head, in the morning, along with a flow of pilgrims pouring out of doors all over Sarria, I elbow my way back onto the Camino with Elena. It is a totally different ambiance today. The fog is like a purdah veil to all the lush beauty beyond, screening also the hundreds of pilgrims ahead.

Before we are out of Sarria, a group of schoolchildren overtakes us with their guide. They are thoroughly enjoying the experience. What a wonderful excuse for playing hooky! Loud and full of beans, they saunter and run after each other, shouting with enthusiasm, until their teacher brings them back gently to a semblance of discipline. They are lovely children. How well I remember those days. Excursions, pilgrimages, what are they after all if not pure escape from the doldrums of schoolwork?

We pass several groups with guides, mostly of retirees with daypacks, and exchange Camino thoughts with them. They all seem in high spirits. Two are from Canada, not too far from me. It is their first day. All of them are amazed that at my age, I have walked from Saint-Jean-Pied-de-Port. "There are hundreds if not thousands of pilgrims my age on the Camino," I tell them. But nothing will diminish their admiration. They think I am brave. I bet in a few days, perhaps even before the end of today, at least some of them will be dreaming of walking the Camino also from Saint-Jean another time, perhaps even from Le-Puy. The seed has been sown. They are probably like I was, totally underestimating their endurance.

Walking with a large group does not appeal to me. I like to walk at my own pace, stop on a whim, connect with different people. I am too much of a free-spirit for group travel, and have always preferred to explore alone or with one friend, off the beaten path. What in the world, I ask myself again, am I doing on the most heavily trodden path in all Europe?

Nature's Many Miracles

Wrapped in thick fog, we are a crowded procession of pilgrims in an enchanted land. At a clearing, before the three-tiered fountain decorated with shells and short lengths of ribbons in all colours, a single clump of hollyhock with about ten proud, tall shoots reaches for the sky. Its four or five pristine, bright yellow flowers call to me. They have hatched out of their stalks like chicks out of eggshells. I want to shout to the pilgrims who are busy chatting or looking at the ground in front of their feet: "Look here. Look at these beautiful flowers." I feel like a five-year-old. "Look at me, Mom, look at me." But it is this beauty I would like to share with them.

The path is easy. No need to watch our step. Elena and I walk in silence with Lizi and Gabriela somewhere near. We are in a dense forest of giant trees with thick, twisted trunks covered in vines. I wish I could spend weeks in their midst. The long branches of an untended apple tree stretch over hundreds of pale green, healthy-looking apples windblown in a large circumference on the ground. Rare is the pilgrim who bothers to go over and pick one. The fruit looks freshly fallen. Surely, the worms must have spared a couple. Elena and I go over and inspect a dozen apples. We pick one and then another and another, only to drop them back with disappointment. Like ill-behaved children, the worms have nibbled each apple, and left them to rot. Not one is intact.

In a reedy area, industrious spiders have woven dozens of webs the size of open umbrellas in the angles between twigs. The wind has shaken the fruit out of its tree near here, yet it has not disturbed these fragile constructions. Or are they as fragile as they look? The white gossamer threads spread from dense crucible-like shapes at the tip of the twigs. At first, I thought they were white flowers until I got closer. "Look," I want to shout again. "Look how beautiful this is." It is almost upsetting to see pilgrims pass by without seeing this amazing work of nature. "Look, please. Look." Happiness and beauty must be shared; it is why we go to a concert with a friend; we watch a ballet performance with a friend; we want to share life with a friend. The joy is not only in seeing; it is in sharing. The musician, the ballet dancer, need an audience as much as the audience needs them. Man is not made to enjoy life alone. Zarathustra was right when he asked the sun: "O great star, what would your happiness be had you not those for whom you shine?" How fortunate I am to be hiking with Elena this morning. As a landscaper, she is sensitive to nature. She likes to slow her step at all the beauty along our path. Although we walk mostly in silence this morning, our steps are synchronized.

A Lonely Old Man

After breakfast, before heading back into thick nature, I spot an old man, an aged urchin, lurking at the side of a high stone wall. He is wearing a soiled, weather-beaten leather jacket over a blue v-neck with stains of last night's dinner and this morning's breakfast. His jeans with their white knees, several sizes too large for him, are gathered and held tight at his waist by a cloth belt. To be kind, I smile and say, "Buenos días." The old man wants to pose with us. Elena is kinder than me; she shows no reluctance. He comes out of hiding and waddles up to her with a walking cane in one hand and a tall branch in the other to which someone has attached a bright orange plastic bowling pin, probably so they will find it when he forgets it in the tall grass. Grabbing Elena's arm, he huddles close to her. The top of his high, dirty, wide-brimmed hat hardly reaches her cheek. He breaks into a wide smile. Elena has made his day. He reluctantly lets go of her arm. He wants to have his photo taken with me. I decline. "*Vamonos*," I say to Elena. All I am willing to offer is a smile and an *Adiós*.

A Pride That Lives On

The low stonewall separating us from the moss-covered forest is also wearing its lush emerald-green coat. I understand more and more why Galicians I have met in Mexico, Cuba, and parts of Central America are so proud of being from this part of Spain. They even pronounce it *Galithia* like in the old country. In reality, they are not from Galicia; it is their ancestors, sometimes many generations removed, who came as immigrants. But they prefer to say: "I am from Galicia" as though it made them superior to those whose

Thinking of Gaudi

Camino encounter

forefathers carted their meagre possessions from arid parts of the peninsula to ships destined for the New World. They might not be superior, but their ancestors left behind a natural paradise. I am walking in it.

Horreos

A mighty chestnut tree heavy with nuts spreads its thick limbs at the entrance to a tiny village near one of the many *horreos* of Galicia. These small granaries have been designated World Heritage. "Just like the Taj Mahal or the Pyramids in Egypt," a proud Galician told me. *Horreos* look like children's playhouses on stilts. They were a clever invention for protecting crops from pests. Their walls, built with slits, provide ventilation, keeping the crop from going moldy; their roof overhang acts as an umbrella, and the tall poles on which they stand prevent animals from climbing into them. Since much of the land belongs to large corporations now, most of the *horreos* are not needed anymore. Some of the owners use them to hang their clothes to dry. Others hang their *jamón ibérico* in them; yet others use them as storage for apples or for tools. Anything goes. As long as the exterior is not altered.

Elena and I snap pictures of our first one with its bright pink and red geraniums at both ends. A dozen steps further, competing for our admiration, pink roses adorn the sides of the path. We automatically stop to smell their perfume. They have a strong, sweet scent; they must not be too hybridized.

The going is laborious this morning, but we have been walking at a relaxed pace. Surrounded by hills and valleys, although we still have lots of energy, we take time to sit on a bench and look back at the tortuous path behind us. Always the same lushness, the same paradise. We are blissfully far from concrete and glass towers here. I think of my son and granddaughter who live in the Rockies in Canada, surrounded by mountains. It's no wonder he fell in love at first sight with the mountains.

The Sky for a Roof

I don't even want to think about what my life would be like surrounded by concrete. I am fortunate to live in a small town with lots of century-old houses and colourful front gardens. In the spring, when they are training their offspring, we never tire of watching our multigenerational squirrel family climb up and down the lofty maple tree outside our window. One of them perches on a branch, tail curled, waiting for us to fetch the camera. We don't think of them as pests anymore, but we have stopped planting tulips. They were digging out the bulbs. We plant flowers they don't like.

On my daily walk at home, I pass ancient weeping willows, locust, oaks, lilac bushes... In springtime, the tall pines echo with the sound of cardinals. We have blue jays, robins, red-wing blackbirds, Baltimore orioles... On humid summer nights, coming back from my evening walk past the old limestone houses near Lake Ontario, fireflies sparkle like diamonds in the trimmed bushes at the front of houses. Nearing my home, I laugh at our obscenely fat neighbourhood raccoon family plodding across the street in search of a late snack. In late summer, the Monarch butterflies dry their wings on the milkweed before their long pilgrimage to Mexico. I could not live in a large metropolis. I need green. And I need lots of it. I need to see the sky at my every step. I want to see cloud formations, starry nights. Cities with palm-sprinkled concrete, skyscrapers, and shopping malls with stores ad infinitum have never appealed to me. I would rather have my toenails pulled out one by one than spend an afternoon in a shopping mall. I will probably never go to Abu Dhabi or to Dubai. Inspired by nature, architects have produced wonders, but they have never surpassed nature. They never will. To a cathedral, I prefer a cathedral forest. I do admire the feats of engineering, but I prefer the miracle of wild roses.

First, mankind knew its smallness under giant trees. Then came the domes of synagogues, the tall spires of churches and cathedrals, the minarets of mosques, making man even smaller. Religion ruled. Then came the Twin Towers, the towers of the oil countries, the skyscrapers of capitalism. On the Camino, we have the sky, 360 degrees of it. That is why I keep returning.

Near the entrance to Ferreiros, a sign in English and Spanish says: 'Delicious homemade food by donation'. Behind a table, a stout woman is busy slicing through local cheese. She also offers large home-made donuts, angelfood cake, fruit... We buy a chunk of cheese, and continue on our way.

The base of a tall cross after the *donativo* is wrapped in ivy. It looks ancient. Its core is a smaller, weather-beaten wooden cross someone has enlarged by encasing it in a tall concrete one. Pilgrims have placed all kinds of stones, pictures of saints or of people, ribbons, and notes on top of its arms. Someone even put a pale green apple alongside the stones. Aha! Someone did pick an apple! Half a dozen small white pouches hang from the cross. The whole thing is quite unsightly. I wonder what pilgrims expect from these. Are they asking for miracles? What about the sheep in the meadow? Are they not miracles?

In Ferreiros, the columbarium by the church looks well tended. Families of the departed have decorated the niches with flowers, fresh or plastic or silk. It is almost a cheerful place. I like this way of remembering the departed. Cemeteries are good places to sit and ponder the meaning of life, its vicissitudes, its unpredictability.

Gourmet *donativo*

Around mid-day, we come upon another *donativo* inside a large barn-like structure without a front wall, and with many tables and chairs. At the end of two end-to-end tables stands a minuscule, shrivelled, ancient woman by an astonishing selection of foods on colourful tablecloths. She moves with difficulty. "Who prepares all this?" I ask as her husband appears from a side door with a plate of freshly fried seafood. "I do," he replies without much enthusiasm. I can hardly believe him. Both he and the woman must be in their ninth decade. Don't they both deserve to sit and put their feet up, look at some old photos, reminisce, and watch a bit of television? How can such an old couple, so apparently worn out by life, go on working so hard?

Elena is eager to reach today's destination, but I just *have* to eat something here. I will catch up to her later. I fill a plate with the old couple's offerings and sit inside the large barn where old straw baskets and large clay urns decorate rough shelves high along the walls. Tools of past trades hang from hooks along with bleached animal horns, dried corn cobs and twisted branches. The quaintness appeals to me. If the hand-written sign at the entrance lacks artistry, the couple's culinary offerings are out of the ordinary. We can choose from heaps of olives, cheeses, spicy sausages, nuts, donuts still hot, boiled eggs, crepes, grapes, bread, something that looks like deep-fried shrimp nuggets, potato chips, little rolled-up sweets, fritters, poached eggs, frittata... What? No eggs Benedict? (I won't ask; I have a feeling their sense of humour has died of old age.)

If the fare is inviting, unfortunately our hosts lack the charisma for such an enterprise. Who can blame them? Smiles come easily to the young and healthy. These two are worn out. Several times, while enjoying my food, I hear the old woman scolding and asking for more money from pilgrims on their way out. Maybe it is the fault of a few lines on the sign near where she stands, collecting donations.

If its possible for you we will appreciate very much
you leave some coins to help other pilgrims during all year.
Thank you so much. Good Pilgrim Way...

Maybe some pilgrims take the word *coin* literally? Julio and his wife deserve more than coins for their gourmet offerings.

Before leaving, I try to make small talk with the woman, complimenting her on the exceptional fare. She thanks me for the donation, but she is not talkative. I thank her again and head back to the Camino without the expected "*Buen Camino.*" There comes a time when one should be able to throw in the towel and rest before the end. I wonder if the old couple can afford to eat without this venture.

Made in India

After many old stone homes beautiful in their decrepitude, and large clumps of tall blue hydrangeas that would stir my husband's envy because he has been trying without much success to turn his from pink to blue, I come to an open pilgrim shelter. Within its three walls are a large area for a fire, two long make-shift benches and a sign enjoining pilgrims to '*rest but please keep clean*'. How sad that such a sign is needed. How frustrating it must be for those who offer hospitality to see their place defaced or disrespected.

At times, I am ashamed of being a pilgrim. We are far from being univer-sally loved. I can only hope that it is hooligans, not pilgrims who deface these shelters.

Outside a large barn, some enterprising person has set large panels with hundreds of shells painted with sayings in many languages. 'A good con-science is the best pillow'. 'Who thinks little errs much'... The barn is an immense shop with a vast selection of colourful Indian imports. A woman is busy non-stop taking money from pilgrims lined up at the cash register. Credit cards accepted. Nothing is lacking here: jewellery, headbands made from free tailors' cuttings, scarves, bags, souvenirs of all kinds, snacks... By now, the pilgrim has been perhaps a whole month without buying... surely it is time to acquire something new. I am not a good customer. I want noth-ing. I ask the woman if she spends her winters in India. "I only work here," she replies. The owner buys from importers. And here, I was thinking of all the fun of spending winters in India going from factory to factory collecting treasures to sell to pilgrims.

After the large shop, I stop at a vibrant patch of cosmos. They stand still in the windless day, their flashes of colour breaking the monotony of the old stone house near them. Lizi is resting at a terrace at the back of a large restaurant. She is having terrible knee problems and worries she won't make it to Santiago. We are both staying at the Pasiño a Pasiño in Portomarín tonight. Slowly we will walk the rest of the way together.

A Town Perched Up High

After the bridge, we have four or five dozen steps to climb before setting foot in Portomarín. Teeming with pilgrims and tourists, this is like no other place we have passed. With a population of only about two thousand, (a hundred years ago, it was triple that) the town is small, compact and elegant although we don't see it until Lizi, limping, and I, out of breath, walk up to the main street with its arcades.

This is not just a town for hiking pilgrims. We are only four stages from Santiago. Many, for whom the destination is what matters, do the pilgrim-age by car. For them, Santiago is like Mecca. Few Muslims walk to Mecca nowadays. In the same way Mohammedans want to visit Islam's holiest city, its Kaaba and its Zamzam Well with its miraculous spring, the pilgrims who come by car want to be near Saint James' resting place inside the cathedral.

If Portomarín is not built helter-skelter like the historical centre of many ancient cities, it is because they have moved the town and rebuilt it in the last century on a practical grid-system high above the river which was flooded to make a reservoir. Some historic buildings, including the San Nicolao church, were lovingly disassembled and rebuilt at the top of the hill. Our albergue, the Pasiño a Pasiño, (One Little Step at a Time) fronts onto an arcade which could trick the visitor into thinking the town has been here for centuries. Our accommodation is top-notch. The young owner has saved us a room with only three beds. Lizi and I have lost Elena en route. We will bump into her later. Meanwhile, across the street at a small drugstore, Lizi invests in a couple of stretchy knee compression sleeves. The clerk takes time to teach her how to wear them for maximum comfort. They will be an excellent investment, allowing her to walk without pain all the way to Santiago.

On a point of land, steps from the drugstore, smack in the middle of a shopping and restaurant area, the church looks forlorn, but it attracts a queue of visitors. Lizi and I make it inside minutes before closing. Igrexa de San Nicolao has its charm, but today, no ray of sunshine floods through the high windows. From outside, even with its arched facade and large rosette, it looks more like a prison, a chunk of the Bastille, than a place of worship. Did it also serve as refuge in case of attack in the old days? The building stands eight or nine stories high. With its castellated roof ramparts, it must have been built with defence in mind. Where are its bells?

Across from the church, at a restaurant table under the arcade, we find Gabriela and another woman who signals for us to join them. I have met the other woman before. She says, "Susan from Denver. We met on a bench at the entrance to Órbigo. I have an adopted daughter." Now I remember! That was a couple of days after León. We shared condensed versions of our lives in fifteen minutes on a bench.

Susan and Gabriela have finished dinner, but they invite us to share their table. The fare here is generous, the prices reasonable. I call for a bottle of wine. When I offer the others a glass, Susan says, "remember, I am an alcoholic." I had forgotten. I am impressed by the way she says it. That is really how it should be. Like being gluten intolerant.

After dinner, Lizi and I find an ancient couple sitting on straight-backed chairs in the lobby of the Pasiño a Pasiño. Staring at their age-stained hands, not talking or reading, they look bored and tired. The owner is not around. I ask them if they are looking for him. "No. He is our grandson. We are waiting for seven Italians." Their grandson had errands to run. Sadly, the old couple will wait almost two hours. The Italian cyclists who had reserved beds won't show up. Neither will they call to cancel. I think about the French couple who vociferated that all Spaniards are thieves. Are they? Really? Sometimes, life is unfair.

Oak and Eucalyptus

Elena is taking it easy this morning. Lizi and I leave ahead of her in a cold, rainy morning with thick fog patches. The Camino is crowded with hundred-kilometre pilgrims. Although their shapes are enshrouded in fog, their chatter can be heard far behind them. There is much to distract us along the narrow paved roads and the few rugged, wet areas sometimes a few inches deep in mud. Our way is lined with blue hydrangeas, tiny pumpkins on window sills, cows being led to pasture, and more *horreos*. I worry about my granny mobiles through the mud. I would not like to walk with wet feet in the chilly morning.

A venerable chestnut tree catches my attention. I have never seen one like it before. It looks so mighty I can't ever imagine the wind toppling it like it often does our tall maples at home. Its bark is coarse and thick. It would take several men fingertip to fingertip to encircle its trunk. Long, irregular, foot-long vertical slits expose its shiny orange wood, like satin inserts in a velvet designer gown. The fat lady would burst out of it and sing her aria that I would not be surprised. The chestnut competes for beauty only with the eucalyptus in their smooth pastel blues and greens, their yellows and pinks. Are they all getting ready for the ball?

The eucalyptus is plentiful around here. It is not native to the Iberian peninsula, but it thrives wherever planted. I had never seen these beauties

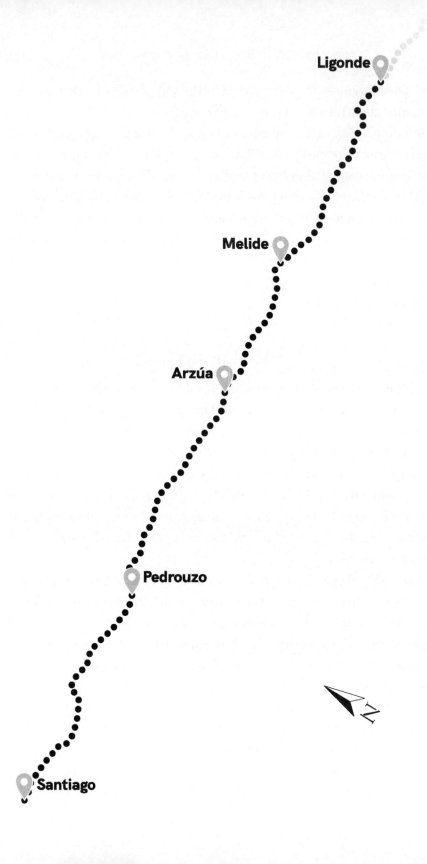

Ligonde

Melide

Arzúa

Pedrouzo

Santiago

N

before, and am by now totally smitten. They grow fast and stand tall. Not everybody loves them, though. As far back as three decades ago, citizens from small municipalities on the Bay of Biscay, north of Portomarín, uprooted the newly planted trees in the night in a protest against what they saw as an invasion of a non-native species proliferating too fast and endangering the natural environment. As should have been expected with conflicts arising from changes in traditional ways of life, the arrival of the eucalyptus on the Iberian continent has been the subject of long, bitter battles. While its proponents point to its inexpensive supply of pulp, others complain their vines and olive plantations are being overtaken by them, and shepherds lament the loss of grazing areas. Who is right? As usual, the ones with the financial power have won. Now, eucalyptus forests thrive in many areas of the Peninsula. Spain is not the only country where this tree has caused controversy. All this saddens me because, not aware of its conflictual impact, I had already fallen in love with it.

By the path, after the eucalyptus, are scattered several waist-high upright sections of logs each topped with a large, oval stone, flat as a basque beret. We are in mushroom area. The artist, in a visual ode to nature, has replicated and magnified its work. Is there a bigger fountain of inspiration than nature?

Pavarotti

At the entrance to Ligonde, we catch up with Susan from Denver. She and Lizi will continue on to Palas de Rei tonight. I have booked a bed in a one-room school, the only place for pilgrims to stay in this tiny village. Isabel, the *hospitalera*, checks me in and, without asking, kindly goes with her car along a snaky road to collect pilgrims' backpacks which have been delivered to a restaurant further ahead. (The transport service does that when a hostel is closed.) I see Elena's backpack in the lot. She will also sleep here tonight. The dorm has ten bunks. It will only be half-full. There is no internet here. We will talk amongst ourselves, write in our diary, or even add a hundred steps to today's hike by exploring around.

Inside the school, it's cold and damp. Outside, the sun shines brightly. There was no rain on the way this afternoon. Here, steam rises from the

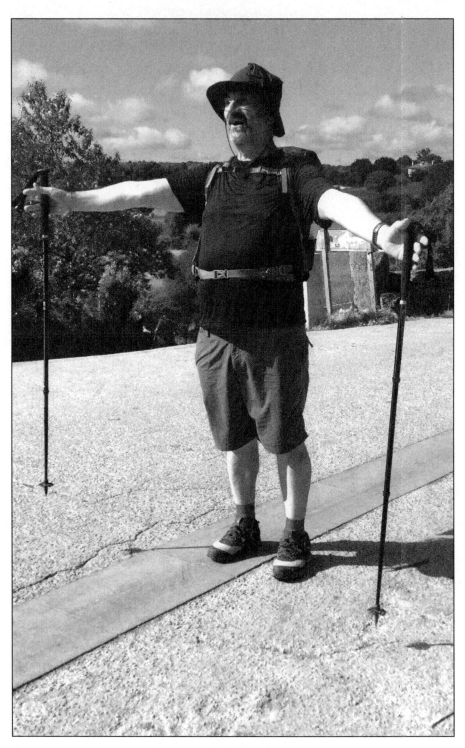

Pavarotti

wet pavement. I am sitting on the front steps, flipping the dry mud off my sneakers, when three Italian pilgrims pass by. One of them is singing *O sole mío*. Bearded and mustachioed like Pavarotti, he even looks like our famous Tenor. Sure, in his red socks and sneakers, he doesn't cut quite as elegant a figure, but I gesture to him to stop and sing for me, and he obliges while his companions disappear down the path across the road. It is not lost on me that the lyrics talk about the sun coming out. In all its years of existence, I wonder how often the song has been sung along the Camino by Italian pilgrims. Tomorrow, I will meet the three men again and our Pavarotti will still be singing, charming other pilgrims. I can see why his companions scooted ahead. His voice carries into the dorm. A French woman and her husband have come out for the free concert. She notices my unusual scarf. "I have one the same," she says. After Pavarotti has left, she adds, "I saw you ahead of me. When I saw your scarf, I thought I must have lost mine, and you had found it." Fortunately, hers, a gift from her son, was in her bag. I bought mine from Bangladeshi *manteros* in Barcelona. I am glad she hasn't lost hers. My reputation could have suffered a blow. I can just imagine trying to defend myself.

Our dorm is half-empty tonight. It is a good thing Isabel, like Olivia at the previous schoolhouse, is paid by the *Ayuntamiento*. She lives in a village near here and looks after the hostel seven days a week. When she goes for her mid-day meal, I stick around to welcome other pilgrims. It is not long before Elena arrives. Later, we will walk to the restaurant for dinner. The steep path through the bush is muddy and slippery. We opt for the road which is all twists and turns. It is deserted now, but a speeding car would be upon us before the driver could spot us. There is no space between the road and the deep ditch. Elena is much braver than I, but I warn her, "No matter what, I am not walking along the road in the dark tomorrow."

Africa or Death

In the morning, the steep trail is dangerously muddy and slippery. With trepidation, I give in and walk our first kilometre briskly along the winding road. And live to tell the tale. We are off to Melide in what looks like relatively easy terrain according to my *vade-me-cum*. Shielded from a fine rain by the canopy of leaves, for most of the morning, we follow a gravel path along a quiet road. We started out today again with hat and gloves. By midday, it is stifling hot and muggy. I refill my water bottle at every fountain and restaurant. Gargantuan black iron ants the size of cows by large patches of blue hydrangea adorn a garden near the restaurant at Portos. They remind me of the gigantic spider in Bilbao. The hydrangeas which obviously thrive in the Galician climate are a pleasing contrast to the sculptures.

Later, in Palas de Rei, by a statue of the Virgin Mary holding the infant Jesus, we bump into Hanne, the young man who has resigned from his work in advertising and is hoping to find inspiration for a new career. It is the first time we see him since we dined together five or six days ago in Pereje with its eight inhabitants. Hanne is enjoying the Camino and taking it easy. I like his laid-back attitude. He is more interested in the journey than in the destination. We are of the same mind, even if I have occasionally forgotten that, and passed a village too quickly only to regret it later.

At Iglesia de San Tirso, we pause to admire the arched stained glass windows with their simple designs in different shades of blue. One depicts communion: a ciborium with the host above it. Another, wheat stalks, symbols of love and charity. Another, the Virgin Mary. Just by the contour and inclination of a veiled woman's head, any Catholic will recognize the Madonna looking with adoration at her infant child. Since Saint-Jean-Pied-de-Port, we have passed many churches without entering, but all three of us are simultaneously drawn to this one. Is it because Elena and I are enjoying Hanne's company that we go in with him? He is, we had both concluded after meeting him in Laguna, the kind of young man a mother likes her daughter to bring home. It doesn't matter that Elena has no daughter and I have only one, and she has already brought home precisely that kind of man.

Hanne stops for a brief prayer inside many of the churches. "Sometimes I light a candle, but not the electric ones," he says. I can't blame him. I don't like them either. I go into the churches to look at the art. It is sometimes quite surprising. I get a stamp and leave a few coins for the upkeep of these wonderful monuments. My *credencial* is getting full and I still have a few days to go. I squeeze in the stamp of a pilgrim in blue. Or perhaps my stamp is of San Daniel Comboni, a saint I have never heard of. In fact, the feature attracting my attention in this small church with its modern interior, its humble pews and organ, its almost total absence of gilt decor, is a tall sculpture of San Daniel Comboni, perched above a carved wooden pedestal in his long black cassock, a heavy golden cross hanging on his chest. In his right hand, the saint is holding the tall crook of the evangelist, topped by Christ's cross. From his left hand hangs a scroll with a picture of Africa and the rather astonishing words: *Africa o Muerte*. (Africa or Death). "Sounds a little fanatic to me," I say to Elena. "It reminds me of Fidel Castro's *Patría o muerte* billboards all over the countryside in Cuba." Even Hanne thinks it's a bit nuts.

"Well, maybe some Galicians are people who would rather die than compromise," I say. "It would fit Fidel Castro. Fidel's ancestors probably came from this area." And Fidel's last name more or less confirms it. Although Elena and I missed the famous *castro* near here, we heard about the ancient fortified villages which gave many Galicians their name. Fidel's father was Galician. He fought in the Spanish-American war of 1898. The old man must have taken the *o muerte* along with the family possessions from Galicia to Cuba and passed it on to his son.

Why is the strange sculpture of Comboni in this tiny village? It is only later in Melide that Xelo, our hospitalera, will fill me in on the story: Saint Daniel Comboni, it turns out, was not Spanish. A multilinguist, (apparently he spoke ten languages) he hailed from the province of Lombardy, Italy. An evangelist, he lived from 1831 to 1881. His mission took him to different countries in Africa where he spread the word of the Gospel, set up schools and clinics, fought for justice and against slavery. His life was cut short during a cholera epidemic. He was canonized in 2003 following his beatification in 1996 on the strength of a miracle: Comboni apparently prevented a Muslim woman from dying in childbirth.

"Three or four years ago the church celebrated 150 years of Comboni's mission," Xelo will say. What ties exactly he had with the area, I will forget to ask, but after starting his evangelical and humanitarian work in Africa, the enterprising missionary had visited many European countries to raise funds for his work. Had he come through here? Who knows? But apparently his followers still fight for human rights in over forty countries.

We are still in *horreo* country. Some of them are quite eye-catching. In this area, a few are still used as corn cribs. One of them stands out from the others. Propped up on a high cement base, its circular wall is made of long interwoven vine branches twisted into a cylindrical shape reminiscent of basketwork and Christmas wreaths. Its protective roof is like a giant, conical, high-peaked, bleached sunhat. Almost every pilgrim ahead of us stops to photograph it. We all like the exceptional. Sometimes we like it so much we forget to see the ordinary beauty around us, the green forests, the cornfields, the dew on the grass, the colourful patch of weeds, the wild herbs, the cows, the sheep, the cats, the stones in the field from which people have built their houses, the clouds... the stars in the night sky, the fingernail moon, the half moon, the Milky Way...

Hanne, Elena and I walk in silence until Puente de San Xoán at Furelos where we bump into our very own Pavarotti, arms stretched wide in a theatrical performance, while his companions walk ahead. *O sole mio* seems to be his repertory. We will pass him one more time. He might be tiring of his celebrity. We won't ask for another encore.

After what seems like an hour of straining uphill, at the entrance to Melide, it's time to part from Hanne. The temperature has reached a high point, and we have stopped too many times. Unfortunately, as we will realize later, we missed the nicest part of this old town. Our hostel is on the very busy main street, and Melide seems to have not one redeeming feature. We walk along the straight, wide, impossible-to-cross road on which heavy trucks trail each other as in a marathon. I am sorry to have missed the old part. The Camino deserves many chances; *Ojalá*, I will return.

Of Weddings and Earthquakes

Fortunately, at Albergue Melide, Eduardo and his wife Xelo, the owners, atone amply for the lack of charm of the busy artery. In an uninspiring location near a garage, once inside, it is a different story. The Melide has none of the antique features I have encountered in Casa Mágica and in a

few other hostels, but it is spacious, spotless, bright, comfortable and welcoming. Before supper, Elena and I relax with a bottle of wine in the quiet
garden in the shade of large umbrellas.

Our hosts, a recently married couple, have decorated the place with their
own touch. In the common area, proudly displayed, is an odd wedding photo.
In the foreground, wearing a traditional wedding dress with a long train,
Xelo holds a large bouquet of red roses. Eduardo's hand is posed amorously
on her waist, and their eyes meet in a beautiful smile. Strangely, they seem
oblivious to the hideous background of scaffolding stretched across the front
of a large building behind them. Later, I will understand the symbolism of the
scaffolding, result of the September 2017 Mexico earthquake that wreaked
havoc in the capital. Upon checking in, I had detected a Mexican accent in
Lala (that is what Xelo calls Eduardo). A look around me now confirms my
intuition. In the large sitting-cum-dining-room by the open kitchen are pictures of Frida Kahlo, and *amate* bark paper art. Eduardo, a Mexican, met
Xelo (a Basque) in Spain while doing the pilgrimage in 2015. Later, Xelo
taught physiotherapy at a university in Mexico where they married.

A fervent catholic, before meeting Lala, Xelo volunteered in Rwanda. I
can tell she is happy for the opportunity to share some of her stories with
me. She tells me at length how kind and thankful the Rwandan families
were. "Some children would bring me three or four dry beans as a thank you
for the little that we could do for them." The memories of those years bring
tears to her eyes. She and Lala married soon after the Mexico earthquake;
the decor behind the wedding picture is a statement. They bought the hostel
since then. "It is a good venture," says Lala. He is even thinking of investing
in a second one near here.

At supper time, the couple prepare a meal for whoever would like to
join. Their offer brings few takers because this is a town with good grocery
stores and restaurants, many of which offer *pulpo (octopus)*, the staple fare
around here.

In the morning, we all comment on how well we have slept, which is
strange since we are on a busy street. Unfortunately, our hosts forgot to
tell us they would not be here, and the kitchen would be locked. It's a bit of
a disappointment since Elena and I had bought eggs to boil before hitting

the Camino, but we easily forgive them, leave the eggs behind and walk out into another misty morning.

Raining *a cántaros*

The sky is heavy, the air cold and foggy. Everyone is bundled up. With capes covering backpacks, we are a parade of bright yellow, green, red or black Quasimodos. I am glad I checked the weather this morning. Already it is drizzling and there is no doubt it will be raining *a cántaros* within the hour.

Before long, we arrive at a devastated forest area. The trees still stand, charred and mournful, their blackened trunks and limbs like macabre ghosts. At their feet, thick bracken pushes through the undergrowth. Like arrogant little rascals, three-foot high pines are staking their claims on their own patches of ground, elbowing their way beside the skeletal trees through the natural vegetation that has taken root again. I can't imagine a fire in this area where high humidity and rain reign supreme. It looks as though the entire ecosystem will be regenerated in no time. It is not the first time I see a burnt forest along the Camino. Chloë and I passed through one between Pamplona and Burgos on our first hike. On that stretch where the climate is dryer than in Galicia, it seemed more natural.

As expected, the sky opens wide. We are grateful for our capes, but the deep puddles are too wide to straddle. By then my shoes are already sodden and muddy. So be it. There is nothing I can do. Fortunately, some kind Friends of the Camino have moved heavy, flat-topped boulders to form a bridge across some shallow streams.

Elena stops by a *horreo*. "People are trusting in this area," she says, pointing to a set of keys dangling from a keyhole in its freshly painted door decorated with a corncob. "The only people they would likely have to worry about are pilgrims," I tell her. But even pilgrims have sticky fingers.

After the *horreo*, some enterprising young woman, under the roof of a tiny kiosk, minds a small vending area. El Pequeño Oasis offers the usual fare plus fat, juicy, ripe figs and wild raspberries. It is the first time I see raspberries here. Although they are offered in a miserly amount, I cannot resist. They are delicious. In three mouthfuls, we have gobbled them up.

Raining a cántaros

At the Parroquia de Boente, lying along the road are piles of kindling and logs waiting for the chain saw and the axe. Thinking of the chimneys puffing merrily in winter, I see my grandfather smoking his pipe in his rocking-chair. How different life was then. Pre-television. Pre-internet. A wood stove, a pipe, a radio perhaps, and family and friends for company. The village is tidy and inviting. Late morning, however, our attention is drawn to a large, impeccable red house with blinds drawn over all the windows. High above the front gate, scarlet roses climb a delicate cast iron arbour. Colourful ceramic tiles decorate the stone pillars at either side of the gate. The message on the first tile is not a happy one: a man furiously bitten at the arm by a nasty Rottweiler, and the caption: *Perro peligroso* (dangerous dog). The man's jeans have already been shredded in three or four places. Offsetting the hostility of the main message, a bird singing in a cage and a climbing vine fill the background. The tile on the other side says: *Aqui vive un hincha del R. Madrid.* Aha! This man is a fan of the Real Madrid. But *hincha* has a bit of an angry connotation. There are lots of friendly Spaniards along the Camino. I have met many of them. But who can blame this resident? At least the artist did not depict the thief with a hiking stick, a gourd, and a backpack from which dangles a shell. I assume the tiles are there as a reaction to past vandalism. Sadly, many of the small villages we pass are prey to vandalism during winter, when few people are around.

We have now passed kilometre 47.281. No thunder or lightning yet, but the rain has started. The atmosphere is definitely electric with groups of exuberant pilgrims. A clamour of voices rises from the muddy path. We are all speaking the same language, all in good spirits and looking forward to Santiago. The scenery, so clean and fresh, could not be more beautiful. Elena, the landscape artist, and I, the rain lover, are in heaven. On our way, in Boente, Albergue El Alemán has set out its sandwich board by the path announcing free swimming pool. That will not attract pilgrims today, but the hostel looks inviting. Doubtless some who started further behind us will fill its beds tonight.

The Milky Way

Before we know it, we have reached Arzúa. It would have been easy to hike further today, but my reservation in Santiago is for two nights ahead. I am sticking to my plans. My granny shoes, socks, feet and the bottom of my trousers are soaked. Elena and I are happy for the opportunity to dry ourselves. It doesn't take us long to realize we have hit the jackpot again tonight.

Across from a lot with palm trees standing like sentinels above a pretty ten-foot high wall, from outside, Albergue Vía Lactea (The Milky Way) presents itself as a rather drab place. Its unadorned grey concrete front wall and concrete balconies jutting out over the sidewalk, the large garage door beside the main entrance, even the shell with the words Vía Lactea could not presage the elegance of the interior. A block away from the main street, it is one of the most elegant hostels on the Camino. I was still commenting on the beauty of our stamps when we noticed the large corridor filled with fine antique furniture, paintings, vases and sculptures. In red ink, in our *credencial*: the contour of a pilgrim with backpack and hiking stick. The artist has captured the motion of the pilgrim well. Elena and I have been rating our stamps. We both agree: this one is in our top five.

The corridor to our dorm is lined with antique chairs. Cast iron sculptures celebrate workers with large harvest baskets. Every object blends nicely with pictures evoking the Camino and pilgrims. On a small dresser along the hallway, someone has placed vases with blue hydrangea and near them, a pretty framed note: *Via Láctea les desea un Buen Camino.* (The Milky Way wishes you a *Buen Camino*.) Our dorm is bright and spacious. They don't offer dinner here. We will use a well-appointed kitchen, the dining-room and enclosed patio.

Arzúa is a busy little town with at least one excellent grocery store near us. Elena and I will prepare a home-cooked meal and share it with other pilgrims. I still have some of my mixture of curry powder. In every town on the Camino, I can pick up a roast chicken and perhaps some fresh grapes or an apple to chop up and add to the mixture. With rice and a salad, we will have a feast.

Humpty Dumpty

Despite the rain and mud, today was easy. Between laundry and supper, Elena and I want to explore the town. A few steps from the hostel, we arrive at the right time to help a fragile old lady who is having difficulty holding a ladder while her husband climbs to the door of their *horreo*. While he grabs keys from his pocket, just as we are standing a few steps away and our eyes are on the two of them, he totters and almost falls backwards. Without our quick reaction and our hands to steady the ladder, all the king's horses and all the king's men couldn't have put him together again. Now, the couple think all Canadians and Russians are the most wonderful people in the world. It reminds me how little it takes to represent a country. It's a good thing old Sausage fingers at the restaurant didn't know where I was from.

Juan Manuel Vidal García

After the *horreo*, a bust of Juan Manuel Vidal García 1885–1936 Alcalde Martyr de Arzúa (mayor, martyr) catches my attention. Vidal García was born in a small village a couple of days' walk south-west of here. An entrepreneur and generous benefactor, he emigrated to Argentina. Successful in his country of adoption, he sent donations for the building of schools in Galicia. Back in his homeland, he set up a company to import farming equipment from Argentina. Councillor of Arzúa in 1924, he was mayor from 1932 to 1936, until he went into hiding following the 1936 uprising marking the beginning of the Civil War. One of the earliest victims of the dictator, two months later, he was executed by a firing squad in Santiago de Compostela. His family was subsequently denied the right to his enterprise. This got me raising my eyebrows at the history of Santiago de Compostela. Its more recent past is rarely part of the narrative destined for the pilgrim. History is always multifaceted. Life cannot be restored, but the victims' honour can be saved. And tyrants can be exposed. It might be too late for heads to fall, but it is still possible to topple statues, erect new ones and send some names to the book of infamy.

Ramón Franco

Nearby, we pass a street sign with the name Ramón Franco and a bust with the same name. The man perhaps in his forties, wears aviator goggles. The name pokes my curiosity. Was Ramón Franco related to the dictator? I imagine the name to be popular in this area where Francisco Franco Bahamonde's family lived. It might be nothing but a coincidence. I must ask around. Alas, I find no one to approach without making a fool of myself. I can be bold but I'm not so forward as to accost someone on the street in the hope that they are history aficionados, nor does Arzúa abound with benches in parks where I could find a couple of old gaffers quietly letting the hours slip by under a palm tree, like the two with whom Elena and I chatted yesterday by the Capela San Roque in Melide. They seemed content watching the day's last straggling pilgrims go by, and to exchange a few pleasantries with us. Ramón Franco might remain an enigma for me.

Back at the Via Lactea, Carmen, our *hospitalera* is busy wiping the kitchen floor which doesn't need wiping. She goes around non-stop, always with a look of pride and satisfaction, making sure everything is spic and span. And it is. She asks if we have everything we need. What a delight it is to be welcomed so generously and in such gracious places by people who love their work. Under the Milky Way, Elena and I will have a heavenly sleep.

General Franco, I will learn from a Galician pilgrim (retired Majorcan teacher) tomorrow, was born in Ferrol on the Bay of Biscay, an hour north of Arzúa. Ramón, of a very different political ilk from his older sibling, became an accomplished pilot, a hero celebrated for his 1928 cross-Atlantic flight in the Plus Ultra, an amphibian aircraft, one year before Lindberg's first trans-Atlantic flight. The Caudillo had tried unsuccessfully to rally him to his cause. But Ramón was on the side of the Republicans.

The charismatic, suave younger brother attracted friends, male and female, like bees to honey, said the teacher. (He talked about Franco's brother as though he had known him personally...) Ramón was fun-loving, adventurous, and surpassed his brother the Dictator in all facets of life. Many Spaniards including our teacher speculate that brotherly jealousy might have been the biggest motive for Franco's ambitions of grandeur. Indeed, I had already read about the rift in the Franco family. Spanish history, from its very beginning, is full of such brotherly enmity. One only has to leaf through books about its royalty. Sibling rivalry, treachery, hate fill their pages. Just like that of many other countries, I suppose.

Ramón died at the controls of his airplane during the Civil War. To this day, historians have not reached a consensus about the cause of the crash. It is difficult to believe that such an accomplished pilot should have perished in a banal flight accident. Some say that the day Ramón disappeared, he was on his way to bomb the port of Valencia or the town of Barcelona. It was raining heavily, the airplane carried a heavy load, a thousand kilos of bombs, he was caught in a storm... The pilot had once said of his brother Francesco that, out of ambition, he would kill his own mother or his own father. Ramón Franco is not the only Spanish republican pilot to have died in this type of suspicious accident. Apparently, he had previously crashed his airplane in a second attempt to cross the Atlantic, and was rescued after five days at sea. But that was before his brother had taken over the country. This time, no one succeeded in rescuing him. Did they even try? Unbridled ambition will turn a man into a monster, concluded the Majorcan. I wonder if the true story of the accident will ever come to light.

99 Bottles of Beer on the Wall

The end is near. Elena is still keen on walking into Santiago with the rising sun at her back. Considering the weather these last days, I would say she is quite the optimist. Pedrouzo will be our last full day together. Galicia lives up to its reputation again. Our warm clothes and rain capes serve us well. Since the weather forecast doesn't presage too much heat, and the terrain doesn't look too punishing, we will take our time leaving in the morning.

The closer we get to Santiago, the smoother the path seems. It is not long before we are walking in a procession with a guard of honour of tall trees on either side of the path, joined again into a lush natural arbour above our heads. Many areas are dense with fog. I am in my element. Even when the crowd is more spread out, we know there are hundreds of pilgrims before and behind us, even if they are invisible or only appear as ghosts. Nature is all it's supposed to be in Galicia. Tree trunks are thick and vegetable gardens teem with large healthy-looking produce. The strange thing is huge cabbages and Brussels sprouts neighbour tilled soil, from which fresh shoots are growing. This is early October. Do they grow vegetables year round?

Before 8:30, a signpost says 30.849 kilometres. Each time we see one, Elena and I wonder why they have it down to the metre. Is this Spanish humour? Near the beginning, there were few of these unmovable cement signs. Apparently there will be more and more all over the Camino to prevent incidents like unfortunately happened a few years ago when a pilgrim was lured off the trail by a sign moved by her psychopath. It did not end well.

One imaginative watering hole has a large garden enclosed within a waist-high stone wall, its top lined with beer bottles. Large trees in the garden also have hundreds of bottles on long nails sticking out of their trunks. As if it weren't enough, high pyramidal wooden structures hold more bottles. Each one has a pilgrim's name on it. There must be thousands of empty bottles all around the garden. A man and a woman were walking ahead of us. "Look at that!" said the woman as she stopped to take a photo. "Well, it's different," said her companion, shaking his head. Like us, I guess they didn't really know what to think of it.

A hundred steps further, another Café competes for customers. The sun is still a fuzzy white sphere. The plastic chairs outside are wet with dew, so even this inviting patio is not tempting. With its stone steps and its sign 'Casa de Boavista' (House with a nice view), I guess the tiny house built of vertical wooden slats, near a garden, and which must have been a large *horreo* is now rented out to pilgrims. It wouldn't surprise me. It looks large enough for a couple of cots. With its artificial pond surrounded by a stone wall, its sculpture of a pilgrim, and its sand-cast candle-burning stand, it looks peaceful and inviting, and does have a *boavista*.

On this leg of the Camino, sprinkled here and there, delicate satiny pink roses stick out through the fog. The belles of the ball, the proud debutantes with their tall slim necks. As often, many pilgrims, intent on getting to destination as soon as possible, seem oblivious to these beauties. Only five hundred Compostelas are doled out daily, which seems unfair to me. Not that I really care. The certificate will only become part of the flotsam and jetsam of my life that my children or grandchildren will feel guilty throwing away.

By mid-morning, Elena and I succumb to the lure of a Café. What a lovely surprise is awaiting us inside: Susan from Denver. She has been walking alone. We will walk together, all three of us, until Pedrouzo. I ask the restaurant owner if I may eat some of my corn cakes with his prosciutto and frittata. "*Claro. No pasa nada,*" he says as if to say "why bother ask?" Later, back on the path, still between high banks, eagle-eyed Elena suddenly hops to one side and returns with a huge mushroom. "*Comida*" (dinner), she announces. Of course, later, when she prepares a mushroom omelet, after my first bite, I can't help but bring my hand to my throat with a look of horror on my face, just the time to get a reaction from her and the others around the table. By now, we are all, consciously or not, full of ourselves for having walked the Camino. We need a bit of comic relief to bring us back to reality. Nietzsche said, "Whenever I climb, I am followed by a dog called Ego." I think our dog called Ego rises with us every morning and goes to bed with us every night. It is perhaps our biggest challenge in life to tame that dog.

Susan has reserved a bed down the street from us. We will hike out together in the morning. At the Trisquel, my dorm is airy and bright. The large picture window beside my bed has a view onto the countryside. The well-appointed kitchen can accommodate many pilgrims at once, and the long dining-room tables are perfect for meeting others. There is also a comfortable sitting area with sofas and a library.

By nine o'clock, all beds are occupied. Many pilgrims are already settled for the night. "I'm out of here at 5 a.m." says one woman to her friend. They have heard about the challenge of obtaining the certificate. The Pilgrim's office in Santiago closes at 1 p.m. Some are catching flights early the day after tomorrow before the office opens. By ten o'clock, everyone is quiet except for three young women, oblivious to the rest of us. "Did you get a massage?" shouts one. "Can you believe we walked a stage and a half today?" "Tomorrow, there'll be a shitload of people on the Camino." "I don't mind, as long as they're respectful and quiet." By 10:30, they finally shut up and turn off the light.

In the morning, they are gone before I wake at 6:30. "Oh, to be young and energetic!" I tell the pilgrim next to me when she points to their beds. "And full of yourself," she replies.

A Pile of Stones

Yesterday afternoon, when I went to buy eggs for our mushroom omelet, I was in my own bubble when I almost bumped into an ancient woman coming out of a grocery store with her purchases. She was short and compact. Her head barely reached my shoulder. Her bag looked so heavy and the curve of her back was so pronounced, I thought for sure she was about to topple over and spread herself and all her groceries onto the sidewalk. I offered her my help. After the faintest hesitation, she accepted. I took the bulging bag, offered her my arm, and she took it. Adjusting my pace to hers, keen on collecting another story, I tried to make a bit of conversation. Her Galician accent was hard for me to understand. I said, "*Sí, sí.*" many more times than I should honestly have. She was a hardy woman with a keen intelligence and a sense of humour. Her hair, of a colour much too uniform for her age, framed a face ravaged by too many years, but from her dark eyes shone an intelligent light. She lived several streets off the Camino.

I asked her if the name O'Pedrouzo meant anything. She seemed to think it was a strange question. I had heard that it translated to 'a pile of stones'. I asked her teasingly if she considered her village to be just a pile of stones. She smiled and raised her eyebrows without saying anything. When I asked what she thought of the pilgrims, she evaded my question, and only said one has to accept life as it presents itself. There was no point in trying to change what we could not change. After a while one could get used to anything. At least, I think that is what she said. At her door, she thanked me not profusely but sincerely for helping carry her bags, as though it was just the civil thing for me to do. And it was.

With about a dozen places to call home for the night, and a profusion of good restaurants, although it does not have the charm of previous villages, O'Pedrouzo is definitely more than just a pile of stones. If it has an interesting history, I saw no sign of it. The only monument I noticed was of a rooster perched up a large stone on top of a tall pillar with the inscription 'Galo Piñeiro o Pino 2017'. I have no idea what that means. Is this rooster the only hero of this place? If a chicken and a rooster can reign supreme over Santo Domingo, I suppose anything is possible. Since I only noticed it after I had returned from accompanying the old woman, it remains a mystery to me for now.

Walking With the Crowd

Elena and I are in fine fettle this morning, my last, her second-last before Santiago. We did not pick our timing well. Like two rats in an army of pestiferous rodents charmed by the Pied Piper, we look at each other as if to say, "Could we not have guessed?" From every door, every street corner, pilgrims appear singly or in groups, in a cacophony of enthusiasm, and too often with their hiking sticks now bared of rubber, click-clicking at every step. Their words echo loudly into the chilly morning air. *"Buen Camino,"* some shout too enthusiastically to others they met perhaps only last night. I hope nobody lives above the shops. I know too well what it is like to live on a street where exuberant young people shout at each other on their way home from the pubs in the small hours of the morning, disturbing your sleep, night after night. It is still early in O'Pedrouzo. Pity the local who had hoped for a few more minutes of sleep this morning. And every morning from April to November.

Susan is waiting outside by the entrance to her hostel. Off we go into the hazy morning with its pink horizon, trying to ignore the others who are probably trying to ignore us. Before long we are walking with an army of pilgrims in small groups of about a dozen. We have many short hills to climb today. We take our time, and especially, we take time to glance at the spectacle of the rising sun behind us. We split for short periods of time, chat with hundred-kilometre pilgrims, exchange a few words, lag behind. Eventually, we are rid of the crowd eager to get their certificates. I have enjoyed talking with some of those pilgrims. They seem less adventurous than we are, but they are all bubbling with enthusiasm. All the ones I talked to seem to have enjoyed the experience. Some of them have been on cruises before; others have taken part in guided tours all over Europe.

Two women, probably in their early fifties, friends since high-school, told me "It was on our bucket list for many years. We had to wait until our kids were grown." They had never travelled outside of the United States before and had to save for many years in order to afford this. Even the cost of their passports was not negligible for their budgets.

None of the ones I talked to had ever ventured alone in a foreign country. Now a few of them are determined to come back and start at Saint-Jean-Pied-de-Port. "Not by myself," said one woman, "but I do want to come back and walk the whole way." I understand.

One septuagenarian with a strong Glaswegian accent told me she was here because her husband died last year. "I am so sorry," I said. She laughed naughtily and without a second of hesitation, replied, "Ach! The Old Stick in the Mud! He would never let me do anything. He's gone now. And not too soon. I'm free to go where I want now." "How long were you married?" I asked. "Fifty-eight years. Fifty-seven years too long," she said. I admire her for calling a spade a spade. Not all marriages are made in heaven.

I asked one man where his group was from. They were mostly British, or at least English-speaking. "You know," he said, shyly, "I've travelled to many countries, but it was always 'this is Monday, it must be Paris' kind of tour. And always in Europe. I'm too chicken to travel on my own." His voice was hesitant. He seemed to consider his lack of adventure a lack of manliness. He had a shy smile, and was not overly handsome, but his features were regular, his eyes deep blue. His head shined where it was bald, but the hair on either side had not yet started greying. He had a small potbelly. I noticed his well-manicured hands, a signet ring. No wedding band. I thought there must be a shy woman somewhere who would love to meet this man. The longer I talked to him, the more comfortable he seemed. It is one advantage of my age. "What do you do for a living?" I asked. He said he worked in a music shop. "Do you play any instrument?" "I play the violin," he said, promptly adding, "but I'm not very good." There was a sadness in his eyes that made me wish I could hug him, as I would hug a friend during a difficult period in their life. He reminded me of Charles Bremer in *Man of Flowers*, an Australian movie from the 80s where a child's love of beauty had led to a life of solitude. He asked me how I enjoyed walking since Saint-Jean. I hope my experience will encourage him to come back. When his group leader gathered her members together before going into a restaurant, I told him, "This is a feather in your cap. Don't belittle your accomplishment. We're all different, you know."

In late morning, Susan, Elena and I are walking together again, escorted on either side of the path by the tall, straight, pastel-coloured eucalyptus with their peeling bark. I wish I did not know about the controversy. Taking pleasure in looking at these beautiful trees is now like enjoying a tasty pork chop next to a table full of vegans. Sometimes you just want to be a happy moron.

The owner of a restaurant down the way serves 'the longest sandwich' in Spain. There are some on the counter where he poses, placing his arm along one. It goes from his fist to his elbow. I wonder how he manages with the drudgery of what I would consider a boring job. He obviously doesn't see it that way. Proud of his success, he is making the best of this invasion of pilgrims which grows each year, which gratifies him more each year. I ask if I can have my corn cakes with his orange juice. *"Claro. No pasa nada,"* he says. I knew it would be OK. Once bitten, twice shy.

Before noon, we slow our steps to better enjoy the dense area of sensuous old trees entwined with vines. But what is Mannequin Pis doing here on the terrace of a restaurant? I suppose there is no rule that says a little hero must stay in his own country. There are lots of Dutch immigrants in Spain. There must be Belgian ones as well. Did one of them start a small business here? After falling in love with the Camino, perhaps? After volunteering? Or after falling in love with a Spanish girl?

I am surprised to find the odd cluster of palm trees. They always seem out of place in this area. I have seen them on the Mediterranean coast. But here? Have they also been transplanted here by some nostalgic person trying to recreate a bit of their sunny paradise from South America? I am getting suspicious about that theory, but with the grey skies, the fog, the drizzle, the rain we have experienced these last days, there doesn't seem to be much chance of them growing naturally here, yet it is no wonder everything is so lush. And I have seen palm trees in Scotland on the coast near the Isle of Sky. It was odd there too. They must like the sea air.

On top of a waist-high wall, six fat, furry golden paws rest on the base of a large metal grate. They belong to three golden retrievers. The dogs are enjoying the parade of pilgrims. Silently, they stare and, every once in a while, a pilgrim darts from a group to pat their heads. "Nice dog" "Hi Pooch" "*Que tal?*" Three furry golden tails wag in unison. These dogs don't lack attention, and they have an endless expanse to run through when they tire of the daily parade. I wish Lizi were with us now; these gentle creatures would help her understand a dog's size does not determine its behaviour.

A few steps further, an old man is repairing a roof. What must it be like to hear this incessant procession of quacking pilgrims? And to know that while you're just doing your work, all eyes are on you? Nearby, behind another low stone wall separating them from the road, a dozen fat sheep graze peacefully. Unlike the dogs, the sheep are oblivious to the daily parade. Without the pilgrims, this would be a quiet village.

I had been looking forward to Monte del Gozo (*gozo* means delight). Sadly, the large monument does nothing to inspire me. What had I expected? To add to my disappointment, we don't see the spires of Santiago from here. "I see nothing. Do you?" I ask Elena. She had also expected something different. Oh well, what does it matter? We take a minute to visit the chapel. The votive candles are the electric kind. Oh my! I find a total lack of anything inspiring around here. "At least, the flowers are real," says Elena, pointing to the many vases at the front of the chapel. She is right. I should not expect everything to always be perfect and to my taste.

Late morning we reach San Lázaro where Elena is staying tonight. Gee! It looks like a concentration camp. Not that it would bother Elena. She lives in a large, charmless apartment building in Yekaterinburg, although I am sure with her enviable artistic touch, her own space must be quite a contrast to the building itself. How spoiled I have become. Some pragmatic architect has designed this humongous dormitory, needed at least during Holy Years when many more pilgrims tramp on the Camino. I am glad I am not staying here. Nuala, the Irish woman I met in Burgos, recommended Seminario Menor in Santiago. I have a reservation there for tonight. She is at

Seminario Mayor beside the cathedral, nursing her bad foot. We have been in touch occasionally since Burgos, and plan on getting together tomorrow or the next day. "Seminario Menor is a bit out of the way," Nuala warned me, "but you will like it." I hope her foot is healing. It doesn't sound good. With her Irish verve, I can't always decipher her messages. I'll soon find out.

Susan and I continue on our way. I don't know what Elena will do here all day. There is not much to see or do. Knowing her, she will make entries into her diary, do a few doodles and communicate with family and friends. She is not easily bored. Russians are rare on the Camino, but she is not afraid to use whatever words she knows of Spanish, German or English to start a conversation. And she has her mascot to keep her company.

Near Santiago, Susan and I are in high spirits. After my disappointment at Monte del Gozo, I try to keep a damper on. I have been on too many approaches to large towns. They are better forgotten. I am ready for it this morning, so what a pleasant surprise it is, nearing Santiago, to find no industrial building, no big-box store. In the distance, the cathedral reigns supreme. Susan will stay here for two nights and I, four. Since we don't need to rush for our certificates, we stop at the first pub on our way. The waiter brings us olives and nuts, compliments of the house, a sure sign the pub is patronized by locals. These freebees are something I missed on the Camino; I had become used to them in other areas of Spain. In some places in Barcelona, it is not rare to even get a generous portion of fried squid, free with a beer. It doesn't matter how much things cost, it always makes you feel special to get something free.

Despite the heat and our tiredness, Susan is radiant. She is like the sun poking through a grey sky on a dull day. Unlike me, she has been carrying her backpack since Saint-Jean-Pied-de-Port. An avid hiker and backpacker all her life, she lives in Denver, and is used to hiking at 5,000 feet. That must have helped a little with the Camino. In Barcelona, next week, she will be celebrating seventeen years of sobriety. She must be proud of her achievements. She should be.

Boru

Nuala

With Susan, Gabriela and Lizi

Muxia

Have Bells, Will Travel

When we, proud pilgrims, arrive in Santiago, full of ourselves, we should consider this: Ali Amil Muhammad ben Amir al'Ma Afiri, (Almanzor for short) decided one day, from his vantage point in Córdoba, to show the Christians in the north who was the boss. While Almanzor was out of sight in Africa, King Bermudos II of León, erroneously thinking he could get away with it, had stopped paying tribute to the Caliphate. He should have known better: Almanzor's conquests were already legendary. With his legions of soldiers, Almanzor decided to put an end to Christian insubordination. Smack in the dog days of summer, galloping across the whole of Spain on his way to Santiago, (already for Christians, a place of pilgrimage, and the most sacred site on the peninsula), his armies captured thousands, the men to be turned into eunuchs for harems or used as labourers, the women chosen for their blue eyes, blond hair, and voluptuous figures, to become wives for high society.

The pilgrimage to Santiago had been popular for about a century. Having had wind of Almanzor's intended visit, and knowing full well he wasn't coming to share a plate of pulpo or to sample Galician wine, the Christians flew the coop. The lucky ones, that is, those who had strong legs or horses. Some say they hid Santiago's tomb in a safe place. Others, that the sepulchre stayed in the church, that Almanzor did not desecrate it. Whatever the truth, when Almanzor arrived, the town was deserted. He reduced to rubble all of Santiago, including the temple. Then, he took the bell (or bells, depending...) and, having it mounted on a large platform, had dozens of Christian slaves carry it to Córdoba in Andalucía, about the same distance as from Saint-Jean-Pied-de-Port to Santiago. All this took place a millennium ago.

The fortunes of history ebb and flow. Two centuries and a half later, the bell did the trek in reverse with Catholics enslaving Muslims to carry it all the way back to Santiago. Apparently the recaptured bell was melted in order to use the bronze to cast a new one which in 1989, after centuries of service, was taken down and now resides in the cathedral's cloister. Doesn't this make my little trek seem like a Sunday afternoon stroll?

Terminus

In front of the cathedral defaced by scaffolding, Susan and I find a gaggle of ebullient pilgrims, backpacks on the ground, hugging, posing, taking photos of each other. They have conquered the Camino. Their cheerful voices rise above the square. The ambiance is electric. Except for me. And perhaps a few others like me. It will take me a while to understand why. For me, the Camino was what mattered: the changing scenery, the people, the villages, the walk, the daily a to b. Whether or not I would reach a destination never mattered too much to me. It was the moment that counted, that I enjoyed, the friends I made along the way, the stories I collected, the spirits of those who had preceded me and lingered in history. It was the way my life was being enriched. For me, Santiago means the return to my role on life's stage at the end of a beautiful interlude. Santiago means goodbyes. I am fortunate to have a loving family to return to. I wonder what it is like for those who must return to an empty house. I have it good both ways.

Looking back now, I can understand the elation of those for whom carrying a heavy bag, walking with blisters, suffering from exhaustion, was a challenge. They deserve to be proud. I can understand the elation of those who felt they had been walking with God, asking for a favour, or less often perhaps, even thanking God for one. I hope wishes are granted. I hope God receives thanks graciously. I understand those for whom the Camino was a time for spiritual reflection, a search for a new direction, a quest. I hope they found the answers they were looking for. I also understand those who sought healing. I sincerely hope they went home healed.

That evening, while the pianist played, with Susan, Gabriela, Lizi and Bori, a reporter we had met briefly a few days before, we celebrated in a restaurant near the cathedral. Tomorrow, Susan was going on a bus tour to Finistere and Muxia. Lizi would be off to Andalucía to vacation with her sister. Bori would be going back to her work in Slovenia.

Gabriela and I had no luck securing seats on the excursion bus with Susan. We met the group in the morning, hoping for a couple of cancellations. When there were none, we made a mad dash for the local bus station twenty minutes away, where the driver welcomed us on board as he was pulling out of the station. Once in our seats, much to my delight, I realized we were on the local bus, the one that pulled into every cove and village. We would at least get a scenic tour.

In Finistere, Gabriela and I walked along the beach and treated ourselves to the most delicious seafood I had ever tasted. Then, she took a direct bus back to Santiago. She would leave for Málaga the next morning and spend a week at the beach with one of her fourteen siblings. I walked two or three kilometres up the hill to the lighthouse where I bumped into Susan and her bus tour, and I took the slow bus back so I could enjoy every bit of the scenery again. I would return to the same restaurant in Finistere two days later with Nuala on an excellent tour with a knowledgeable guide. Our favorite stop would be Muxia with its tragic history of the oil spill, its giant sculpture commemorating the thousands of international volunteers who came to clean and restore the shoreline.

I was ready to return home now. It would be good to be with my family again. Before my train back to Pamplona, Nuala and I would have time to explore Santiago off the beaten track. What a treat it was to have a private room. I could leave my belongings all over the place. I was glad she had suggested the Seminario Menor. We enjoyed breakfasts at her hotel, and I cooked us dinner up the hill.

Sadly, the Camino was not to end on a cheerful note for everyone. On my last evening, as I was preparing a salad at the long kitchen counter, I heard a middle-aged woman weeping. Her sobs were getting louder and louder. Bent over the counter, her tears fell in large drops in a puddle on the stainless steel. I went to her, put my arm around her shoulder, and asked if I could help. She picked up her cell phone, entered Korean characters into a translation App, and showed me the screen: 'My father died.' I was shocked. She had obviously just received the news. I put my arms around her and let her cry. After only a few seconds, she picked up her phone again and wrote something else. 'Suicide.' I couldn't believe it. It was all too brutal. Too unreal. Why couldn't he at least wait until she got home? I held her in my arms. When her sobs abated somewhat, I asked a young man to please go to the common room and find some Korean women to help comfort her.

Before he could find anyone, a Korean man arrived and asked what was wrong. He shook his head, thanked me and took her away to another area.

I knew nothing of that woman; I had never met her before. It seemed a cruel irony, a nasty twist of fate, that this should happen now. Often, people come on the Camino to heal. I have no idea why she was here. Was it a quest for her father's healing? She would be going home with pain rather than a cure. In that moment, I felt angry. I felt all the unfairness of life. I understood once again there is no point in looking for the meaning of life. Just live it to the fullest. *Carpe diem.*

Epilogue

In September 2021, during the Covid pandemic, Andrea and I returned to the Camino. It was quiet. Many changes had occurred. The albergue and restaurant in Zariquiegui, the Jardín de Muruzábal, the Casa Mágica in Villatuerta were all closed. In front of the church in Zariquiegui, several friendly officers of the Guardia Civil were giving out information about an app in case of emergency. The large windows of Hostal Burgos were papered over and full of graffiti. I don´t know whether it will open again. In Valverde, heavyhearted, I spotted a large 'For Sale' sign at the deserted Casa del Camino where I had first met Elena and the hospitaleros had been so kind to me. But all was not bad. I discovered so many wonderful new albergues and small hotels, including charming Pensión Santa Rosa in Samos, and award-winning Mercadoiro with its fine antiques and history of (now defunct) linen production.

When I hurt my foot and could not hike for several days, at O'Cebreiro, I met a generous woman called Camino (her real name). From Vigo, she took time off from her usual life in order to help pilgrims. Two days in a row, she drove Lluc, a Majorcan writer also in physical distress, and me, to our separate destinations, asking nothing in return.

I will never cease to be amazed at the wonderful connections the Camino provides. Back home, through FaceTime, I was able to cheer up Elena, my Russian Camino friend while despite being vaccinated she was ill with Covid and in hospital in Yekaterinburg.

I can't imagine ever tiring of the Camino.

Printed in Great Britain
by Amazon

26722989R00192